PEARSON CUSTOM LIBRARY

PEARSON

Cover Art: Jerry Driendl/Getty Images, Inc.; Steve Bloom/Getty Images, Inc.; "Cheetah" courtesy of Marvin Mattelson/ Getty Images; "Tabs" courtesy of Andrey Prokhorov/iStockphoto; "Open Doors" courtesy of Spectral-Design/iStockphoto; "Compass" courtesy of Laurent Hamels/Getty Images; "Fortune Teller" courtesy of Ingvald Kaldhussaeter/iStockphoto; "Ladder of Success" courtesy of iStockphoto; "Global Communication in Blue" courtesy of iStockphoto. Additional images courtesy of Photodisc/Getty Images, Photodisc, Stockbyte/Getty Images, Digital Vision/Getty Images, Pearson Learning Solutions, and brandXpictures.

Pearson Learning Solutions, 501 Boylston Street, Suite 900, Boston, MA 02116
A Pearson Education Company
www.pearsoned.com

Printed in the United States of America.
V0UD

PEARSON

ISBN 10: 1-269-76139-0
ISBN 13: 978-1-269-76139-0

Table of Contents

Looking at Computers: Understanding the Parts

Looking at Computers: Understanding the Parts

Understanding Digital Components

Understanding Your Computer

OBJECTIVES

1. What exactly is a computer, and what are its four main functions?
2. What is the difference between data and information?
3. What are bits and bytes, and how are they measured?

Sound Byte: Binary Numbers

Active Helpdesk: Understanding Bits and Bytes

Input Devices and Output Devices

OBJECTIVES

4. What devices can I use to get data into the computer?
5. What devices can I use to get information out of the computer?

Active Helpdesk: Using Output Devices

Processing, Storage, and Connectivity

Processing, Memory, and Storage

OBJECTIVES

6. What's on the motherboard?
7. Where are information and programs stored?

Sound Byte: Virtual Computer Tour

Ports and Power Controls

OBJECTIVES

8. How are devices connected to the computer?
9. What's the best way to turn my computer on and off, and when should it be done?

Active Helpdesk: Exploring Storage Devices and Ports

Sound Byte: Port Tour: How Do I Hook It Up?

Setting It All Up

OBJECTIVE

10. How do I set up my computer to avoid strain and injury?

Sound Byte: Healthy Computing

The information in this text is written for Windows 8.1. If you are still running Windows 8, your screens and task instructions may vary slightly.

For all media in this chapter go to **pearsonhighered.com/techinaction** or **MyITLab**.

(Login/Shutterstock; Zadorozhnyi Viktor/Shutterstock; rukanoga/Fotolia; Lola & Bek/ImageZoo/Alamy)

HOW COOL IS THIS?

The **touch experience** is pretty common on computing devices now, making the mouse appear almost passé. But what about manipulating your computer like Tony Stark did in *Iron Man 3* by **waving your hands** in the air? Leap Motion has released a controller that senses how you move your hands to allow you to control your computing device **using just gestures**…no touching the screen needed! The inventors of this device were inspired by the **Holodeck technology** as envisioned in *Star Trek*. Although current apps aren't designed to make optimal use of this technology, many experts agree that **gesture interfaces** are the wave of the future. And you won't need to clean your fingerprints off your screens any longer! *(Leap Motion, Inc.; Courtesy of Leap Motion, Inc.)*

Scan here for more info

Understanding Digital Components

Becoming computer literate is important. But where do you start? You've no doubt gleaned some knowledge about computers just from being a member of society. However, even if you have used a computer before, do you really understand how it works, what all its parts are, and what those parts do?

understanding your COMPUTER

Let's start our look at computers by discussing what a computer does and how its functions make it such a useful machine.

Computers Are Data Processing Devices

Strictly defined, a **computer** is a data processing device that performs four major functions:

1. **Input:** It gathers data, or allows users to enter data.
2. **Process:** It manipulates, calculates, or organizes that data into information.
3. **Output:** It displays data and information in a form suitable for the user.
4. **Storage:** It saves data and information for later use.

What's the difference between data and information? People often use the terms *data* and *information* interchangeably. Although they may mean the same thing in a simple conversation, the distinction between data and information is an important one.

In computer terms, **data** is a representation of a fact, a figure, or an idea. Data can be a number, a word, a picture, or even a recording of sound. For example, the number 7135553297 and the names Zoe and Richardson are pieces of data. Alone, these pieces of data probably mean little to you. **Information** is data that has been organized or presented in a meaningful fashion. When your computer provides you with a contact listing that indicates that Zoe Richardson can be reached at (713) 555-3297, the data becomes useful—that is, it becomes information.

How do computers interact with data and information? Computers are excellent at **processing** (manipulating, calculating, or organizing) data into information. When you first arrived on campus, you probably were directed to a place where you could get an ID card. You most likely provided a clerk with personal data that was entered into a computer. The clerk then took your picture with a digital camera (collecting more data). All of the data was then processed appropriately so that it could be printed on your ID card (see Figure 1). This organized output of data on your ID card is useful information.

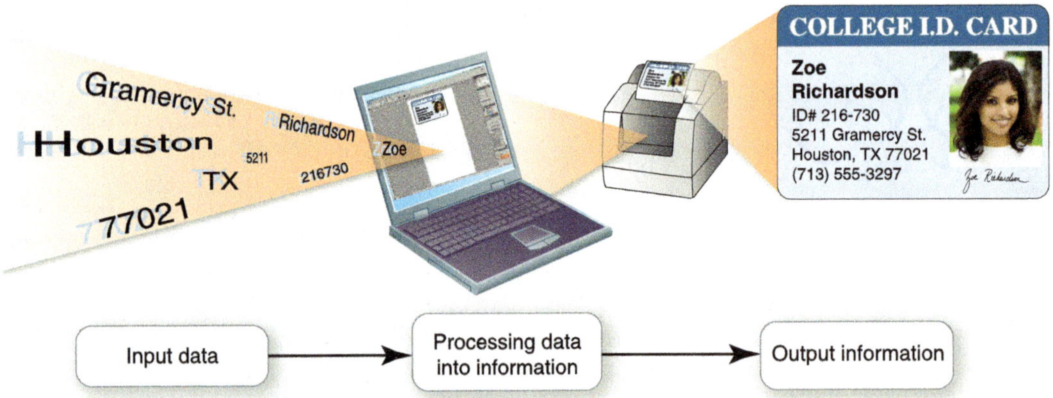

FIGURE 1 Computers process data into information. *(Michaeljung/Shutterstock)*

SOUND BYTE

Binary Numbers

This Sound Byte helps remove the mystery surrounding binary numbers. You'll learn about base conversion between decimal, binary, and hexadecimal numbers using colors, sounds, and images.

ACTIVE HELPDESK

Understanding Bits and Bytes

In this Active Helpdesk call, you'll play the role of a helpdesk staffer, fielding calls about the difference between data and information, what bits and bytes are, and how bytes are measured.

Bits and Bytes: The Language of Computers

How do computers process data into information? Unlike humans, computers work exclusively with numbers (not words). To process data into information, computers need to work in a language they understand. This language, called **binary language**, consists of just two digits: 0 and 1. Everything a computer does, such as processing data, printing a report, or editing a photo, is broken down into a series of 0s and 1s. Each 0 and 1 is a **binary digit**, or **bit** for short. Eight binary digits (or bits) combine to create one **byte**. In computers, each letter of the alphabet, each number, and each special character (such as @, pronounced "at") consists of a unique combination of eight bits, or a string of eight 0s and 1s. So, for example, in binary language, the letter *K* is represented as 01001011. This is eight bits, or one byte.

What else can bits and bytes be used for? Bits and bytes not only are used as the language that tells the computer what to do, they are also used to represent the *quantity* of data and information that the computer inputs and outputs. Word processing files, digital pictures, and even software are represented inside computing devices as a series of bits and bytes. These files and applications can be quite large, containing thousands or millions of bytes.

To make it easier to measure the size of such files, we need units of measure larger than a byte. Kilobytes, megabytes, and gigabytes are therefore simply larger amounts of bytes. As shown in Figure 2, a **kilobyte (KB)** is approximately 1,000 bytes, a **megabyte (MB)** is about 1 million bytes, and a **gigabyte (GB)** is around 1 billion bytes. Today, personal computers are capable of storing **terabytes (TB)** of data (around 1 trillion bytes), and many business computers can store up to a **petabyte (PB)** (1,000 terabytes) of data. The Google search engine processes more than 1 PB of user-generated data per *hour*!

How does your computer process bits and bytes? Your computer uses hardware and software to process data into information that lets you complete tasks such as writing a letter or playing a game. **Hardware** is any part of the computer you can physically touch. However, a computer needs more than just hardware to work. **Software** is the set of computer programs that enables the hardware to perform different tasks.

There are two broad categories of software: *application software* and *system software*. **Application software** is the set of programs you use on a computer to help you carry out tasks such as writing a research paper. If you've ever typed a document, created a spreadsheet, or edited a digital photo, for example, you've used application software.

System software is the set of programs that enables your computer's hardware devices and application software to work together. The most common type of system software is the **operating system (OS)**—the program that controls how your computer system functions. It manages the hardware, such as the monitor and printer, and provides a means by which users can interact with the computer. Most likely, the computer you own or use at school runs a version of Windows as the system software. However, if you're working on an Apple computer, you're probably running OS X.

Types of Computers

What types of computers are popular for personal use? There are two basic designs of computers: portable and stationary. For portable computers, a number of options exist:

- In 2010, Apple introduced the iPad, which created a new class of portable computers. A **tablet computer**, such as the iPad or Samsung Galaxy Tab, is a portable computer integrated into a flat multitouch-sensitive screen. It uses an onscreen virtual keyboard, but you can connect separate keyboards to it via Bluetooth or wires.
- A **laptop** or **notebook computer** is a portable computer that has a keyboard, monitor, and other devices integrated into a single compact case.
- A **netbook** is a small, lightweight laptop computer that is generally 7 to 10 inches wide and has a longer battery life than a laptop. These have been losing market share to tablet devices.
- An **ultrabook** is a full-featured but lightweight laptop computer designed to compete with the MacBook Air. Ultrabooks feature low-power processors and solid-state drives and try to reduce their size and weight to extend battery life without sacrificing performance.
- A **tablet (or convertible) PC** is similar to a laptop computer, but the monitor swivels and folds flat (see Figure 3a). This allows it to function both as a conventional laptop and as a tablet computer using its touchscreen.

A **desktop computer** is intended for use at a single location, so it's stationary. Most desktop computers consist of a separate case or tower (called the **system unit**) that

FIGURE 2

How Much Is a Byte?

NAME	NUMBER OF BYTES	RELATIVE SIZE
Byte (B)	1 byte	One character of data (8 bits, or binary digits)
Kilobyte (KB)	1,024 bytes (2^{10} bytes)	1,024 characters, or about 1 page of plain text
Megabyte (MB)	1,048,576 bytes (2^{20} bytes)	 About 4 books (200 pages, 240,000 characters)
Gigabyte (GB)	1,073,741,824 bytes (2^{30} bytes)	 About 4,500 books, or over twice the size of Sir Isaac Newton's library (considered very large for the time)
Terabyte (TB)	1,099,511,627,776 bytes (2^{40} bytes)	About 4.6 million books, or about the number of volumes in the Rutgers University Library
Petabyte (PB)	1,125,899,906,842,624 bytes (2^{50} bytes)	 About 4.7 billion books, which would fill the Library of Congress (the United States' largest library) 140 times!
Exabyte (EB)	1,152,921,504,606,846,976 bytes (2^{60} bytes)	About 4.8 trillion books, which, if stored as they are in the Library of Congress, would occupy about 11,000 square miles, or an area almost the size of the state of Maryland
Zettabyte (ZB)	1,180,591,620,717,411,303,424 bytes (2^{70} bytes)	 The library required to house the 4.9 quadrillion books equal to a ZB of data would occupy about 11.3 million square miles, or an area about 1 million square miles larger than all of North America

(Ninice64/Fotolia; Georgios Kollidas/Fotolia; D.aniel/Fotolia; Flavijus Piliponis/Fotolia)

FIGURE 3 (a) A convertible PC has a monitor that swivels to become a touch-sensitive input device; (b) an all-in-one computer does not need a separate tower. *(© JeKh – Fotolia.com; PRNewsFoto/Apple/AP Images)*

houses the main components of the computer plus peripheral devices. A **peripheral device** is a component, such as a monitor or keyboard, that connects to the computer. An **all-in-one computer**, such as the Apple iMac (Figure 3b) or HP TouchSmart, eliminates the need for a separate tower because these computers house the computer's processor and memory in the monitor. Many all-in-one models, such as the TouchSmart, also incorporate touch-screen technology.

Are there other types of computers? Although you may never come into direct contact with the following types of computers, they are still very important and do a lot of work behind the scenes of daily life:

- A **mainframe** is a large, expensive computer that supports many users simultaneously. Mainframes are often used in businesses that manage large amounts of data, such as insurance companies, where many people are working at the same time on similar operations, such as claims processing. Mainframes excel at executing many computer programs at the same time.
- A **supercomputer** is a specially designed computer that can perform complex calculations extremely rapidly. Supercomputers are used when complex models requiring intensive mathematical calculations are needed (such as weather forecasting or atomic energy research). Supercomputers are designed to execute a few programs as quickly as possible, whereas mainframes are designed to handle many programs running at the same time but at a slower pace.
- An **embedded computer** is a specially designed computer chip that resides in another device, such as your car or the electronic thermostat in your home. Embedded computers are self-contained computer devices that have their own programming and that typically don't receive input from you or interact with other systems (see Figure 4).

FIGURE 4 This robot vacuum includes an embedded computer. *(Jirsak/Shutterstock)*

Even your smartphone is a computer. Today's **smartphones** offer many features you probably use day to day, including a wide assortment of apps, media players, high-quality cameras, and web connectivity. And just like your laptop computer, your smartphone has a CPU, memory, and storage. Examples of smartphones include the iPhone and the HTC One.

Each part of your computer has a specific purpose that coordinates with one of the functions of the computer—input, processing, output, or storage (see Figure 5). Additional devices, such as modems and routers, help a computer communicate with the Internet and other computers to facilitate the sharing of documents and other resources. Let's begin our exploration of hardware by looking at your computer's input devices. ■

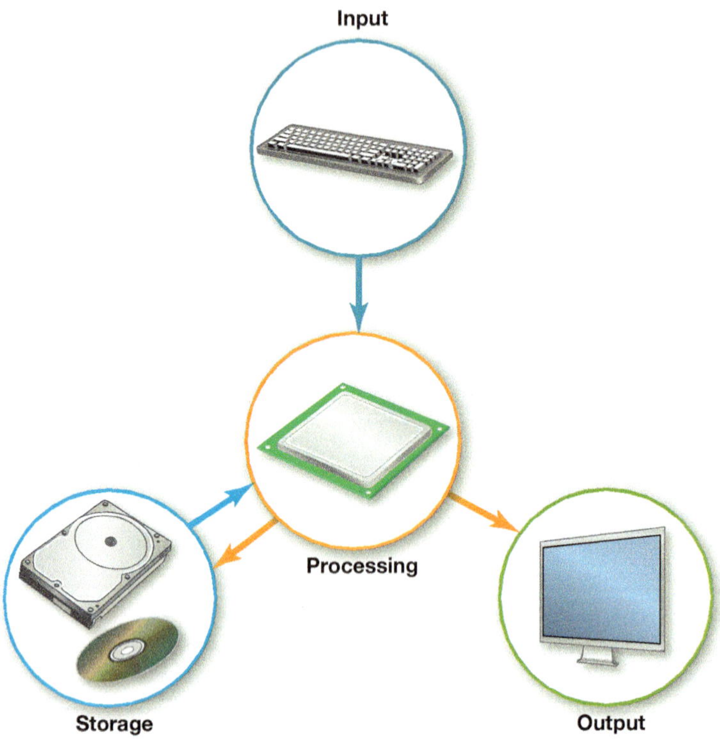

FIGURE 5 Each part of the computer serves a special function.

BITS&BYTES

Putting Your Computer to Work . . . While You Sleep

Complex scientific research, such as human genome exploration, requires vast computing power. Software has been developed to tie individual computing devices (including tablets and smartphones) in a grid to enable them to work together. This effectively creates a cheap supercomputer that many not-for-profit research organizations use to research problems that will benefit the greater good...and your computer can help. Visit the World Community Grid (**worldcommunitygrid.org**) and download its software. Once installed on your device, it allows your computer to work on research during the many times when your CPU is idle (or at least not working to its full potential). Your computing device can participate in exciting research projects on new drugs, sustainable water, and cancer. So tell your computer to get to work!

FIGURE 6 Help solve complex problems by adding your computer to the World Community Grid. *(adimas/Fotolia)*

input DEVICES

An **input device** lets you enter data (text, images, and sounds) and instructions (user responses and commands) into your computer. A **keyboard** is an input device you use to enter typed data and commands, and a **mouse** is used to enter user responses and commands.

There are other input devices as well. Microphones input sounds, scanners input nondigital data (such as magazine articles and old photographs) by turning it into a digital form, and digital cameras input digital images. A **stylus** is an input device that looks like a pen, which you use to tap commands or draw on a screen. We'll explore these and other input devices next.

FIGURE 7 Virtual keyboards are found on tablets and other touch-screen devices. *(PhotoNonStop/Glow Images)*

Keyboards

What is the most common way to input data and commands? Most computing devices, such as smartphones and tablets, now respond to touch. **Touch screens** are display screens that respond to commands initiated by touching them with your finger or a stylus. Touch-screen devices use a virtual keyboard (see Figure 7) that displays on screen when text input is required. These keyboards show basic keyboard configurations and use special keys to switch to numeric, punctuation, and other special keys.

Are all keyboards the same? Whether onscreen touch keyboards or physical keyboards, the most common keyboard layout is a standard **QWERTY keyboard**. This keyboard layout gets its name from the first six letters in the top-left row of alphabetic keys and is the standard English-language keyboard layout. The QWERTY layout was originally designed for typewriters and was meant to slow typists down and prevent typewriter keys from jamming. Although the QWERTY layout is considered inefficient because it slows typing speeds, efforts to change to more efficient layouts, such as that of the Dvorak keyboard (see the Bits and Bytes on the next page), have not been met with much public interest.

What alternatives are there to an onscreen touch keyboard? Touchscreen keyboards are not always convenient when a great deal of typing is required. Most computing devices can accept physical keyboards as an add-on accessory. Wired keyboards plug into a data port on the computing device. Wireless keyboards send data to the computer using a form of wireless technology that uses *radio frequency (RF)*. A radio transmitter in the keyboard sends out signals that are received either by a receiving device plugged into a port on the device or by a Bluetooth receiving device located in the device. You've probably heard of **Bluetooth technology** if you use a headset or earpiece with your cell phone. Bluetooth is a wireless transmission standard that lets you connect devices such as smartphones, tablets, and laptops to peripheral devices such as keyboards and headsets. Often, wireless keyboards for tablets are integrated with a case to protect your tablet (see Figure 8a).

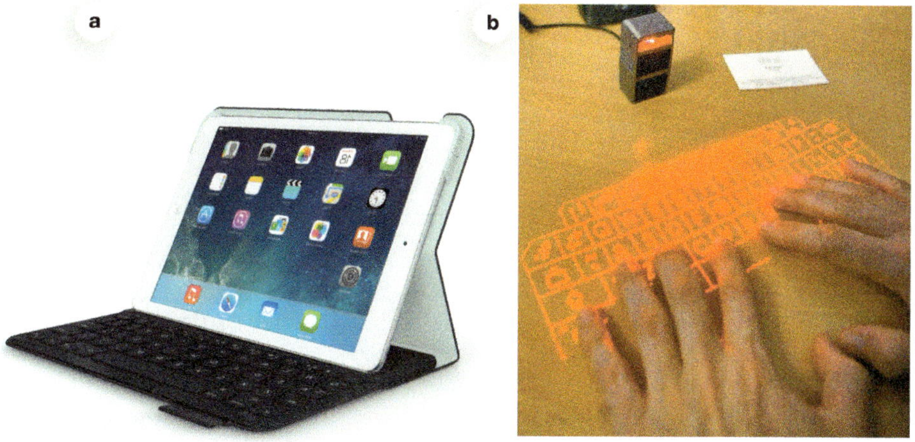

FIGURE 8 (a) Cases with integrated physical keyboards make tablets more typing-friendly. (b) The virtual laser keyboard projects the image of a QWERTY keyboard on any surface. Sensors detect typing motions, and data is transmitted to a computing device via Bluetooth technology. *(Logitech; Martin Meissner/AP Images)*

BITS&BYTES

Switching Your Keyboard Layout

The Dvorak keyboard is an alternative keyboard layout that puts the most commonly used letters in the English language on "home keys"—the keys in the middle row of the keyboard. The Dvorak keyboard's design reduces the distance your fingers travel for most keystrokes, increasing typing speed.

But did you know that you can change your keyboard from the QWERTY layout to the Dvorak layout without buying a new keyboard? You can use the Windows operating system to customize the keyboard by changing the keyboard layout. The keyboard layout then controls which characters appear on the screen when you press the keys on your keyboard. If you suffer from a repetitive strain injury such as carpal tunnel syndrome, you may find it useful to switch to the Dvorak keyboard layout. You can also switch layouts to conform to different foreign languages. Instructions for changing keyboard layouts are shown in Figure 9.

You might also find it useful to cover the keys on the keyboard with stickers of the corresponding characters of the newly configured layout so that the characters on your keyboard match up to the new layout.

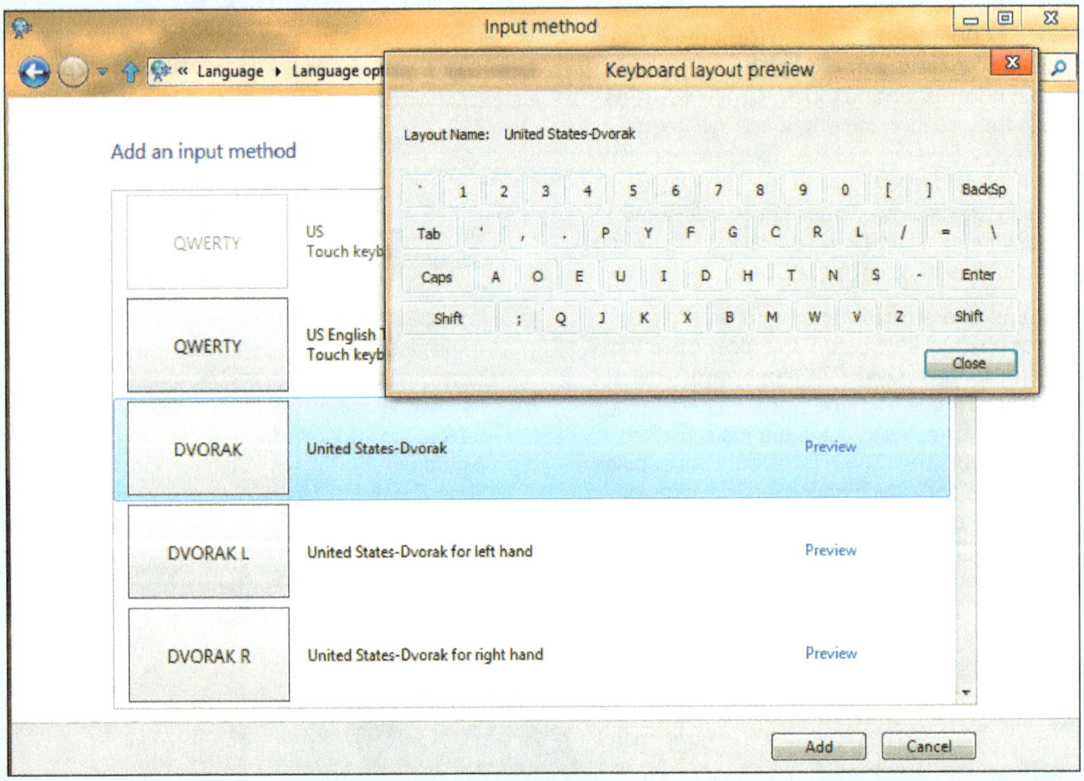

FIGURE 9 You can customize the layout of your keyboard using the Windows operating system.

>To change the keyboard layout in Windows 8.1, open Control Panel, click **Change input methods** *in the Clock, Language, and Region section. Click the* **Options link**. *Click the* **Add an input method** *link. Scroll to find the appropriate keyboard and click the* **Preview link** *to view it. Then left-click the keyboard, and click* **Add**.

Flexible keyboards are a terrific alternative if you want a full-sized keyboard for your laptop, netbook, or tablet. You can roll one up, fit it in your backpack, and plug it into a USB port when you need it. Another compact keyboard alternative is the Magic Cube *virtual laser keyboard* (see Figure 8b) from Cellulon, which is about the size of a cell phone. It projects an image of a keyboard onto any flat surface, and sensors detect the motion of your fingers as you "type." Data is transmitted to the device via Bluetooth. The keyboard works with the latest iPhones, iPads, and Android devices.

How can I use my keyboard most efficiently? All keyboards have the standard set of alphabetic and numeric keys that you regularly use when typing. As shown in Figure 10, many keyboards for laptop and desktop computers have additional keys that perform special functions. Knowing how to use the special keys shown in Figure 10 will help you improve your efficiency.

Mice and Other Pointing Devices

What kinds of mice are there? The mouse type you're probably most familiar with is the **optical mouse**. An optical mouse uses an internal sensor or laser to detect the mouse's movement. The sensor sends signals to the computer, telling it where to move the pointer on the screen. Optical mice don't require a mouse pad, though you can use one to enhance the movement of the mouse on an uneven surface or to protect your work surface from being scratched.

If you have special ergonomic needs or want to customize the functionality of your mouse, there are plenty of options. Most mice have two or three buttons that let you execute commands and open shortcut menus. (Mice for Macs sometimes have only one button.) As shown in Figure 11, many mice, such as the Cyborg R.A.T. 9 Gaming Mouse, have additional programmable buttons and wheels that let you quickly maneuver through web pages or games. In addition, the R.A.T. 9 is customizable to fit any size hand and grip style by allowing for length and width adjustments. Aside from gamers, many people use customizable mice to reduce susceptibility to repetitive strain injuries.

How do wireless mice work? Wireless mice usually connect the same way that wireless keyboards do—either through Bluetooth or a receiver that plugs into a USB port. Wireless mice have receivers that often clip into the bottom of the mouse for easy storage when not in use.

Why would I want to use a mouse with a touch-screen device? If you're using a conventional keyboard with your touch-screen device, it's often easier to perform actions with a mouse rather than taking your hands off the keyboard and reaching to touch the screen. In addition, there are new kinds of mice that are designed with touch-screen computers

FIGURE 10 Keyboards have a variety of keys that help you work more efficiently. (Note that on Macs, function keys are slightly different: The Control function is the Apple key or Command key, and the Alt function is the Option key.)
(Artur Synenko/Shutterstock)

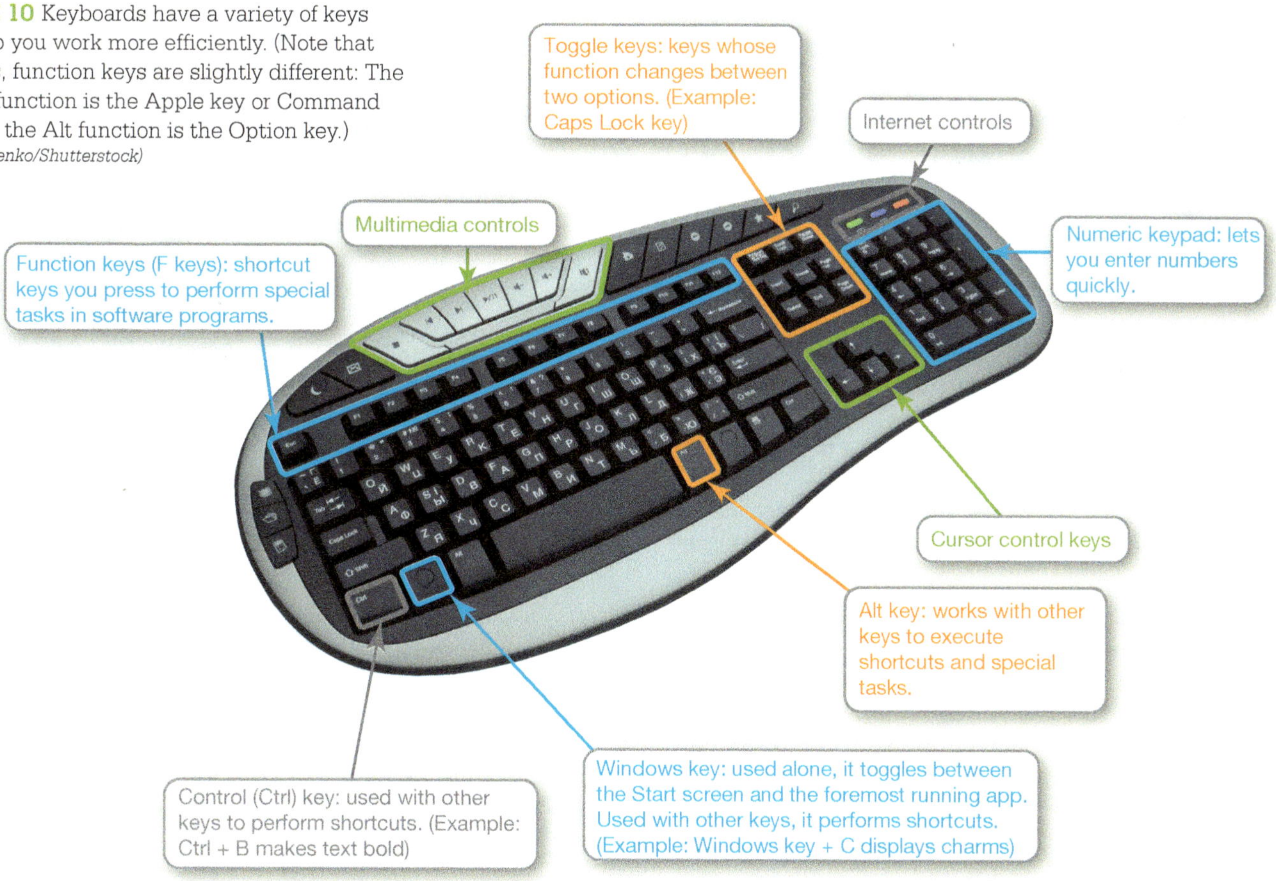

BITS&BYTES

Keystroke Shortcuts

Did you know that you can combine certain keystrokes to take shortcuts within an application, such as Microsoft Word, or within the operating system itself? The following are a few of the most helpful Windows-based shortcuts. For more, visit **support.microsoft.com**. For a list of shortcuts for Macs, see **apple.com/support**.

TEXT FORMATTING	FILE MANAGEMENT	CUT/COPY/PASTE	WINDOWS CONTROLS
Ctrl+B applies (or removes) **bold** formatting to/from selected text.	**Ctrl+O** opens the Open dialog box.	**Ctrl+X** cuts (removes) selected text and stores it in the Clipboard.	**Alt+F4** closes the current window.
Ctrl+I applies (or removes) *italic* formatting to/from selected text.	**Ctrl+N** opens a new document.	**Ctrl+C** copies selected text to the Clipboard.	**Windows Key+Tab** displays open Windows 8 apps.
Ctrl+U applies (or removes) underlining to/from selected text.	**Ctrl+S** saves a document.	**Ctrl+V** pastes selected text (previously cut or copied) from the Clipboard.	**Windows Key+L** locks the computer.
	Ctrl+P opens the Print dialog box.		**Windows Key+F** opens the Search bar in Files mode.

FIGURE 11 Customizable mice offer programmable buttons and adjustable fittings to meet most any need. *(Cyborg)*

in mind. For example, the Logitech Touch Mouse is a multitouch wireless mouse that allows you to perform a variety of touch-screen tasks (see Figure 12). Unlike older mice, there are no specifically defined buttons. The top surface of this mouse is the button. You use one, two, or three fingers to perform touch-screen tasks such as scrolling, switching through open apps, and zooming. The mouse also allows you to perform traditional mouse tasks, such as moving the cursor when you move the mouse.

FIGURE 12 The Logitech Touch Mouse features multitouch technology that lets you perform a variety of touch-screen tasks using the surface of the mouse by tapping, clicking, and using various finger movements. *(© Hugh Threlfall / Alamy)*

Are touch pads considered mice? Most laptops have an integrated pointing device, such as a **touch pad** (or **trackpad**), a small, touch-sensitive area at the base of the keyboard. Mac laptops include multitouch trackpads, which don't have buttons but are controlled by various one-, two-, three-, and four-finger actions. For example, scrolling is controlled by brushing two fingers along the trackpad in any direction. Most touch pads are sensitive to taps, interpreting them as mouse clicks. Most laptops also have buttons under or near the pad to record mouse clicks.

What input devices are used with games? Game controllers such as joysticks, game pads, and steering wheels are also considered input devices because they send data to the computer. Game controllers, which are similar to the devices used on gaming consoles such as the Xbox One and the PlayStation, are also available for use with computers. They have buttons and miniature pointing devices that provide input to the computer. Most game controllers, such as those for Rock Band and the Wii system, are wireless to provide extra mobility.

Image Input

What are popular input devices for images? Digital cameras, camcorders, and cell phones are common devices for capturing pictures and video and are all considered input devices. These devices can connect to your computer with a cable, transmit data wirelessly, or transfer data automatically through the Internet. **Scanners** can also input images. They work similarly to a photocopy machine; however, instead of generating the image on paper, they create a digital image, which you can then print, save, or e-mail.

How do I capture live video from my computing device? A **webcam** is a small camera that sits on top of your computer monitor (connected to your computer by a cable) or is built into a laptop, tablet, or smartphone. Although webcams are able to capture still images, they're used mostly for capturing and transmitting live video. Videoconferencing technology lets a person using a device equipped with a webcam and a microphone transmit video and audio across the Internet. Video call sites such as Skype and ooVoo (see Figure 13) make it easy to videoconference with as many as 12 people. You can also exchange files, swap control of computers, and text message during the call. There is also a mobile application to make it easy to conference on the go.

FIGURE 13 Videoconferencing is simplified with software from **ooVoo.com**.
(Courtesy of ooVoo, LLC.)

DIG DEEPER How Touch Screens Work

Touch-screen technology was developed in 1971 and used primarily with ATMs and fast-food order displays. The technology for monitors and other displays was made popular by the iPod Touch in 2007 and is now in many smartphones, tablets, and laptop and desktop monitors. Windows 8 finally brought the touch-screen interface to Windows users. But how do touch-screen monitors know where you're touching? How do they know what you want them to do?

The basic idea behind touch screens is pretty straightforward—when you place your finger or stylus on a screen, it changes the physical state of the screen and registers your touch. The location of your touch is then translated into a command. Three basic systems are used to recognize a person's touch: *resistive, capacitive,* and *surface acoustic wave*. All of these systems require the basic components of a touch-responsive glass panel, controller, and software driver, combined with a display and computer processor.

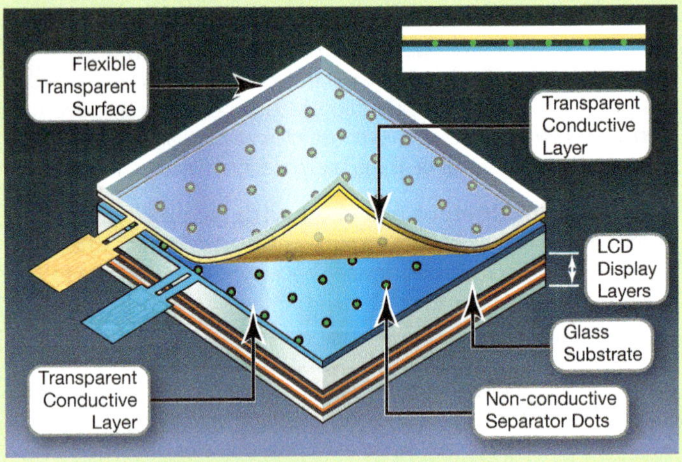

FIGURE 14 Some basic touch screens use a capacitive system to detect touches and translate them into meaningful commands that are understood by the computer's operating system.

The *resistive system* maps the exact location of the pressure point created when a user touches the screen. The *capacitive system* (see Figure 14) uses the change in the electrical charge on the glass panel of the monitor, which is created by the user's touch, to generate a location. The third technology, *surface acoustic wave system,* uses two transducers (electrical devices that convert energy from one form to another) that are placed along the *x* and *y* axes of the monitor's glass plate. Reflectors, which are also placed on the glass, are used to reflect an electric signal sent from the sending transducer to the receiving transducer. The receiving transducer determines whether the signal has been disturbed by a touch event and locates the touch instantly. With all three systems, the display's software driver then translates the touch into something the operating system can understand, similar to how a mouse driver translates a mouse's movements into a click or drag.

Sound Input

How do my computing devices benefit from accepting sound input? In addition to letting others hear you in a videoconference, equipping your device to accept sound input opens up a variety of possibilities. You can conduct audio conferences with work colleagues, chat with friends or family over the Internet, record podcasts, and more. Inputting sound to your computer requires using a **microphone** (or **mic**), a device that lets you capture sound waves (such as your voice) and transfer them to digital format on your computer. Most laptop and tablet computers come with built-in microphones.

What types of add-on microphones are available? For specialized situations, built-in microphones don't always provide the best performance. You may want to consider adding other types of microphones, such as those shown in Figure 16, to your system for the best results. ■

Because the resistive system uses pressure to register a touch, it doesn't matter if the touch is created by a finger or another device. On the other hand, a capacitive system must have conductive input, so generally a finger is required. The surface acoustic wave system allows touches by any object.

The iPhone introduced another complexity to the touch-screen system—a multitouch user interface. In addition to just pressing the screen in one location, multitouch technology can process multiple simultaneous touches on the screen. For example, pinching or spreading out your thumb and finger together makes the display zoom out and in, respectively. The features of each touch, such as size, shape, and location, are also determined.

A touch-sensitive screen, like the one used with the iPhone and iPad and with many other smartphones and tablets, arranges the capacitors in a coordinate system so the circuitry can sense changes at each point along the grid (see Figure 15). Consequently, every point on the grid generates its own signal when touched, and can do so even as another signal is being generated simultaneously. The signals are then relayed to the device's processor. This allows the device to determine the location and movement of simultaneous touches in multiple locations.

After detecting the position and type of touch occurring on the display, the device's processor combines this information with the information it has about the application in use and what was being done in the application when the touch occurred. The processor relays that information to the program in use, and the command is executed. All this happens seemingly instantaneously.

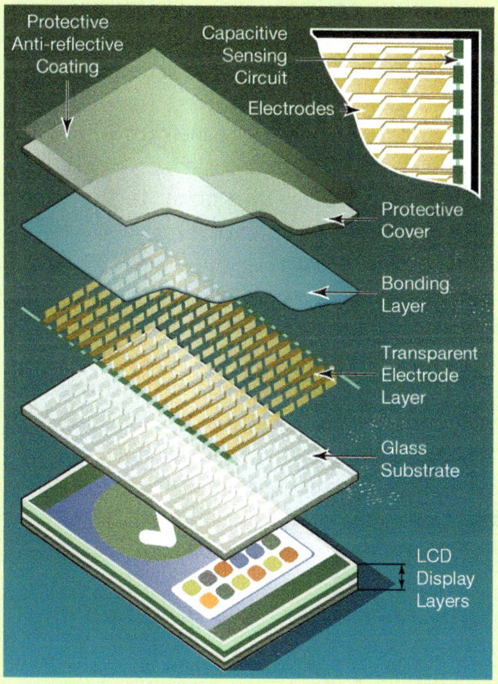

FIGURE 15 Multitouch screens use a coordinate-based grid to arrange the capacitors so the circuitry can detect and respond to multiple touches occurring at the same time.

FIGURE 16

Types of Microphones

MICROPHONE TYPE	ATTRIBUTES	BEST USED FOR	MICROPHONE TYPE	ATTRIBUTES	BEST USED FOR
Close Talk 	• Attached to a headset (allows for listening) • Leaves hands free	• Video conferencing • Phone calls • Speech recognition software	**Unidirectional** 	• Picks up sounds from only one direction	• Recordings with one voice (podcasts)
Omnidirectional 	• Picks up sounds equally well from all directions	• Conference calls in meeting rooms	**Clip-on (Lavalier)** 	• Clips to clothing • Available as wireless	• Presentations requiring freedom of movement • Leaves hands free for writing on whiteboards

(Yuri Arcurs/Fotolia; Blue Microphones; Sumnersgraphicsinc/Fotolia; Feliks Gurevich/Shutterstock)

ethics in IT

What Is Ethical Computing?

You've probably heard news stories about people using computers to unleash viruses or commit identity theft. You may also have read about students who were prosecuted for illegally sharing copyrighted material, such as songs and videos. These are both examples of *unethical* behavior while using a computer. However, what constitutes *ethical* behavior while using a computer?

Loosely defined, *ethics* is a system of moral principles, rules, and accepted standards of conduct (see Figure 17). So what are the accepted standards of conduct when using computers? The Computer Ethics Institute has developed the Ten Commandments of Computer Ethics, which is widely cited as a benchmark for companies developing computer usage and compliance policies for employees. These guidelines are applicable for schools and students, as well. The ethical computing guidelines listed below are based on the Computer Ethics Institute's work:

FIGURE 17 Strive to take the "high road" and behave ethically by not claiming others' work as your own intellectual output. *(Andy Dean Photography/Shutterstock)*

Ethical Computing Guidelines

1. Avoid causing harm to others when using computers.
2. Do not interfere with other people's efforts at accomplishing work with computers.
3. Resist the temptation to snoop in other people's computer files.
4. Do not use computers to commit theft.
5. Agree not to use computers to promote lies.
6. Do not use software (or make illegal copies for others) without paying the creator for it.
7. Avoid using other people's computer resources without appropriate authorization or proper compensation.
8. Do not claim other people's intellectual output as your own.
9. Consider the social consequences of the products of your computer labor.
10. Only use computers in ways that show consideration and respect for others.

The United States has enacted laws that support some of these guidelines, such as Guideline 6, the breaking of which would violate copyright laws, and Guideline 4, which is enforceable under numerous federal and state larceny laws. Other guidelines, however, require more subtle interpretation as to what behavior is unethical because there are no laws designed to enforce them.

Consider Guideline 7, which covers unauthorized use of resources. The school you attend probably provides computer resources for you to use for coursework. But if your school gives you access to computers and the Internet, is it ethical for you to use those resources to run an online business on the weekends? Although it might not be technically illegal, you're tying up computer resources that other students could use for their intended purpose: learning and completing coursework. (This behavior also violates Guidelines 2 and 10.)

Throughout this text, we touch on many topics related to these guidelines. So keep them in mind as you study, and think about how they relate to the actions you take as you use computers in your life.

output DEVICES

An **output device** lets you send processed data out of your computer in the form of text, pictures (graphics), sounds (audio), or video. The most common output device is a **monitor** (sometimes referred to as a **display screen**), which displays text, graphics, and video as soft copies (copies you can see only on screen). Another common output device is the **printer**, which creates hard copies (copies you can touch) of text and graphics. Speakers and earphones (or earbuds) are the output devices for sound.

Monitors

What are the different types of monitors? The most common type of monitor is a **liquid crystal display (LCD)**. An LCD monitor, also called a flat-panel monitor, is light and energy efficient. Some newer monitors use **light-emitting diode (LED)** technology, which is more energy efficient and may have better color accuracy and thinner panels than LCD monitors. LCD flat-panel monitors have replaced cathode ray tube (CRT) monitors. CRT monitors are considered **legacy technology**, or computing devices that use techniques, parts, and methods that are no longer popular. Although legacy technology may still be functional, it has been replaced by newer technological advances.

Organic light-emitting diode (OLED) displays use organic compounds that produce light when exposed to an electric current. Unlike LCDs and LEDs, OLEDs do not require a backlight to function and therefore draw less power and have a much thinner display, sometimes as thin as 3 mm. They are also brighter and more environmentally friendly than LCDs. Because of their lower power needs, OLED displays run longer on a single battery charge than do LEDs, which is why OLED technology is probably the technology used in your cell phone, iPod, and digital camera.

Companies like Samsung are now working on transparent OLED display screens (see Figure 18). These screens allow you to see what is behind the screen while still being able to display information on the screen. These types of screens present interesting possibilities for augmented reality. *Augmented reality (AR)* is a view of a real-world environment whose elements are *augmented* (or supplemented) by some type of computer-generated sensory input such as video, graphics, or GPS data. For instance, if you had a transparent screen on your smartphone and held it up to view street signs that were in English, you could possibly have your phone display the signs in another language. Currently, applications like this exist but require the use of a camera as well as your screen. But transparent screens will eliminate the need for the camera.

How do LCD monitors work? Monitor screens are grids made up of millions of tiny dots, called **pixels**. When these pixels are illuminated by the light waves generated by a fluorescent panel at the back of your screen, they create the images you see on the screen or monitor. Each pixel is actually made up of three red, blue, and green subpixels; some newer LCD TVs on the market have even added a fourth color: yellow. LCD monitors are made of two or more sheets of material filled with a liquid crystal solution (see Figure 19). A fluorescent panel at the back of the LCD monitor generates light waves. When electric current passes through the liquid crystal solution, the crystals move around and either block the fluorescent light or let the light shine through. This blocking or passing of light by the crystals causes images to form on the screen. The various combinations of red, blue, and green make up the components of color we see on our monitors.

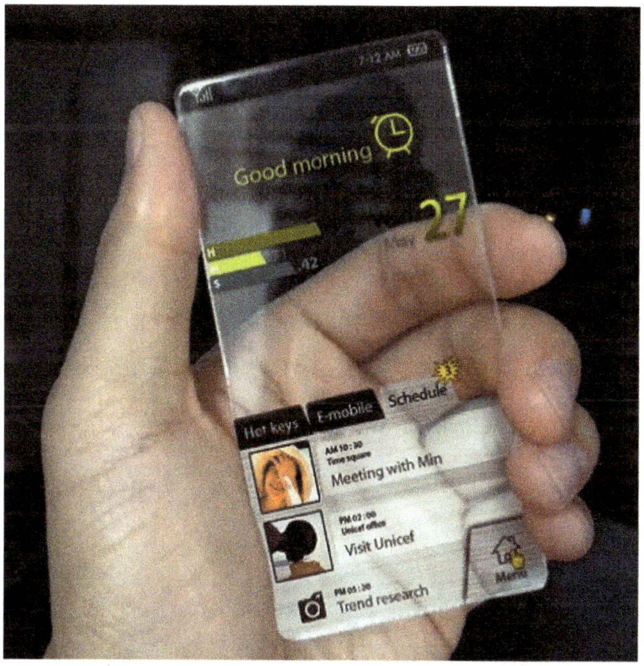

FIGURE 18 Because they don't need a backlight, OLED displays can be made transparent. *(PhotoAlto/Milena Boniek/Getty Images)*

What factors affect the quality of an LCD monitor? When choosing an LCD monitor, the most important factors to consider are aspect ratio and resolution. The **aspect ratio** is the width-to-height proportion of a monitor. Traditionally, aspect ratios have been 4:3, but newer monitors are available with an aspect ratio of 16:9 to accommodate HD format video. The screen **resolution**, or the clearness or sharpness of the image, reflects the number of pixels on the screen. An LCD monitor may have a native (or maximum) resolution of 1600 × 1200, meaning it contains 1,600 vertical columns with 1,200 pixels

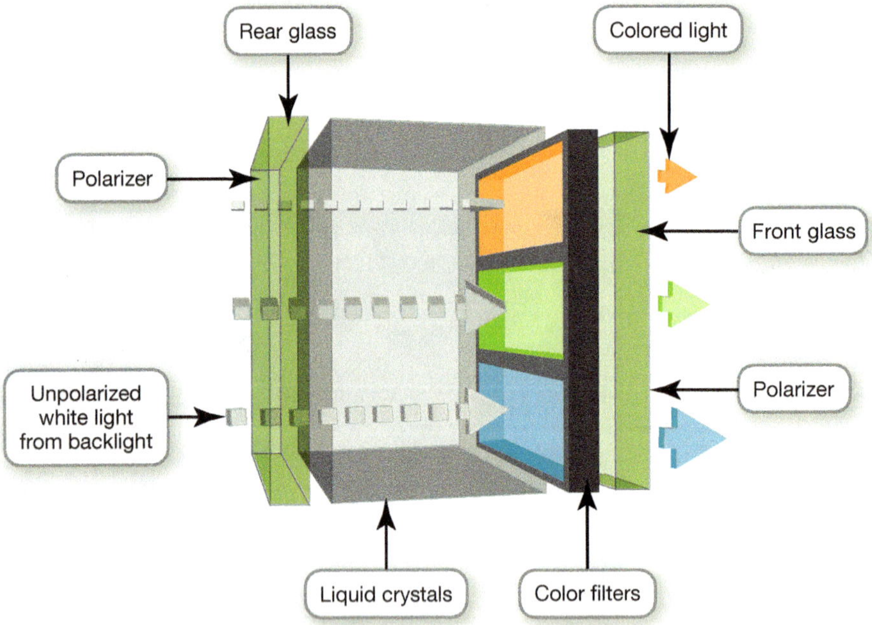

FIGURE 19 A magnification of a single pixel in an LCD monitor.

in each column. The higher the resolution, the sharper and clearer the image will be, but generally, the resolution of an LCD monitor is dictated by the screen size and aspect ratio. Although you can change the resolution of an LCD monitor beyond its native resolution, the images will become distorted. Generally, you should buy a monitor with the highest resolution available for the screen size (measured in inches). Figure 20 lists these and other factors to consider when judging the quality of an LCD monitor.

Is a bigger screen size always better? The bigger the monitor, the more you can display, and depending on what you want to display, size may matter. In general, the larger the panel, the larger number of pixels it can display. For example, a 27-inch monitor can display 2560 × 1440 pixels, whereas a 21.5-inch monitor may only be able to display 1680 × 1050 pixels. However, most new monitors have at least the 1920 × 1080 resolution required to display Blu-ray movies.

Larger screens can also allow you to view multiple documents or web pages at the same time, creating the effect of using two separate monitors side by side. Buying two smaller monitors might be cheaper than buying one large monitor. For either option—a big screen or two separate screens—check that your computer has the appropriate video hardware to support these display devices.

What other features should I look for in an LCD monitor? Some monitors, especially those on laptop

FIGURE 20

Factors to Consider When Shopping for a Monitor

FACTOR	POSSIBLE PROBLEMS	LOOK FOR
Aspect ratio: Width-to-height proportion of a screen	• An odd aspect ratio may make images look distorted	• Ratios of 4:3 or 16:9 (HDTV)
Screen resolution: Number of pixels displayed on the screen	• Low screen resolution = unclear image • High resolution on a small size monitor results in image being too small	• Highest resolution monitor is capable of displaying (make sure you are comfortable viewing that size image)
Contrast ratio: Difference in light intensity between brightest white and darkest black a monitor can produce	• Ratio too low results in colors fading when adjusting brightness	• Ratios between 400:1 and 1,000:1
Viewing angle: Distance in degrees from which you can move to the side of (or above or below) a monitor before the image degrades	• Angle too low means people not sitting directly in front of the monitor will see a poor image	• 150 degrees or more is preferable
Brightness: Greatest amount of light showing when the monitor is displaying pure white (measured in candelas per square meter [cd/m^2] or *nits*)	• Image will be hard to see in bright rooms if brightness level is too low	• 300 cd/m^2 or greater
Response time: Time it takes for a pixel to change color (in milliseconds)	• High response time results in images appearing jerky	• Seek lowest possible response time if viewing live action sports

BITS&BYTES

Testing and Calibrating Your PC Monitor

Most new PC monitors don't need color or tint adjustments, but some can benefit from a few tweaks that will ultimately enhance your video experience. This might be especially important if you're a web designer, digital photographer, or graphics professional. In those professions especially, you want to make sure the colors are displayed on the monitor as accurately as possible. Before you start the calibration process, check that your monitor is set to the "native" resolution (usually the recommended setting). Some monitors have their own calibration program; otherwise, you can work through the adjustments manually or use the display utility in your operating system.

If you're running Windows, you can use the Display Color Calibration utility found by displaying the Control Panel and then clicking Appearance and Personalization. Click Display, and then in the Navigation Pane, click Calibrate color. The Display Color Calibration utility will check the gamma, brightness, contrast, and color balance settings. Gamma describes the relationship between the varying levels of brightness a monitor can display. Brightness determines how dark colors appear on your display. When brightness is set too high, dark colors appear washed out. Contrast determines how white and light colors display. (Note that most laptop computers don't have controls to adjust contrast.) Color balance makes adjustments to the red, blue, and green controls.

computers, come with built-in features such as speakers, webcams, and microphones. A built-in multiformat memory card reader is convenient for displaying images directly on the monitor or for downloading pictures quickly from a camera memory card to your PC. Another nice feature to look for in a desktop LCD monitor is a built-in USB port. This feature lets you connect extra peripherals easily without reaching around the back of the PC.

How do I show output to a large group of people? A **projector** lets you project images from your computing device onto a wall or viewing screen. Projectors are commonly used in business and education settings such as conference rooms and classrooms. Many projectors are small and lightweight, and some, such as the 3M MPro 150 (see Figure 21), are small enough to fit in the palm of your hand. These portable projectors are ideal for businesspeople who have to make presentations at client locations. ***Entertainment projectors,*** such as the Discovery Expedition, include stereo speakers and an array of multimedia connectors, making them a good option for use in the home to display TV programs, DVDs, digital images, or video games in a large format. If your computing device is equipped with an HDMI port, you can also choose to connect your computer directly to an HDTV.

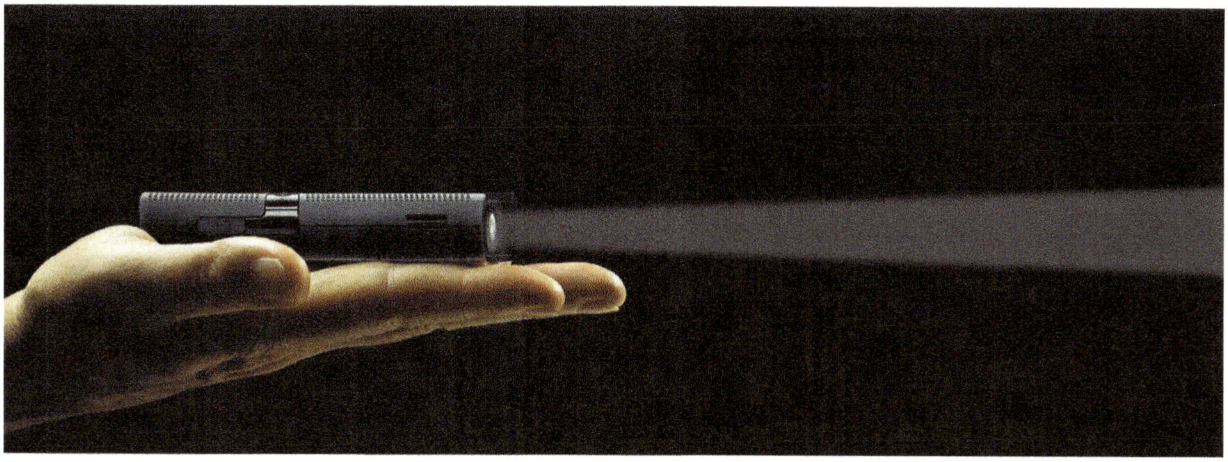

FIGURE 21 Inexpensive projectors are showing up more frequently in business and the home to provide large images for movie viewing and gaming. *(3M)*

Printers

What are the different types of printers? There are two primary categories of printers: inkjet and laser, both of which are considered nonimpact printers. A **nonimpact printer** such as an inkjet printer sprays ink or uses laser beams to transfer marks onto the paper. An **impact printer** has tiny hammer-like keys that strike the paper through an inked ribbon to make marks on the paper. For most users, impact printers are legacy technology.

What are the advantages of inkjet printers? An **inkjet printer** (see Figure 22) is the type of printer found in many homes. These printers are popular because they're affordable and produce high-quality printouts quickly and quietly. Inkjet printers work by spraying tiny drops of ink onto paper and are great for printing black-and-white text as well as color images. In fact, when loaded with the right paper, higher-end inkjet printers can print images that look like professional-quality photos. One thing to consider when buying an inkjet printer is the type and cost of the ink cartridges the printer needs. Some printers use two cartridges: black and color. Others use four or more cartridges: typically, black, magenta, cyan, and yellow.

Why would I want a laser printer? A **laser printer** uses laser beams and static electricity to deliver toner (similar to ink) onto the correct areas of the page (see Figure 23). Heat is used to fuse the toner to the page, making the image permanent. Laser printers are often used in office or classroom settings because they print faster than inkjet printers and produce higher-quality printouts. Black-and-white laser printers have also been common in homes for a decade. Over the past few years, the price of color laser printers has fallen dramatically, making them price competitive with high-end inkjet printers. Thus, color laser printers are a viable option for the home. If you print a high volume of pages, consider a laser printer. When you include the price of ink or toner in the overall cost, color laser printers can be more economical than inkjets.

FIGURE 23 Laser printers print quickly and offer high-quality printouts. *(Courtesy of Xerox Corporation)*

What's the best way to print from portable devices such as tablets and smartphones? Wireless printers are a good option for home networks as they let several people print to the same printer from different devices and any location in the home. There are two types of wireless printers: WiFi and Bluetooth. Both WiFi and Bluetooth printers have a range of up to approximately 300 feet. WiFi, however, sends data more quickly than Bluetooth.

Wireless printers are also great for printing from portable devices. If you're using a device running Apple's iOS (such as an iPhone), AirPrint makes printing easy. AirPrint is a feature of iOS that facilitates printing to AirPrint-compatible wireless printers, and many printers produced today are AirPrint compatible.

For non-Apple mobile devices (or if your printer isn't compatible with AirPrint), you should try other solutions, such as Presto by Collobos Software and ThinPrint Cloud Printer by Cortado. Once you install one of these apps on your portable device, you can send documents to printers that are connected to PCs and Macs on your home network. It makes printing from mobile devices as simple as hitting print on your laptop.

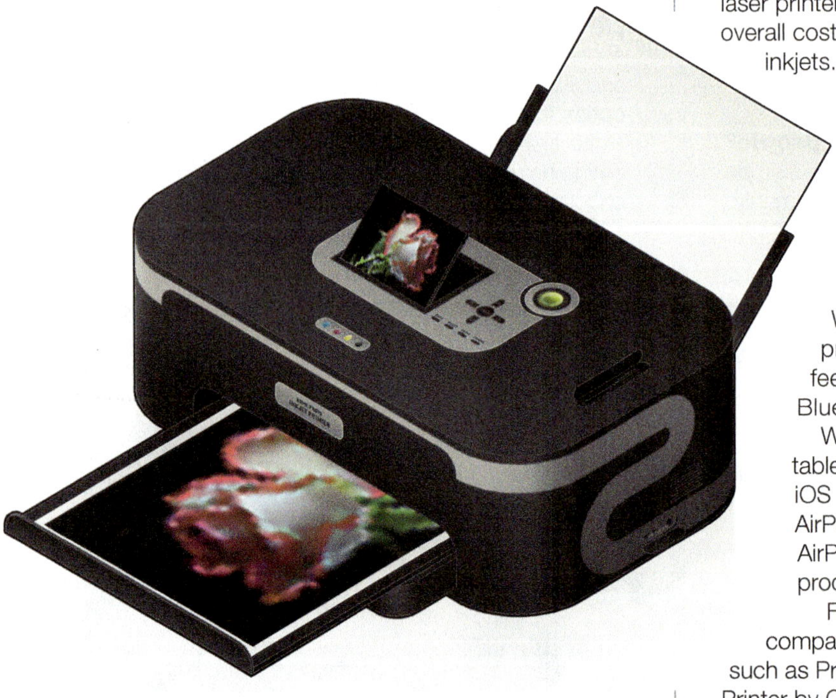

FIGURE 22 Inkjet printers are popular among home users, especially with the rise of digital photography. Many inkjet printers are optimized for printing photos from digital cameras. *(The Vectorminator/Shutterstock)*

a

b

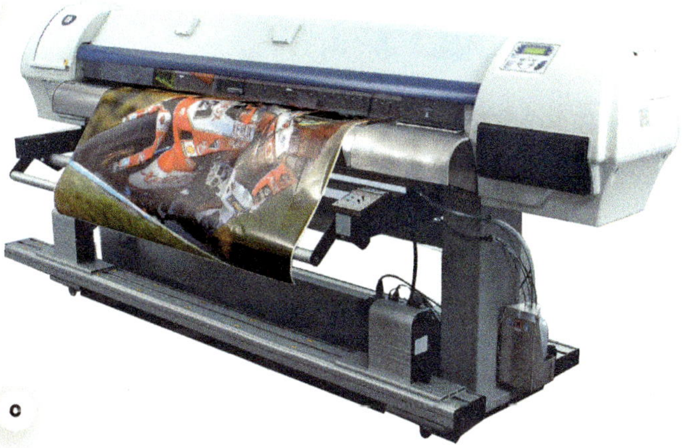

c

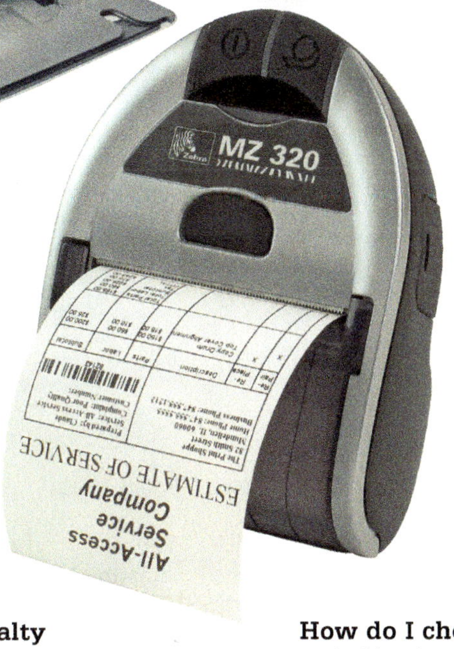

FIGURE 24 Specialty printers: (a) all-in-one printer, (b) plotter, (c) thermal printer. *(Adisa/Fotolia; Provided Courtesy of Xerox Corporation; Zebra Technologies)*

Can I carry my printer with me? Although some inkjet printers are small enough to be considered portable, you may want to consider a printer designed for portability. These compact printers can connect to your computer, tablet, or smartphone via Bluetooth technology or through a USB port. Portable printers are often compact enough to fit in a briefcase or backpack, are lightweight, and can run on batteries as well as AC power.

Are there any other types of specialty printers? Although you'll probably use laser or inkjet printers most often, you might also encounter several other types of printers (shown in Figure 24):

- An **all-in-one printer** combines the functions of a printer, scanner, copier, and fax into one machine. Popular for their space-saving convenience, all-in-one printers may use either inkjet or laser technology.
- A **plotter** prints oversize pictures that require the drawing of precise and continuous lines, such as maps and architectural plans. Plotters use a computer-controlled pen that provides a greater level of precision than the series of dots that laser or inkjet printers make.
- A **thermal printer** works either by melting wax-based ink onto ordinary paper (a process called *thermal wax transfer printing*) or by burning dots onto specially coated paper (a process called *direct thermal printing*). Thermal printers are used in stores to print receipts and in airports for electronic ticketing, and many models feature wireless technology. Thermal printers are also popular for mobile printing in conjunction with smartphones and tablets.

How do I choose the best printer? Your first step is to decide what your primary printing need is. If you're planning to print color photos and graphics, an inkjet printer or color laser printer is a must, even though the cost per page will be higher. If you'll be printing mostly black-and-white, text-based documents or will be sharing your printer with others, a black-and-white laser printer is best because of its speed and overall economy for volume printing. It's also important to determine whether you want just a printer or a device that prints and scans, copies, or faxes (an all-in-one). In addition, you should decide whether you need to print from mobile devices.

Once you have narrowed down the *type* of printer you want, you can use the criteria listed in Figure 25 to help you determine the best model to meet your needs.

> **ACTIVE HELPDESK**
> **Using Output Devices**
> In this Active Helpdesk call, you'll play the role of a helpdesk staffer, fielding calls about different output devices.

Sound Output

What are the output devices for sound? Most computers include inexpensive **speakers**, which are the output devices for sound. These speakers are sufficient to play the standard audio clips you find on the web and usually for letting you participate in videoconferencing or phone

BITS&BYTES

Does It Matter What Paper I Print On?

The quality of your printer is only part of what controls the quality of a printed image. The paper you use and the printer settings that control the amount of ink used are equally important.

- If you're printing text-only documents for personal use, using low-cost paper is fine. You also may want to consider selecting draft mode in your printer settings to conserve ink. However, if you're printing more formal documents, such as business correspondence, you may want to choose a higher-quality paper (determined by the paper's weight, whiteness, and brightness) and adjust your print setting to "normal" or "best."
- The weight of paper is measured in pounds, with 20 pounds being standard. A heavier paper may be best for projects such as brochures, but be sure to check that your printer can handle the added thickness of the paper.
- The degree of paper whiteness is a matter of personal preference. Generally, the whiter the paper, the brighter the printed color. However, for documents that are more formal, you may want to use a creamier color.
- The brightness of paper usually varies from 85 to 94. The higher the number, the brighter the paper, and the easier it is to read printed text.
- Opacity, or the "show through" of ink from one side of the paper to the other, is especially important if you're printing on both sides of the paper.

If you're printing photos, paper quality can have a big impact on your results. Photo paper is more expensive than regular paper and comes in a variety of textures ranging from matte to high gloss. For a photo-lab look, high-gloss paper is the best choice. Semigloss (often referred to as satin) is good for formal portraits, while a matte surface is often used for black-and-white photo printing.

calls over the Internet. However, if you plan to digitally edit audio files or are particular about how your music sounds, you may want a more sophisticated speaker system, such as one that includes subwoofers (special speakers that produce only low bass sounds) and surround-sound speakers. A **surround-sound speaker** is a system of speakers and audio processing that envelops the listener in a 360-degree field of sound. In addition, wireless speaker systems are available to help you avoid cluttering up your rooms with speaker wires.

FIGURE 25

Major Printer Attributes

ATTRIBUTE	CONSIDERATIONS
Speed 	• Print speed is measured in *pages per minute (PPM)*. • Black-and-white documents print faster than color documents. • Laser printers often print faster than inkjets.

Resolution 	• Resolution refers to a printer's image clarity.
	• Resolution is measured in *dots per inch (dpi)*.
	• Higher dpi = greater level of detail and clarity.
	• Recommended dpi:
	  • Black-and-white text: 300
	  • General purpose images: 1200
	  • Photos: 4800

Color Output 	• Printers with separate cartridges for each color produce the best quality output. • Inkjet and laser color printers generally have four cartridges (black, cyan, magenta, and yellow). • Higher-quality printers have six cartridges (the four above plus light cyan and light magenta). • With separate cartridges, you only need to replace the empty one.
Cost of Consumables 	• Consumables are printer cartridges and paper. • Printer cartridges can exceed the cost of some printers. • Consumer magazines such as *Consumer Reports* can help you research costs.

(Freshidea/Fotolia; Michael Nivelet/Fotolia; ThomasAmby/Fotolia; Tomislav Forgo/Fotolia)

If you work in close proximity to other employees or travel with a laptop, you may need to use headphones or earbuds to avoid distracting other people. Both devices plug into the same jack on the computing device to which speakers connect. Studies of users of portable media players have shown that hearing might be damaged by excessive volume, especially when using earbuds because they fit into the ear canals. Exercise caution when using these devices. ■

Before moving on to Part 2:

- **Watch Replay Video 1**.
- Then check your understanding of what you've learned so far.

check your understanding//

For a quick review to see what you've learned so far, answer the following questions. Visit **pearsonhighered.com/techinaction** to check your answers.

multiple choice

1. Which of the following is NOT one of the four major functions of a computer?
   - **a.** input
   - **b.** processing
   - **c.** storage
   - **d.** indexing
2. A large, expensive computer that supports many users simultaneously and that businesses use to manage large amounts of data is
   - **a.** a mainframe computer.
   - **b.** a supercomputer.
   - **c.** an embedded computer.
   - **d.** none of the above.
3. Which of the following is both an input device and an output device?
   - **a.** a touch-screen monitor
   - **b.** an optical mouse
   - **c.** speakers
   - **d.** a laser printer
4. What printer produces the highest-resolution images?
   - **a.** inkjet
   - **b.** thermal
   - **c.** laser
   - **d.** impact
5. Which is NOT important to consider when buying a monitor?
   - **a.** screen resolution
   - **b.** viewing angle
   - **c.** color depth
   - **d.** aspect ratio

true–false

_____ **1.** Data is information that has been organized.

_____ **2.** A gigabyte is around 1 billion bytes.

critical thinking

1. **Computer of the Future**

   Think about how mobile our computing devices have become and the convergence of different devices such as cameras, phones, and computers. What do you think the computer of the future will be like? What capabilities will it have that computers currently don't have? Do you see desktop or laptop computers becoming obsolete in the near future?

2. **Integrating Tablets into the Workplace**

   Currently, laptop and desktop computer dominate most workplaces while tablet computers are relegated mostly to personal use. What types of businesses do you think are ready for a broader use of tablet computers for their employees? What changes in current tablets do you think are required to make them more functional in the workplace?

3. **Ethics Violations**

   Review the Ethics in IT section in this chapter. Which of the Ten Ethical Computing Guidelines do you think students violate most often? Why do you think these violations occur, and what do you think could be done to reduce or eliminate such unethical behaviors?

Continue »

TRY THIS What's Inside My Computer?

Understanding what capabilities your current computer has is one of the first steps toward computer literacy. In this exercise, you'll learn how to explore the components of your Windows computer.

Step 1 To gather information about the storage devices on your computer, on the Start screen, click **File Explorer** (previously called Windows Explorer) to switch to the Desktop and display File Explorer. In the navigation pane, click **Computer** to display information about your computer's drives.

Step 2 The File Explorer Computer screen displays information about internal storage devices (such as internal hard drives), optical storage devices (such as DVD drives), and portable storage devices (such as flash drives and external hard drives). The total amount of usable storage space, as well as the amount of space actually free (unused), on the devices is shown.

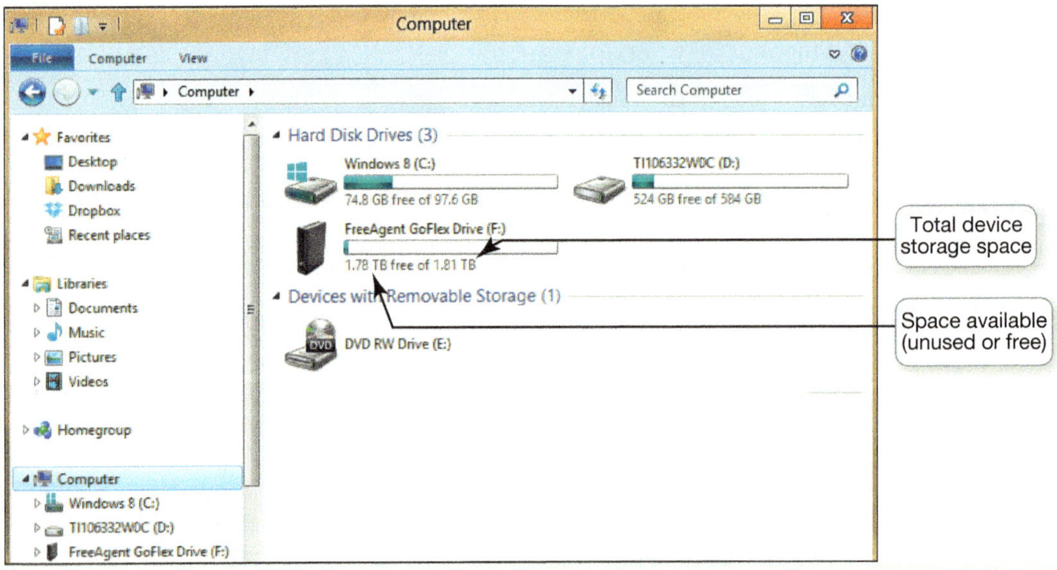

Step 3 To display the System screen, click the **Computer** tab on the File Explorer Ribbon, and then click the **Properties** button.

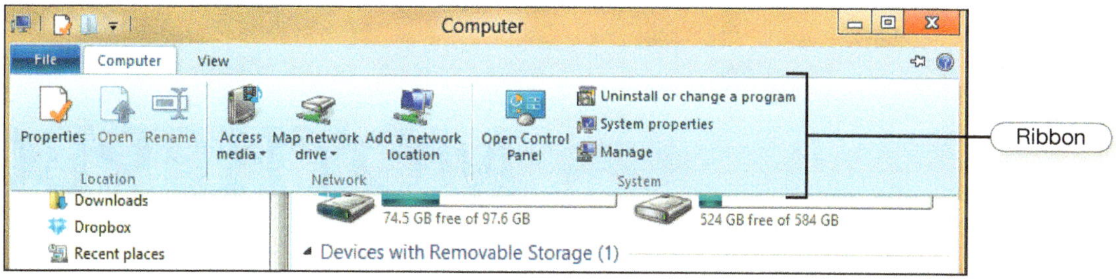

Step 4 You can gather quite a bit of information from the System screen, such as:

- Version of Windows
- Type of processor
- Speed of the processor
- Amount of RAM installed
- System type (32-bit or 64-bit)

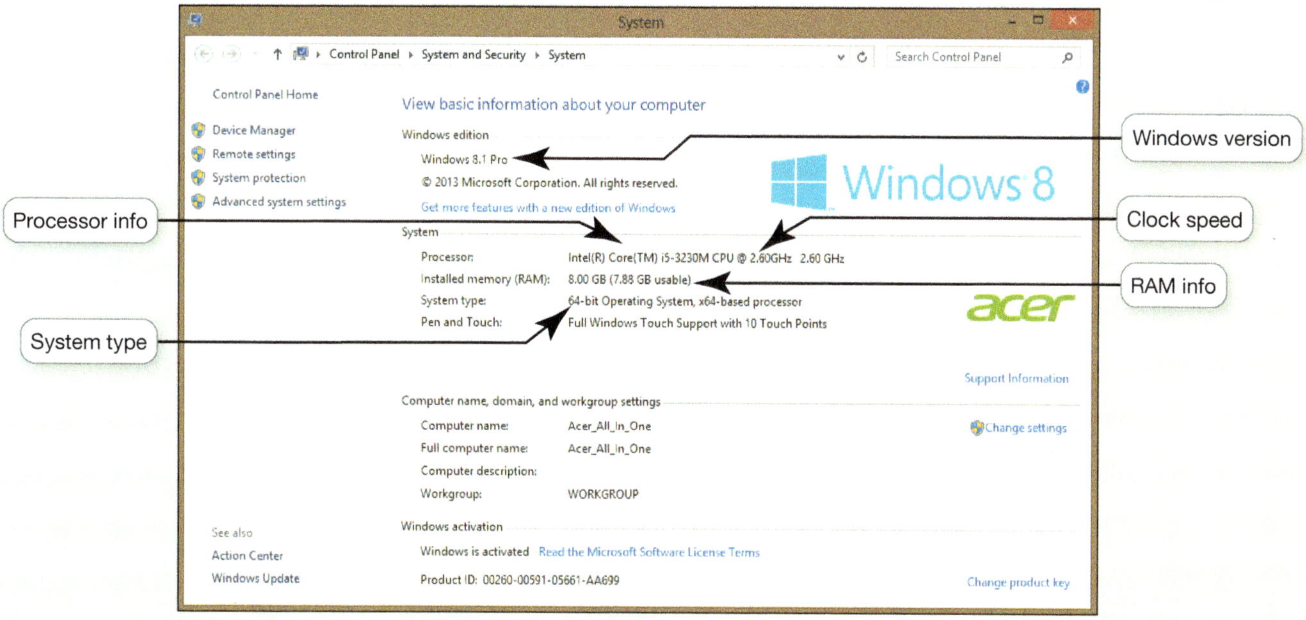

Processing, Storage, and Connectivity

So far, we have explored the components of your computer that you use to input and output data. But where does the processing take place, and where is the data stored? And how does your computer connect with peripherals and other computers?

processing and memory on the MOTHERBOARD

The **motherboard** is the main circuit board that contains the central electronic components of the computer, including the computer's processor (CPU), its memory, and the many circuit boards that help the computer function (see Figure 26). On a desktop, the motherboard is located inside the system unit, the metal or plastic case that also houses the power source and all the storage devices (CD/DVD drive and hard drive). In a laptop or all-in-one computer, the system unit is combined with the monitor and the keyboard into a single package.

What's on the motherboard besides the CPU and memory? The motherboard also includes slots for **expansion cards** (or **adapter cards**), which are circuit boards that provide additional functionality. Typical expansion cards found in the system unit are sound and video cards. A **sound card** provides a connection for the speakers and microphone, whereas a **video card** provides a connection for the monitor. Laptops and tablets have video and sound capabilities integrated into their motherboards. High-end desktops use expansion cards to provide video and sound capabilities.

Other expansion cards provide a means for network and Internet connections. A **network interface card (NIC)**, which enables your computer to connect with other computers or to a cable modem to facilitate a high-speed Internet connection, is often integrated into the motherboard. Lastly, some expansion cards provide additional USB and FireWire ports.

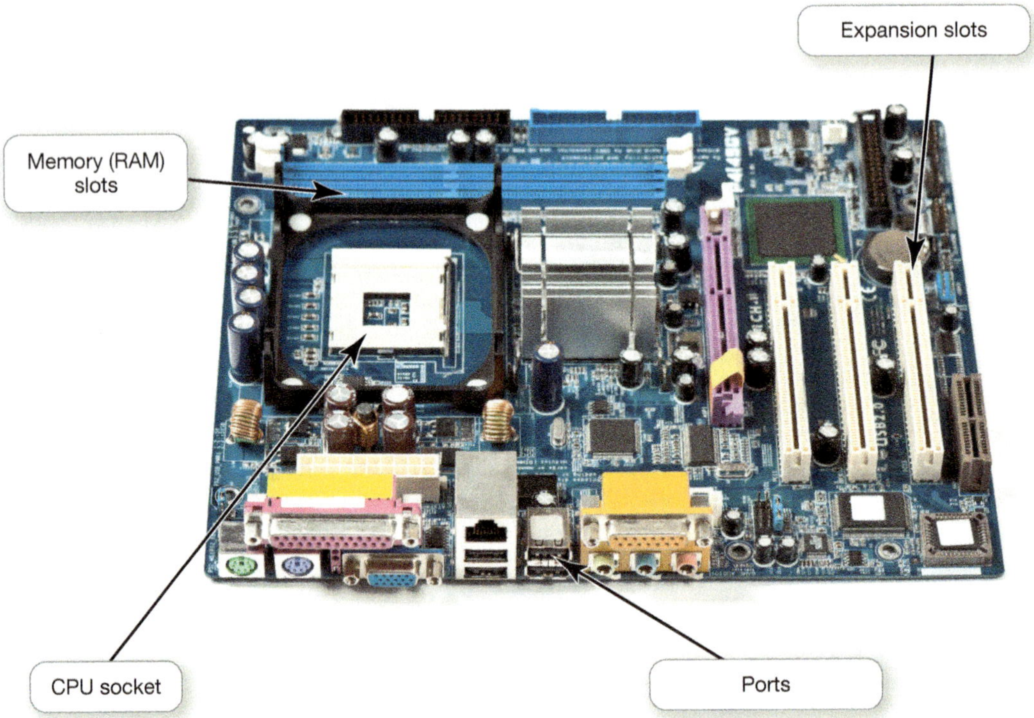

FIGURE 26 A motherboard contains the socket for the computer's processor (CPU), the memory (RAM) modules, ports, and slots for expansion cards. *(S.Dashkevych/Shutterstock)*

Memory

What exactly is RAM? Random access memory (RAM) is the place in a computer where the programs and data the computer is currently using are stored. RAM is much faster to read from and write to than the hard drive and other forms of storage. The processor can request the RAM's contents, which can be located, opened, and delivered to the CPU for processing in a few nanoseconds (billionths of a second). If you look at a motherboard, you'll see RAM as a series of small cards (called *memory cards* or *memory modules*) plugged into slots on the motherboard (see Figure 26).

Because the entire contents of RAM are erased when you turn off the computer, RAM is a temporary or **volatile storage** location. To save data permanently, you need to save it to your hard drive or to another permanent storage device such as a CD or flash drive.

Does the motherboard contain any other kinds of memory besides RAM? In addition to RAM, the motherboard contains a form of memory called **read-only memory (ROM)**. ROM holds all the instructions the computer needs to start up when it's powered on. Unlike data stored in RAM, which is volatile storage, the instructions stored in ROM are permanent, making ROM a **nonvolatile storage** location, which means the data isn't erased when the power is turned off.

Processing

What is the CPU? The **central processing unit (CPU,** or **processor)** is sometimes referred to as the "brains" of the computer because it controls all the functions performed by the computer's other components and processes all the commands issued to it by software instructions. Modern CPUs can perform as many as tens of billions of tasks per second without error, making them extremely powerful components.

How is processor speed measured? Processor speed is measured in units of hertz (Hz). Hertz is a measurement of machine cycles per second. A machine cycle is the process of the CPU getting the data or instructions from RAM and decoding the instructions into something the computer can understand. Once the CPU has decoded the instructions, it executes them and stores the result back in system memory. Current systems run at speeds measured in **gigahertz (GHz)**, or billions of machine cycles per second. Therefore, a 3.8 GHz processor performs work at a rate of 3.8 billion machine cycles per second. It's important to realize, however, that CPU processor speed alone doesn't determine the performance of the CPU.

What else determines processor performance? Although speed is an important consideration when determining processor performance, CPU performance is also affected by other factors. One factor is the number of *cores,* or processing paths, a processor has. Initially, processors could handle only one instruction at a time. Now, processors have been designed so that they can have two, four, or even eight different paths, allowing them to process more than one instruction at a time (see Figure 27). Applications such as virus protection software and the operating system, which are always running behind the scenes, can have their own processor paths, freeing up the other paths to run other applications such as a web browser, Word, or iTunes more efficiently.

Besides the number of cores, what other factors determine processing power? The "best" processor will depend on your particular needs and is not always the processor with the highest processor speed and the greatest number of cores. Intel, one of the leading manufacturers of computer processor chips, has created a pictorial rating system for CPU chips. Intel uses one to five stars to illustrate the relative computing power of each type of CPU within the Intel line of processors. ■

> SOUND BYTE
> **Virtual Computer Tour**
> In this Sound Byte, you'll take a video tour of the inside of a desktop system unit. From opening the cover to locating the power supply, CPU, and memory, you'll become more familiar with what's inside your computer.

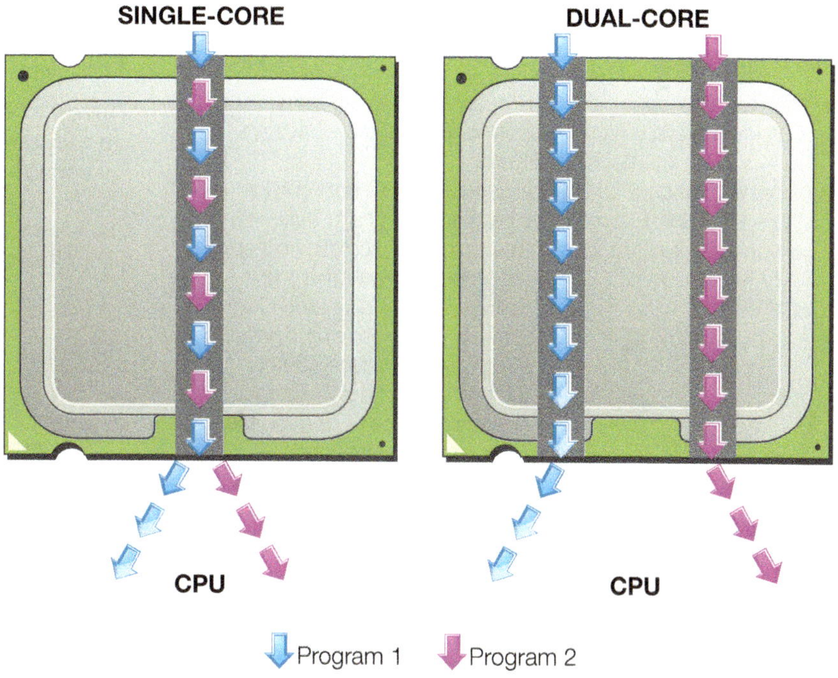

FIGURE 27 With multi-core processors, CPUs can work in parallel, processing two or more separate programs at the same time instead of switching back and forth between them.

storing data and INFORMATION

Because RAM is volatile storage, it can't be used to store information indefinitely. To save your data and information permanently, you need to save it to a nonvolatile storage device, such as a hard drive, cloud storage location, DVD, or flash drive.

Hard Drives

Are there different kinds of hard drives? The **hard disk drive (HDD,** or **hard drive)** is your computer's primary device for permanent storage of software and documents. The hard drive is a nonvolatile storage device. An **internal hard drive** resides within the system unit and usually holds all permanently stored programs and data. Today's internal hard drives (see Figure 28) have capacities of as much as 8 TB or more. **External hard drives** offer similar storage capacities but reside outside the system unit and connect to the computer via a port.

The most common type of hard drive has moveable parts—spinning platters, a moving arm with a read/write head—that can fail and lead to devastating disk failure. However, the **solid-state drive (SSD)** has recently become a popular option for ultrabooks and laptop storage. SSDs have no moving parts, so they're more efficient, run with no noise, emit little heat, and require little power. In addition, they're less likely to fail after being bumped or dropped.

Permanent storage devices are located in your desktop or laptop computer in a space called a **drive bay**. There are two kinds of drive bays:

1. *Internal drive bays* cannot be seen or accessed from outside the system unit. Generally, internal drive bays are reserved for internal hard drives.
2. *External drive bays* can be seen and accessed from outside the system unit. External drive bays house CD and DVD drives, for example. On desktop computers, sometimes there are empty external drive bays that can be used to install additional drives. These extra spaces are covered by a faceplate on the front panel. Laptop computers generally do not give you the ability to add additional drives. Such expansion is done by attaching an external drive to the computer through a USB port.

FIGURE 28 Internal hard drives are a computer's primary nonvolatile storage. *(Ragnarock/Shutterstock)*

Cloud Storage

How can I easily access my files if I constantly switch between devices? You may find yourself using multiple devices, such as a smartphone, laptop, and a tablet, at different times during the day. Invariably, you'll find you need access to a current version of a file that is stored on a device other than the one you're using. If your devices are connected to the Internet, cloud storage provides a convenient option.

Cloud storage refers to using a service that keeps your files on the Internet (in the "cloud") rather than storing your files solely on a local device. Using a cloud storage service requires that you install software/an app on your device. A popular web-based application for storing files on the cloud is Dropbox. Dropbox supports computers running Windows, OS X, and Linux as well as many smartphones and tablets. After installing the Dropbox software on your devices, any files you save in the Dropbox folder are accessible to all your other devices via the Internet. You can also share folders in Dropbox with other Dropbox users, making it ideal for group projects.

For example, when you save a history term paper to Dropbox on your laptop, the Dropbox software also copies the paper up onto a computer attached to the web. Now when you grab your smartphone and head off to class, you can access the paper created on your laptop through the Internet connection on your smartphone and make changes to it if necessary.

Dropbox storage capacity is limited to between 2 GB and 8 GB for free accounts. Other cloud storage alternatives include Microsoft OneDrive which provides 7 GB of free space, and Apple iCloud and Google Drive, which each offer 5 GB of free storage.

Portable Storage Options

How can I take my files with me without relying on cloud storage? For large portable storage needs, there are portable external hard drives, which are small enough to fit into your pocket and have storage capacities of 4 TB (or larger). These devices are lightweight and enclosed in a protective case. They attach to your computer via a USB port (see Figure 29).

FIGURE 29 Smaller, portable external hard drives enable you to take a significant amount of data and programs on the road with you. *(Inga Nielsen/Shutterstock)*

BITS&BYTES

Taking Care of Flash Drives

Although they're fairly rugged and can withstand much abuse, flash drives can fail. Therefore, it's important to know how to care for your flash drive to extend its life and keep your data safe.

1. Don't expose your flash drive to moisture or extreme temperatures.
2. Keep the end covered or closed when not in use. This prevents dust and other particles from interfering with the connections.
3. Never "defragment" a flash drive, as doing so can reduce its life expectancy.
4. A flash drive has a limited amount of writes in its lifetime. Depending on the device, it could be 10,000 or 100,000, which seems like a lot. However, over years of extensive use, the number of writes will add up. It's best to make edits to documents on the computer and then transfer the finished document to your flash drive.
5. Remove the flash drive correctly. All files and folders must be closed, with no active documents running, before the device is removed. To properly eject the device, use the "Safely remove hardware" feature in the taskbar, or select Eject from Windows Explorer (called File Explorer in Windows 8). (Mac users should select Eject from the Finder menu.) If you find that you can't eject the flash drive using these methods, power down the computer before removing the drive.

A **flash drive** (sometimes referred to as a **jump drive**, **USB drive**, or **thumb drive**) uses solid-state flash memory, storing information on an internal memory chip. When you plug a flash drive into your computer's USB port, it appears in the operating system as another disk drive. You can write data to it or read data from it as you would a hard drive. Because a flash drive contains no moving parts, it's quite durable. It's also tiny enough to fit in your pocket. Despite their size, flash drives can have significant storage capacity—currently as much as 256 GB. Often, flash drives are combined with other devices such as pens or pocketknives (see Figure 30) for added convenience.

New wireless flash drives, like the SanDisk Connect, are also appearing on the market to make transferring files from portable devices easier. Although they look like normal flash drives, these wireless drives can connect to your portable devices via WiFi after installing the appropriate app. Up to eight devices can be connected to the flash drive at once, and the drive can even stream media to three devices simultaneously. So your friend could be watching a movie stored on the flash drive while you're uploading pictures from your phone.

Another convenient means of portable storage is a **flash memory card**, such as an SD card. Like the flash drive, memory cards use solid-state flash memory. Most desktops and laptops include slots for flash memory cards, but if your computer is not equipped, there are memory card readers that you can plug into a USB port. Flash memory cards let you transfer digital data between your computer and devices such as digital cameras, smartphones, tablets, video cameras, and printers. Although incredibly small—some are even smaller than the size of a postage stamp—these memory cards have capacities that exceed the capacity of a DVD. Figure 31 compares the storage capacities of hard drives and flash drives.

FIGURE 30 Flash drives are a convenient means of portable storage and come in many different shapes and sizes. *(ekler/Shutterstock)*

FIGURE 31

Hard Drive and Flash Drive Storage Capacity

DRIVE TYPE	IMAGE	TYPICAL CAPACITY	DRIVE TYPE	IMAGE	TYPICAL CAPACITY
Solid-state drive (SSD)		5 TB or more	Flash drive	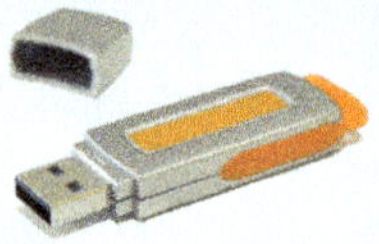	256 GB or more
External portable hard drive		4 TB or more	Flash memory card		128 GB
Mechanical internal hard drive		As much as 8 TB or more			

(Oleksiy Mark/Shutterstock; Julia Ivantsova/Shutterstock; D. Hurst/ Alamy; Cphoto/Fotolia; © Gene Blevins/ZUMAPRESS.com)

Optical Storage

What other kinds of storage devices are available? Most desktop and laptop computers come with at least one **optical drive** that can read from and maybe even write to CDs, DVDs, or Blu-ray discs. Data is saved to such discs as tiny pits that are burned into the disc by a high-speed laser. **Compact discs (CDs)** were initially created to store audio files. **Digital video (or versatile) discs (DVDs)** are the same size and shape as CDs but can store up to 14 times more data than CDs.

What if you want even more storage capacity? Blu-ray is the latest incarnation of optical storage to hit the market. **Blu-ray discs (BDs)**, which are similar in size and shape to CDs and DVDs, can hold as much as 50 GB of data—enough to hold approximately 4.5 hours of movies in high-definition (HD) digital format. Many systems are now available with BD-ROM drives and even Blu-ray burners. External BD drives are another inexpensive way to add HD storage capacity to your system. Figure 32 shows the storage capacities of the various optical storage media. ■

FIGURE 32

Optical Storage Media Capacities

MEDIUM TYPE	TYPICAL CAPACITY
Blu-ray (dual layer)	50 GB
Blu-ray	25 GB
DVD DL (dual layer)	8.5 GB
DVD	4.7 GB
CD	700 MB

connecting peripherals to the COMPUTER

Throughout this chapter, we have discussed peripheral devices that input, store, and output data and information. A **port** is a place through which a peripheral device attaches to the computer so that data can be exchanged between it and the operating system. Although peripherals may connect to devices wirelessly, ports are still often used for connections.

High-Speed and Data Transfer Ports

What is the fastest data transfer port available on today's computing devices? Thunderbolt is the newest input/output technology on the market. It was developed by Intel using fiber optic technology and can achieve blazingly fast transfer speeds of up to 10 Gb/s. **Thunderbolt ports** (see Figure 33) are very useful for laptops and ultrabooks because one Thunderbolt port can allow you to connect up to six different peripherals to your computer. Apple was the first computer maker to integrate the ports into their hardware although other manufacturers are now following suit.

What is the most common port on digital devices? A **universal serial bus (USB) port** is the port type most commonly used to connect input and output devices to the computer. This is mainly because of the ready availability of USB-compatible peripherals. USB ports can connect a wide variety of peripherals, including keyboards, printers, mice, smartphones, external hard drives, flash drives, and digital cameras, to computing devices. The current USB 3.0 standard provides transfer speeds of 4.8 Gbps and charges devices faster than previous USB ports. USB ports come in three different configurations (see Figure 34), which allows them to be integrated into all different sizes of devices.

What other types of data transfer ports are there? You may also see other ports, such as **FireWire 800**, especially on Apple computers. The current standard, FireWire 800, provides a fast transfer rate of 800 Mbps. Devices such as external hard drives and digital video cameras benefit from the speedy data transfer capabilities of FireWire. As more peripherals are released with Thunderbolt capabilities, we should see FireWire declining in popularity.

FIGURE 33 Thunderbolt ports are slim and speedy, making them popular on today's ultrabooks and laptops. *(David Paul Morris/ Bloomberg via Getty Images)*

FIGURE 34 USB connector types (from left to right): standard, micro and mini. *(© Nikita Buida – Fotolia.com; © de_marco – Fotolia.com)*

Connectivity and Multimedia Ports

Which ports help me connect with other computers and the Internet? Another set of ports on your computer helps you communicate with other computers. A **connectivity port** can give you access to networks and the Internet. To find a connectivity port, look for a port that resembles a standard phone jack but is slightly larger. This port is called an **Ethernet port**. Ethernet ports transfer data at speeds up to 10,000 Mbps. You can use an Ethernet port to connect your computer to a cable modem, or to a network.

How do I connect monitors and multimedia devices? Other ports on the back and sides of the computer include audio and video ports. Audio ports are where you connect headphones, microphones, and speakers to the computer. Whether you're attaching a monitor to a desktop computer, or adding a second, larger display to a laptop computer, you'll use a video port. HDMI ports are now the most common video port on computing devices.

A **high-definition multimedia interface (HDMI) port** is a compact audio–video interface that allows both HD video and uncompressed digital audio to be carried on one cable. Because HDMI can transmit uncompressed audio and video, there's no need to convert the signal, which could ultimately reduce the quality of the sound or picture. All currently available monitors, DVD players, televisions, and game consoles have at least one HDMI port (see Figure 35).

> **ACTIVE HELPDESK**
> **Exploring Storage Devices and Ports**
> In this Active Helpdesk call, you'll play the role of a helpdesk staffer, fielding calls about the computer's main storage devices and how to connect various peripheral devices to the computer.

FIGURE 35 HDMI is the latest digital connector type for HD monitors, televisions, and home theater equipment. *(Feng Yu/Shutterstock)*

What ports might I encounter on older computers and peripherals? The **video graphics array (VGA) port** and the **digital video interface (DVI) port** are two ports to which older LCD monitors and televisions connect (see Figure 36). Some Apple computers still feature a Mini DisplayPort for connection of video peripherals. Adapters are available for the Mini DisplayPort that allow the connection of older DVI and VGA devices.

Adding Ports: Expansion Cards and Hubs

What if I don't have all the ports I need? If you're looking to add the newest ports to an older desktop computer or to expand the number of ports on it, you can install special expansion cards (Figure 37) into an open expansion slot on the motherboard to provide additional ports.

Another alternative is adding an expansion hub (shown in Figure 38). An expansion hub is a device that connects to one port, such as a USB port, to provide additional ports. It works like the multiplug extension cords used with electrical appliances. ■

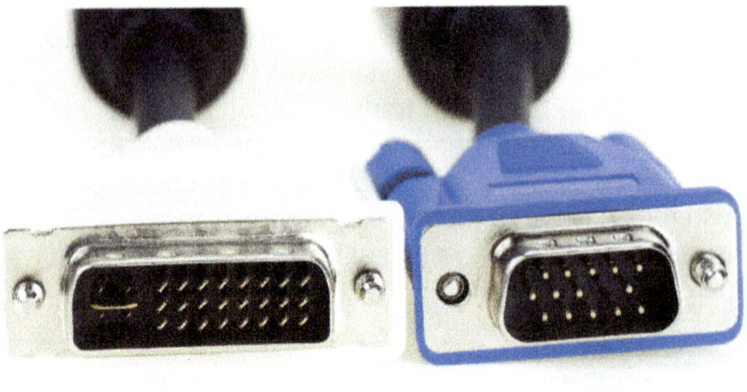

FIGURE 36 DVI (left) and VGA (right) cables are used to connect older LCD monitors and televisions to computing devices. (Marek Kosmal/Fotolia)

FIGURE 37 Expansion cards fit into slots on the motherboard in a desktop computer. *(Andrew Kitching/Alamy)*

FIGURE 38 If you don't have enough USB ports to support your USB devices, consider getting an expansion hub, which can add four or more USB ports to your system. *(Norman Chan/ Fotolia)*

SOUND BYTE

Port Tour: How Do I Hook It Up?

In this Sound Byte, you'll take a tour of both a desktop system and a laptop system to compare the number and variety of available ports. You'll also learn about the different types of ports and compare their speed and expandability.

power CONTROLS

What's the best way to turn my computer on and off? The **power supply**, which is housed inside the system unit, transforms the wall voltage to the voltages required by computer chips. Powering on your computer from a completely turned off state, such as when you start your computer in the morning, is called a **cold boot**. In Windows 8, you can turn your computer off by pressing the computer's power button or by using the Shut Down option from the power icon found under Settings on the Charms bar.

Should I turn off my computer every time I'm done using it? Some people say you should leave your computer on at all times. They argue that turning your computer on and off throughout the day subjects its components to stress because the heating and cooling process forces the components to expand and contract repeatedly. Other people say you should shut down your computer when you're not using it. They claim that it's not as environmentally friendly and that you'll end up wasting money on electricity from the computer running all the time.

Modern operating systems include power-management settings that allow the most power-hungry components of the system (the hard drive and monitor) to shut down after a short idle period. With the power-management options of Windows 8, for example, you only need to shut down your computer completely when you need to repair or install hardware in the system unit or move it to another location. However, if you use your computer only for a little while each day, it would be best to power it off completely after each daily use.

Can I "rest" my computer without turning it off completely? In Windows 8, the main method of power management is Sleep. When your computer enters **Sleep mode**, all of the documents, applications, and data you were using remain in RAM (memory), where they're quickly accessible when you restart your computer.

In Sleep mode, the computer enters a state of greatly reduced power consumption, which saves energy. To put your computer into Sleep mode in Windows 8, display the Charms bar, click (or touch) the Settings option, then click the Power option and select the Sleep option. To wake up your computer, press a key or the power button. In a few seconds, the computer will resume with exactly the same programs running and documents displayed as when you put it to sleep.

If you don't ever want to completely turn off your computer, you can change what happens when you press the power button or close the lid on your laptop. By accessing the Power Options System Settings window (see Figure 39), you can decide if you want your computer to Sleep, Hibernate, or Shut

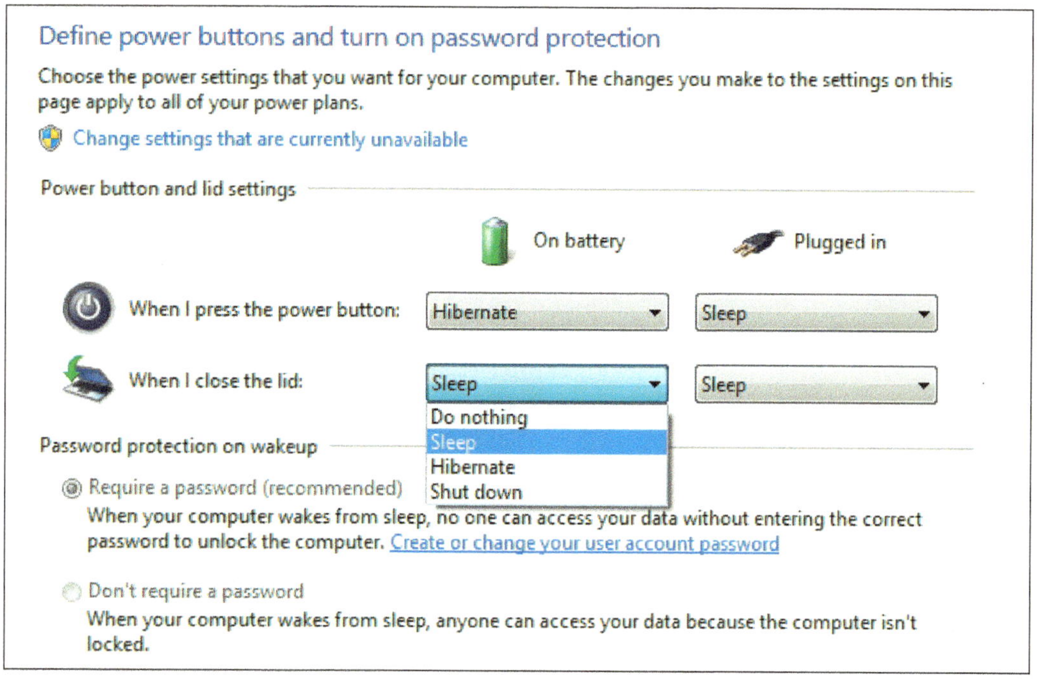

FIGURE 39 You can determine what happens when you click the power button on your computer or close the lid through the Power Options System Settings screen.

>*To access Power Options System Settings, display the Control Panel, click* **Hardware and Sound,** *and then select* **Change what the power buttons do** *under Power Options.*

Down when you press the power button. The **Hibernate** option is similar to Sleep except that your data is stored on your hard drive instead of in RAM and your computer is powered off. This uses much less battery power than Sleep and is a good choice if you won't be using your laptop for a long time and won't have the opportunity to charge it. However, Sleep is still a good option to choose if you just won't be using your computer for a short time. You may want to set your computer so it sleeps when you close the lid but hibernates when you press the power button, giving you quick access to either option.

What's the Restart option in Windows for? If you're using Windows 8, you have the option to restart the computer when you display the Charms bar, click (or touch) Settings, then click the Power button (see Figure 40). Restarting the system while it's powered on is called a **warm boot**. You might need to perform a warm boot if the operating system or other software application stops responding or if you've installed new programs. It takes less time to perform a warm boot than to power down completely and then restart all your hardware. ■

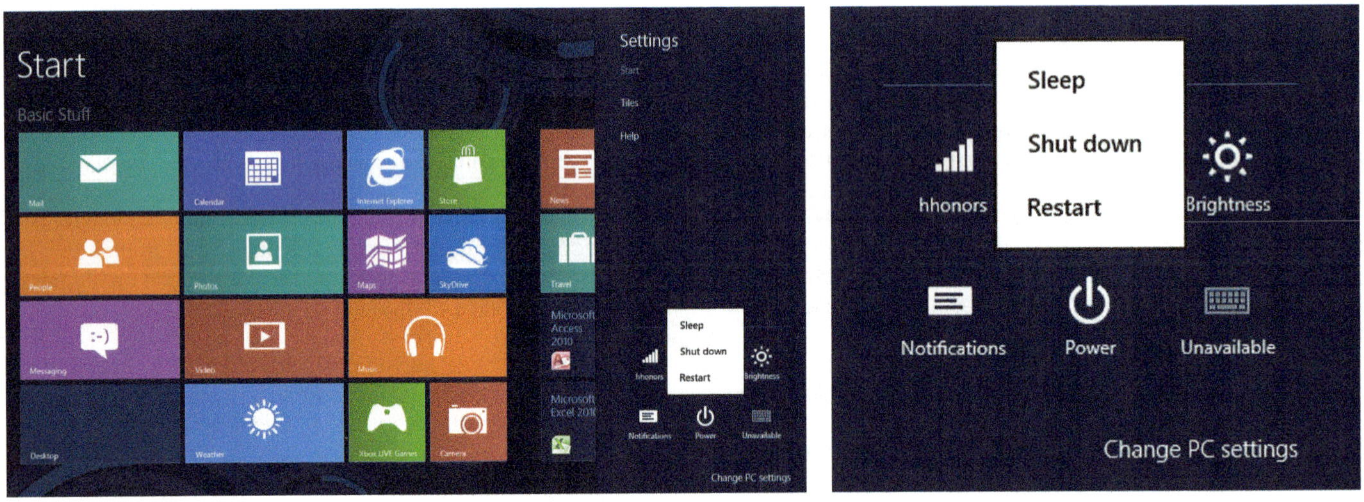

FIGURE 40 The Settings panel in Windows 8 presents several power options. For a warm boot, choose **Restart**. To power down the computer completely, choose **Shut down**. To put your computer into a lower power mode, select **Sleep**.

>To select a particular power option, display the Charms bar, click ***Settings****, then click the* ***Power*** *button.*

setting it ALL UP

It's important that you understand not only your computer's components and how they work together but also how to set up these components safely. **Ergonomics** is the science that deals with the design and location of machines and furniture so that the people using them aren't subjected to an uncomfortable or unsafe experience. In terms of computing, ergonomics refers to how you set up your computer and other equipment to minimize your risk of injury or discomfort.

Why is ergonomics important? Studies suggest that teenagers, on average, spend 31 hours online each week. When you factor in other computer uses such as typing school reports and playing video games, there is great potential for injury. The repetitive nature of long-term computer activities can place too much stress on joints and pull at the tendons and muscles, causing repetitive stress injuries such as carpal tunnel syndrome and tendonitis. These injuries can take months or years to develop to a point where they become painful, and by the time you notice the symptoms, the damage has already taken place. If you take precautionary measures now, you may prevent years of unnecessary pain later.

How can I avoid injuries when I'm working at my computer? As Figure 41 illustrates, it's important to arrange your monitor, chair, body, and keyboard in ways that will help you avoid injury, discomfort, and eyestrain. The following additional guidelines can help keep you comfortable and productive:

- **Position your monitor correctly.** Studies suggest it's best to place your monitor at least 25 inches from your eyes. Experts recommend that you position your monitor either at eye level or at an angle 15 to 20 degrees below your line of sight.
- **Purchase an adjustable chair.** Adjust the height of your chair so that your feet touch the floor (or use a footrest to get the right position). The back support needs to be adjustable

FIGURE 41 Using proper equipment that is adjusted correctly helps prevent repetitive strain injuries while working at a computer.

so that you can position it to support your lumbar (lower back) region. You should also be able to move the seat or adjust the back so that you can sit without exerting pressure on your knees. If your chair doesn't adjust, place a pillow behind your back to provide support.

- **Assume a proper position while typing.** Improperly positioned keyboards are one of the leading causes of repetitive stress injuries in computer users. Your wrists should be flat (not bent) with respect to the keyboard, and your forearms should be parallel to the floor. Additionally, your wrists should not be resting on the keyboard while typing. You can adjust the height of your chair or install a height-adjustable keyboard tray to ensure a proper position. Specially designed ergonomic keyboards such as the one shown in Figure 42 can help you achieve the proper wrist position.
- **Take breaks.** Remaining in the same position for long periods of time increases stress on your body. Shift your position in your chair and stretch your hands and fingers periodically. Likewise, staring at the screen for long periods can lead to eyestrain, so rest your eyes by periodically taking them off the screen and focusing them on an object at least 8 feet away.
- **Ensure the lighting is adequate.** Ensuring that you have proper lighting in your work area minimizes eyestrain. Eliminate sources of direct glare (light shining directly into your eyes) or reflected glare (light shining off the computer screen) and ensure there is enough light to read comfortably. If you still can't eliminate glare from your computer screen, you can buy an antiglare screen to place over your monitor.

Is ergonomics important when using mobile devices? Working with mobile computing devices presents interesting challenges when it comes to injury prevention. For example, many users work with laptops resting on their laps, placing the monitor outside of the optimal line of sight and thereby increasing neck strain. Figure 43 provides guidelines on preventing injuries when computing on the go.

So, whether you're computing at your desk or on the road, consider the ergonomics of your work environment. Doing so will help you avoid injury and discomfort.

What devices are available for people with disabilities? People who have physical challenges sometimes need special devices to access computers. For visually impaired users, voice recognition is an input option. For those users whose visual limitations are less severe, keyboards with larger keys are available. Keyboards that display on a touch screen or specialized input consoles (see Figure 44a) can make input easier for individuals who can't type with their hands: The user presses the keys with a pointing device. There are also keyboards, such as those made by Maltron, designed for individuals who can use only one hand (see Figure 44b).

People with motor control issues may have difficulty with pointing devices. To aid such users, special trackballs are available that can be easily manipulated with one finger and can be attached to almost any surface, including a wheelchair. When arm motion is severely restrained, head-mounted pointing devices can be used. Generally, these involve a camera mounted on the computer monitor and a device attached to the head (often installed in a hat). When the user moves his or her head, the camera detects the movement and moves the cursor. In this case, mouse clicks are controlled by a switch that can be manipulated by the user's hands or feet or even by using an instrument that fits into the mouth and senses the user blowing into it. ■

FIGURE 42 Ergonomic keyboards, like the Truly Ergonomic Mechanical Keyboard shown here, which help users type with straight wrists and contain built-in wrist rests, facilitate proper hand position and minimize wrist strain. *(Truly Ergonomic Ltd.)*

SOUND BYTE
Healthy Computing

In this Sound Byte, you'll see how to set up your workspace in an ergonomically correct way. You'll learn the proper location of the monitor, keyboard, and mouse, as well as ergonomic features to look for when choosing the most appropriate chair.

FIGURE 43

Preventing Injuries While on the Go

	SMARTPHONE REPETITIVE STRAIN INJURIES	PORTABLE MEDIA PLAYER HEARING DAMAGE	SMALL-SCREEN VISION ISSUES	LAP INJURIES	TABLET REPETITIVE STRAIN INJURIES
	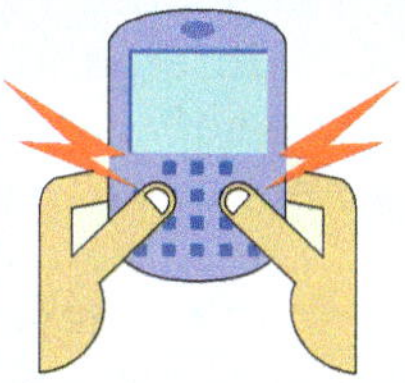	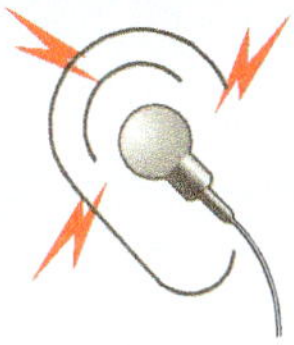	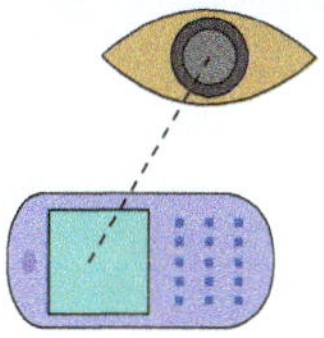		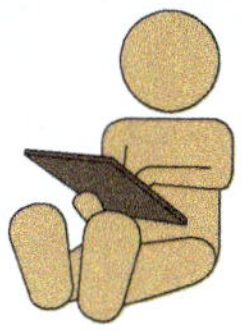
Malady	Repetitive strain injuries (such as DeQuervain's tendonitis) from constant typing of instant messages	Hearing loss from high-decibel sound levels in earbuds	Blurriness and dryness caused by squinting to view tiny screens on mobile devices	Burns on legs from heat generated by laptop	Pain caused from using tablets for prolonged periods in uncomfortable positions
Preventative measures	Restrict length and frequency of messages, take breaks, and perform other motions with your thumbs and fingers during breaks to relieve tension.	Turn down volume (you should be able to hear external noises, such as people talking), use software that limits sound levels (not to exceed 60 decibels), and use external, over-ear style headphones instead of earbuds.	Blink frequently or use eye drops to maintain moisture in eyes, after 10 minutes take a break and focus on something at least 8 feet away for 5 minutes, use adequate amount of light, and increase the size of fonts.	Place a book, magazine, or laptop cooling pad between your legs and laptop.	Restrict the length of time you work at a tablet, especially typing or gaming. Use the same ergonomic position you would use for a laptop when using a tablet.

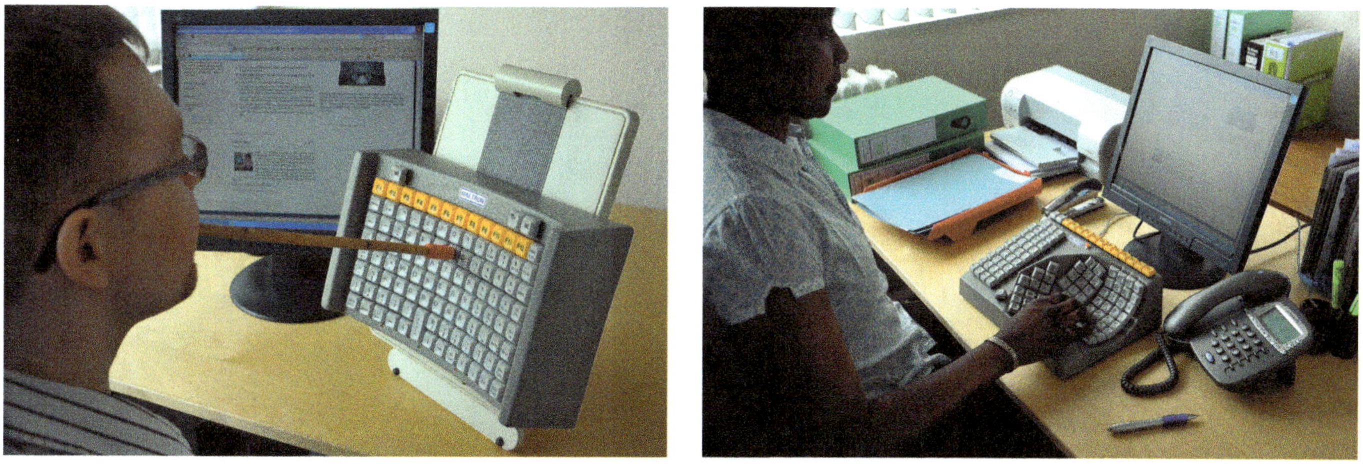

FIGURE 44 (a) Input consoles for people who can't type with their hands and (b) keyboards designed for one-handed use make computer interaction easier for individuals with disabilities. *(Maltron; Maltron)*

trends in IT

Innovations in Printing

With the advent of the computer, many speculated that ours would become a paperless society. Instead of saving printed documents and other output as was done prior to the PC, information would be saved in a digital state: hard drives replacing filing cabinets, online photo buckets replacing photo albums and scrapbooks, and e-books replacing our favorite texts. Hard drive capacities do enable us to save more content, and online storage systems enable us to save pictures and other files to the "cloud." Additionally, e-book readers have increased in popularity. But has this push toward digital content begun to make the printer obsolete? Surprisingly, no. People still have a deep-rooted need to see, feel, mark, share, or use their digital images or information in a physical form. New technologies that push the boundaries of printing, such as printing from the cloud and 3-D printing, are being developed and refined.

Cloud Printing

To print a document from a desktop or laptop computer, you must have a printer associated with your computer. Usually this is not a problem because at home, at school, or in the office, there is generally one printer, and all the PCs connected to it have the software and cables or wireless capabilities needed to use it. But what happens if you want to print something from your smartphone or tablet? Common solutions have been to e-mail the document to yourself or transfer the document to a web-based storage service such as Dropbox so that a printer-connected computer could access it. Another solution is Google Cloud Print, a service that lets you configure your printers so you can access them from mobile devices.

Google Cloud Print uses cloud-ready printers (see Figure 45) that are now available from manufacturers such as HP, Kodak, and Epson. These printers connect directly to the Internet and register themselves with Google Cloud Print without needing to be connected to a computer. Once a printer is registered with Cloud Print, printing jobs can be sent to it from mobile devices (such as tablets and smartphones) using the Internet. Conventional printers that you already own can

FIGURE 45 Cloud-ready printers only need an Internet connection to be accessed from any mobile device.

also be registered with Cloud Print, although they require connection to the Internet through a computer.

3-D Printing

Printing a 3-D model of a proposed building or new prototype is common for architects and engineers. The process builds a model one layer at a time from the bottom up. The procedure begins by spreading a layer of powder on a platform. Then, depending on the technology, the printer uses nozzles similar to those in an inkjet printer to spray tiny drops of glue at specific places to solidify the powder, or the powder is solidified through a melting process. The printer repeats solidifying layers of powder until the model is built to specifications. This technology has spurred the manufacturing of a variety of consumer goods, from toys to clothing (see Figure 46). Shapeways (**shapeways.com**) uses 3-D printing to enable anyone to turn his or her 3-D designs into real physical models. Then, those models can be personalized, bought, or sold through Shapeways's online community.

3-D printing is being used in the medical community as well. Bespoke Innovations (**bespokeinnovations.com**) is using 3-D printing to create prosthetic limbs with more lifelike form and textures as well as to give the recipient the ability to further personalize the prosthetic to include tattoos! And researchers at Wake Forest Institute for Regenerative Medicine have developed a way to use similar inkjet technologies to build heart, bone, and blood vessel tissues in the lab. They have also developed a way to "print" restorative cells directly into a soldier's wound at the site where the injury occurred, thus significantly improving the soldier's chances of survival.

Taking traditional technologies, such as inkjet printing, and applying them to solve current human struggles is a long and tedious process, but without these pioneers experimenting with different applications, society would advance a lot more slowly.

FIGURE 46 3-D printing is being used to fabricate parts for machines on demand. *(Tomas Mikula/Shutterstock)*

Before moving on to the Chapter Review:

- **Watch Replay Video 2**.
- Then check your understanding of what you've learned so far.

check your understanding//

For a quick review to see what you've learned so far, answer the following questions. Visit **pearsonhighered.com/techinaction** to check your answers.

multiple choice

1. Which is the fastest data transfer port available today?
   - **a.** USB
   - **b.** Thunderbolt
   - **c.** FireWire
   - **d.** VGA
2. Which optical storage media can hold the most data?
   - **a.** DVD
   - **b.** CD
   - **c.** Blu-ray
   - **d.** a flash memory card
3. Which of these are considered volatile storage?
   - **a.** flash drive
   - **b.** ROM
   - **c.** RAM
   - **d.** hard drive
4. Which of these is NOT a storage device?
   - **a.** flash drive
   - **b.** solid-state drive
   - **c.** internal hard drive
   - **d.** Thunderbolt drive
5. Proper ergonomics helps prevent repetitive strain injuries
   - **a.** only when using tablet computers.
   - **b.** only when using desktop computers.
   - **c.** in all types of computing devices.
   - **d.** except when using mobile computing devices.

true–false

_____ **1.** Both RAM and ROM are located on the motherboard.

_____ **2.** The number of cores in a CPU is the only measure of a processor's expected performance.

critical thinking

1. Cloud Storage Alternatives

Hard drives are great for storing data on your computer, but there are many reasons why you might want to have access to your data wherever you go. Research various types of available cloud storage (such as Dropbox and OneDrive). Which service do you think is most appropriate for students (and why)? What service would you recommend to a small business that has three physical locations and 50 employees (and why)?

2. iPad

The Apple iPad has been enthusiastically accepted because of its multitouch screen; useful apps; two cameras; and small, light frame. If the CEO of Apple asked you for your advice as to what to include in the next version of the iPad, what would you suggest? What features would make tablets even more appealing to students?

Continue

Chapter Review

summary//

Understanding Your Computer

1. What exactly is a computer, and what are its four main functions?

- Computers are devices that process data. They help organize, sort, and categorize data to turn it into information.
- The computer's four major functions are: (1) input: gather data, or allow users to enter data; (2) process: manipulate, calculate, or organize that data; (3) output: display data and information in a form suitable for the user; and (4) storage: save data and information for later use.

2. What is the difference between data and information?

- Data is a representation of a fact or idea. The number 3 and the words *televisions* and *Sony* are pieces of data.
- Information is data that has been organized or presented in a meaningful fashion. An inventory list that indicates that "three Sony televisions" are in stock is processed information. It allows a retail clerk to answer a customer query about the availability of merchandise. Information is more powerful than raw data.

3. What are bits and bytes, and how are they measured?

- To process data into information, computers need to work in a language they understand. This language, called *binary language*, consists of two numbers: 0 and 1.
- Each 0 and each 1 is a binary digit, or bit. Eight bits create one byte.
- In computers, each letter of the alphabet, each number, and each special character consists of a unique combination of eight bits (one byte)—a string of eight 0s and 1s.
- For describing large amounts of storage capacity, the terms *megabyte* (approximately 1 million bytes), *gigabyte* (approximately 1 billion bytes), *terabyte* (approximately 1 trillion bytes), and *petabyte* (1,000 terabytes) are used.

Input Devices and Output Devices

4. What devices can I use to get data into the computer?

- An input device enables you to enter data (text, images, and sounds) and instructions (user responses and commands) into a computer.
- You use keyboards to enter typed data and commands, whereas you use the mouse to enter user responses and commands.
- Touch screens are display screens that respond to commands initiated by a touch with a finger or a stylus.
- Images are input into the computer with scanners, digital cameras, camcorders, and smartphones.
- Live video is captured with webcams and digital video recorders.
- Microphones capture sounds. There are many different types of microphones, including desktop, headset, and clip-on models.

5. What devices can I use to get information out of the computer?

- Output devices enable you to send processed data out of your computer. It can take the form of text, pictures, sounds, or video.
- Monitors display soft copies of text, graphics, and video, whereas printers create hard copies of text and graphics.
- There are two primary categories of printers: inkjet and laser. Specialty printers are also available. These include all-in-one printers, plotters, and thermal printers. When choosing a printer, you should be aware of factors such as speed, resolution, color output, and cost.
- Speakers are the output devices for sound. Most computers include speakers; more-sophisticated systems include subwoofers and surround sound.

Processing, Memory, and Storage

6. What's on the motherboard?

- The motherboard, the main circuit board of the system, contains a computer's CPU, which coordinates the functions of all other devices on the computer. The performance of a CPU is affected by the speed of the processor (measured in GHz), the amount of cache memory, and the number of processing cores.

- RAM, the computer's volatile memory, is also located on the motherboard. RAM is where all the data and instructions are held while the computer is running.
- ROM, a permanent type of memory, is responsible for housing instructions to help start up a computer.
- The motherboard also houses slots for expansion cards, which have specific functions that augment the computer's basic functions. Typical expansion cards are sound and video cards.

7. Where are information and programs stored?

- To save programs and information permanently, you need to save them to the hard drive or to another permanent storage device such as a DVD or flash drive, or to the cloud.
- The hard drive is your computer's primary device for permanent storage of software and files. The hard drive is a nonvolatile storage device, meaning it holds the data and instructions your computer needs permanently, even after the computer is turned off.
- Mechanical hard drives have spinning platters on which data is saved, whereas newer solid-state drives (SSDs) use solid-state memory, similar to that used with flash drives.
- External hard drives are essentially internal hard drives that have been made portable by enclosing them in a protective case and making them small and lightweight.
- Cloud storage refers to nonvolatile storage locations that are maintained on the Internet (in the "cloud") by companies such as Dropbox. Storing your data in the cloud allows you to access it from almost any computing device that is connected to the Internet.
- Optical drives that can read from and write to CD, DVD, or Blu-ray discs are another means of permanent, portable storage. Data is saved to CDs, DVDs, and Blu-ray discs as pits that are burned into the disc by a laser.
- Flash drives are another portable means of storing data. Flash drives plug into USB ports.
- Flash memory cards let you transfer digital data between your computer and devices such as digital cameras, smartphones, video cameras, and printers.

Ports and Power Controls

8. How are devices connected to the computer?

- There is a wide variety of ports that allow you to hook up peripheral devices (such as your monitor and keyboard) to your system.
- The fastest type of port used to connect devices to a computer is the Thunderbolt port.
- The most common type of port used to connect devices to a computer is the USB port.
- FireWire ports provide additional options for data transfer.
- Connectivity ports, such as Ethernet ports, give you access to networks and the Internet.
- HDMI ports are the most common multimedia port. They are used to connect monitors, TVs, and gaming consoles to computing devices and handle both audio and video data.
- Audio ports are where you connect headphones, microphones, and speakers to computing devices.

9. What's the best way to turn my computer on and off, and when should it be done?

- Power on your computer from a completely turned-off state. In Windows 8, you can turn your computer off by pressing the computer's power button or by using the Shut Down option from the power icon found under Settings on the Charms bar.
- With the power-management options of Windows 8, for example, you only need to shut down your computer completely when you need to repair or install hardware in the system unit or move it to another location. However, if you use your computer only for a little while each day, it would be best to power it off completely after each daily use.

Setting It All Up

10. How do I set up my computer to avoid strain and injury?

- *Ergonomics* refers to how you arrange your computer and equipment to minimize your risk of injury or discomfort.
- Ergonomics includes positioning your monitor correctly, buying an adjustable chair, assuming a proper position while typing, making sure the lighting is adequate, and not looking at the screen for long periods. Other good practices include taking frequent breaks and using specially designed equipment such as ergonomic keyboards.
- Ergonomics is also important to consider when using mobile devices.

Be sure to check out the companion website for additional materials to help you review and learn, including a Tech Bytes Weekly newsletter—**pearsonhighered.com/techinaction.** And don't forget the Replay Videos.

key terms //

all-in-one computer
all-in-one printer
application software
aspect ratio
binary digit (bit)
binary language
Bluetooth technology
Blu-ray disc (BD)
byte
central processing unit (CPU, or processor)
cloud storage
cold boot
compact disc (CD)
computer
connectivity port
data
desktop computer
digital video (or versatile) disc (DVD)
digital video interface (DVI) port
drive bay
embedded computer
ergonomics
Ethernet port
expansion cards (or adapter cards)
external hard drive
FireWire 800
flash drive (jump drive, USB drive, or thumb drive)
flash memory card
gigabyte (GB)
gigahertz (GHz)
hard disk drive (HDD, or hard drive)
hardware
Hibernate
high-definition multimedia interface (HDMI) port
impact printer
information
inkjet printer
input device
internal hard drive
keyboard
kilobyte (KB)
laptop (or notebook) computer
laser printer
legacy technology
light-emitting diode (LED)
liquid crystal display (LCD)
mainframe
megabyte (MB)
microphone (mic)
monitor (display screen)
motherboard
mouse
netbook
network interface card (NIC)
nonimpact printer
nonvolatile storage
operating system (OS)
optical drive
optical mouse
organic light-emitting diode (OLED) displays
output device
petabyte
peripheral device
pixel
plotter
port
power supply
printer
processing
projector
QWERTY keyboard
random access memory (RAM)
read-only memory (ROM)
resolution
scanner
Sleep mode
smartphone
software
solid-state drive (SSD)
sound card
speakers
stylus
supercomputer
surround-sound speaker
system software
system unit
tablet computer
tablet (or convertible) PC
terabyte (TB)
thermal printer
Thunderbolt port
touch pad (trackpad)
touch screen
ultrabook
universal serial bus (USB) port
video card
video graphics array (VGA) port
volatile storage
warm boot
webcam

making the transition to . . . next semester//

1. **Watching Device Demos**

   YouTube is a great resource for product demonstrations. Open your browser, navigate to YouTube (**youtube.com**), and search on any type of computer peripheral discussed in this chapter to see if you can find a demonstration of a cool product.

   How helpful are these demonstrations? Make a video demonstration of a computing device you have and post it to your course management system or present it to your classmates (as specified by your instructor).

2. **Communicating with the Computer**

   You're involved in many group projects at school. Between your work, your classes, and other outside responsibilities, you're finding it difficult to meet in person. Investigate the devices you would need to be able to have virtual group meetings.

3. **Ultrabook or Tablet**

   You need a new computing device for school. Consider the following:

   a. Explain the differences between a tablet and an ultrabook.

   b. What advantages would an ultrabook provide you for your academic career?

   c. What advantages would a tablet (such as an iPad) provide to you in the classroom? At home?

   d. Which device do you think is better suited to your needs? Explain fully.

making the transition to . . . the workplace//

1. **Backing Up Your Work**

   You've embarked on a position as a freelance editor. You'll be using your own computer. Until now, you haven't worried too much about backing up your data. Now, however, it's extremely important that you back up all your work frequently. Research the various backup options available, including cloud backup services, external hard drives, and portable flash storage. What are the size limitations of each? What are the initial and ongoing costs of each? How frequently do the options allow you to perform backups? Which option would you choose, and why?

2. **What Hardware Will You Use?**

   When you arrive at a new position for a company, your employer will most likely provide you with a computer. Based on the career you're in now or are planning to pursue, answer the following questions:

   a. What kind of computer system would the company mostly likely provide to you—desktop, laptop, tablet PC, or something else? How does that compare with the type of system with which you prefer to work?

   b. If you were required to use a type of computer you'd never used before (such as a Mac instead of a PC), how would you go about learning to use the new computer?

   c. What other devices might your employer provide? Consider such items as smartphones or peripherals such as printers. How important is it for these devices to conform to the latest trends?

   d. Should you be able to use employer-provided equipment, such as a smartphone, for personal benefit? Does your answer differ if you have to pay for part or all of the device?

team time//

Which Mobile Device Is the Best?

Problem

You've joined a small business that's beginning to evaluate its technology setup. Because of the addition of several new sales representatives and other administrative employees, the company needs to purchase many new computers. You're trying to decide which mobile devices would be better—laptop computers, tablet computers (iPads), smartphones with large screens (phablets), or a combination of these devices.

Task

Split your class into teams of three and assign the following tasks:

- Member A explores the benefits and downfalls of laptop computers.
- Member B explores the benefits and downfalls of smartphones with large screens (phablets).
- Member C explores the benefits and downfalls of tablet computers.

Process

1. Think about what the technology goals are for the company and what information and resources you will need to tackle this project.
2. Research and then discuss the components of each system you're recommending. Are any components better suited for the particular needs of certain types of employees (sales representatives versus administrative staff)? Consider all the input, output, processing, and storage devices. Are any special devices or peripherals required?
3. Consider the different types of employees in the company. Would a combination of devices be better than a single solution? If so, what kinds of employees would get which type of device?
4. As a team, write a summary position paper. Support your system recommendation for the company. Each team member should include why his or her type of computer will be part of the solution or not.

Conclusion

Laptops, smartphones with large screens (phablets), and tablet computers have their own merits as computing systems. Being aware of the options in the marketplace, knowing how to analyze the trade-offs of different designs, and recognizing the different needs each type of computer fulfills allows you to become a better consumer as well as a better computer user.

ethics project //

Green Computing

Ethical conduct is a stream of decisions you make all day long. In this exercise, you'll research and then role-play a complicated ethical situation. The role you play may or may not match your own personal beliefs, but your research and use of logic will enable you to represent whichever view is assigned. An arbitrator will watch and comment on both sides of the arguments, and together, the team will agree on an ethical solution.

Background

Green computing—conducting computing needs with the least possible amount of power and impact on the environment—is on everyone's minds. Although it's hard to argue with an environmentally conscious agenda, the pinch to our pocketbooks and the loss of some comforts sometimes make green computing difficult. Businesses, including colleges, need to consider a variety of issues and concerns before jumping into a complete green overhaul.

Research Areas to Consider

- End-of-life management: e-waste and recycling
- Energy-efficient devices
- Renewable resources used in computer manufacturing
- Costs of green computing
- Government funding and incentives

Process

1. Divide the class into teams.
2. Research the areas cited above and devise a scenario in which your college is considering modifying its current technology setup to a more green information technology (IT) strategy.
3. Team members should write a summary that provides background information for their character—for example, environmentalist, college IT administrator, or arbitrator—and that details their character's behaviors to set the stage for the role-playing event. Then, team members should create an outline to use during the role-playing event.
4. Team members should arrange a mutually convenient time to meet for the exchange, using a virtual meeting tool or by meeting in person.
5. Team members should present their case to the class or submit a PowerPoint presentation for review by the rest of the class, along with the summary and resolution they developed.

Conclusion

As technology becomes ever more prevalent and integrated into our lives, more and more ethical dilemmas will present themselves. Being able to understand and evaluate both sides of the argument, while responding in a personally or socially ethical manner, will be an important skill.

Glossary

all-in-one computer A desktop system unit that houses the computer's processor, memory, and monitor in a single unit.

all-in-one printer Combines the functions of a printer, scanner, copier, and fax into one machine.

application software The set of programs on a computer that helps a user carry out tasks such as word processing, sending e-mail, balancing a budget, creating presentations, editing photos, taking an online course, and playing games.

aspect ratio The width-to-height proportion of a monitor.

binary digit (bit) A digit that corresponds to the on and off states of a computer's switches. A bit contains a value of either 0 or 1.

binary language The language computers use to process data into information, consisting of only the values 0 and 1.

Bluetooth (technology) A type of wireless technology that uses radio waves to transmit data over short distances (approximately 3–300 feet depending on power); often used to connect peripherals such as printers and keyboards to computers or headsets to cell phones.

Blu-ray disc (BD) A method of optical storage for digital data, developed for storing high-definition media. It has the largest storage capacity of all optical storage options.

byte Eight binary digits (bits).

central processing unit (CPU, or processor) The part of the system unit of a computer that is responsible for data processing; it is the largest and most important chip in the computer. The CPU controls all the functions performed by the computer's other components and processes all the commands issued to it by software instructions.

cold boot The process of starting a computer from a powered-down or off state.

compact disc (CD) A method of optical storage for digital data; originally developed for storing digital audio.

computer A data-processing device that gathers, processes, outputs, and stores data and information.

connectivity port A port that enables a computing device to be connected to other devices or systems such as networks, modems, and the Internet.

data Numbers, words, pictures, or sounds that represent facts, figures, or ideas; the raw input that users have at the start of a job.

desktop computer A computer that's intended for use at a single location. A desktop computer consists of a case that houses the main components of the computer, plus peripheral devices.

digital video (or versatile) disc (DVD) A method of optical storage for digital data that has greater storage capacity than compact discs.

digital video interface (DVI) port Video interface technology that newer LCD monitors, as well as other multimedia devices such as televisions, DVD players, and projectors, use to connect to a PC.

drive bay A special shelf inside a computer that is designed to hold storage devices.

embedded computer A specially designed computer chip that resides inside another device, such as a car. These self-contained computer devices have their own programming and typically neither receive input from users nor interact with other systems.

ergonomics How a user sets up his or her computer and other equipment to minimize risk of injury or discomfort.

Ethernet port A port that's slightly larger than a standard phone jack and that transfers data at speeds of up to 10,000 Mbps; used to connect a computer to a DSL or cable modem or to a network.

expansion card (adapter card) A circuit board with specific functions that augment the computer's basic functions and provide connections to other devices; examples include the sound card and the video card.

external hard drive A hard drive that is enclosed in a protective case to make it portable; the drive is connected to the computer with a data transfer cable and is often used to back up data.

FireWire 800 An interface port that transfers data at 800 Mbps.

flash drive A drive that plugs into a universal serial bus (USB) port on a computer and that stores data digitally. Also called a USB drive, jump drive, or thumb drive.

flash memory card A form of portable storage; this removable memory card is often used in digital cameras, smartphones, video cameras, and printers.

gigabyte (GB) About a billion bytes.

gigahertz (GHz) One billion hertz.

hard disk drive (HDD) The computer's nonvolatile, primary storage device for permanent storage of software and documents.

hardware Any part of a computer or computer system you can physically touch.

hibernate A power-management mode that saves the current state of the current system to the computer's hard drive.

high-definition multimedia interface (HDMI) A compact audio–video interface standard that carries both high-definition video and uncompressed digital audio.

impact printer A printer that has tiny hammer-like keys that strike the paper through an inked ribbon, thus making a mark on the paper. The most common impact printer is the dot-matrix printer.

information Data that has been organized or presented in a meaningful fashion; the result, or output that users require at the end of a job.

inkjet printer A nonimpact printer that sprays tiny drops of ink onto paper.

input device A hardware device used to enter, or input, data (text, images, and sounds) and instructions (user responses and commands) into a computer. Some input devices are keyboards and mice.

internal hard drive A hard drive that resides within the computer's system unit and that usually holds all permanently stored programs and data.

keyboard A hardware device used to enter typed data and commands into a computer.

kilobyte (KB) A unit of computer storage equal to approximately 1,000 bytes.

laptop (or notebook) computer A portable computer with a keyboard, a monitor, and other devices integrated into a single compact case.

laser printer A nonimpact printer known for quick and quiet production and high-quality printouts.

legacy technology Comprises computing devices, software, or peripherals that use techniques, parts, and methods from an earlier time that are no longer popular.

light-emitting diode (LED) A newer, more energy-efficient technology used in monitors. It may result in better color accuracy and thinner panels than traditional LCD monitors.

liquid crystal display (LCD) The technology used in flat-panel computer monitors.

mainframe A large, expensive computer that supports hundreds or thousands of users simultaneously and executes many different programs at the same time.

megabyte (MB) A unit of computer storage equal to approximately 1 million bytes.

microphone (mic) A device that allows you to capture sound waves, such as those created by your voice, and to transfer them to digital format on your computer.

monitor (display screen) A common output device that displays text, graphics, and video as soft copies (copies that can be seen only on screen).

motherboard A special circuit board in the system unit that contains the central processing unit, the memory (RAM) chips, and the slots available for expansion cards; all of the other boards (video cards, sound cards, and so on) connect to it to receive power and to communicate.

mouse A hardware device used to enter user responses and commands into a computer.

netbook A computing device that runs a full-featured operating system but that weighs two pounds or less.

network interface card (NIC) An expansion card that enables a computer to connect other computers or to a cable modem to facilitate a high-speed Internet connection.

nonimpact printer A printer that sprays ink or uses laser beams to make marks on the paper. The most common nonimpact printers are inkjet and laser printers.

nonvolatile storage Permanent storage, as in read-only memory (ROM).

operating system (OS) The system software that controls the way in which a computer system functions, including the management of hardware, peripherals, and software.

optical drive A hardware device that uses lasers or light to read from, and even write to, CDs, DVDs, or Blu-ray discs.

optical mouse A mouse that uses an internal sensor or laser to control the mouse's movement. The sensor sends signals to the computer, telling it where to move the pointer on the screen.

organic light-emitting diode (OLED) displays Displays that use organic compounds to produce light when exposed to an electric current. Unlike LCDs, OLEDs do not require a backlight to function and therefore draw less power and have a much thinner display, sometimes as thin as 3 mm.

output device A device that sends processed data and information out of a computer in the form of text, pictures (graphics), sounds (audio), or video.

petabyte (PB) 10^{15} bytes of digital information.

peripheral device A device such as a monitor, printer, or keyboard that connects to the system unit through a data port.

pixel A single point that creates the images on a computer monitor. Pixels are illuminated by an electron beam that passes rapidly back and forth across the back of the screen so that the pixels appear to glow continuously.

plotter A large printer that uses a computer-controlled pen to produce oversize pictures that require precise continuous lines to be drawn, such as maps and architectural plans.

port An interface through which external devices are connected to the computer.

power supply A power supply regulates the wall voltage to the voltages required by computer chips; it's housed inside the system unit.

printer A common output device that creates tangible or hard copies of text and graphics.

processing Manipulating or organizing data into information.

projector A device that can project images from your computer onto a wall or viewing screen.

QWERTY keyboard A keyboard that gets its name from the first six letters on the top-left row of alphabetic keys on the keyboard.

random access memory (RAM) The computer's temporary storage space or short-term memory. It's located in a set of chips on the system unit's motherboard, and its capacity is measured in megabytes or gigabytes.

read-only memory (ROM) A set of memory chips, located on the motherboard, which stores data and instructions that cannot be changed or erased; it holds all the instructions the computer needs to start up.

resolution The clearness or sharpness of an image, which is controlled by the number of pixels displayed on the screen.

scanner A type of input device that inputs images into computers.

sleep mode A low-power mode for electronic devices such as computers that saves electric power consumption and saves the last-used settings. When the device is "woken up," work is resumed more quickly than when cold booting the computer.

solid-state drive (SSD) A storage device that uses the same kind of memory that flash drives use but that can reach data in only a tenth of the time a flash drive requires.

sound card An expansion card that attaches to the motherboard inside the system unit and that enables the computer to produce sounds by providing a connection for the speakers and microphone.

speakers Output devices for sound.

stylus A pen-shaped device used to tap or write on touch-sensitive screens.

supercomputer A specially designed computer that can perform complex calculations extremely rapidly; used in situations in which complex models requiring intensive mathematical calculations are needed (such as weather forecasting or atomic energy research).

surround-sound speaker A system of speakers set up in such a way that it surrounds an entire area (and the people in it) with sound.

system software The set of programs that enables a computer's hardware devices and application software to work together; it includes the operating system and utility programs.

system unit The metal or plastic case that holds all the physical parts of the computer together, including the computer's processor (its brains), its memory, and the many circuit boards that help the computer function.

tablet computer A mobile computer, such as the Apple iPad or Samsung Galaxy Tab, integrated into a flat multitouch-sensitive screen. It uses an onscreen virtual keyboard, but separate keyboards can be connected via Bluetooth or wires.

tablet PC A laptop computer designed specifically to work with handwriting-recognition technology.

Terabyte (TB) 1,099,511,627,776 bytes or 2^{40} bytes.

thermal printer A printer that works either by melting wax-based ink onto ordinary paper (in a process called *thermal wax transfer printing*) or by burning dots onto specially coated paper (in a process called *direct thermal printing*).

Thunderbolt port A high speed input/output port; Thunderbolt 2 provides two channels of 20 Gbps capacity on one port.

touch pad (trackpad) A small, touch-sensitive screen at the base of a laptop keyboard that's used to direct the cursor.

touch screen A type of monitor (or display in a smartphone or tablet computer) that accepts input from a user touching the screen.

ultrabook A full-featured but lightweight laptop computer that features a low-power processor and a solid-state drive; it tries to reduce its size and weight to extend battery life without sacrificing performance.

universal serial bus (USB) port A port that can connect a wide variety of peripheral devices to the computer, including keyboards, printers, mice, smartphones, external hard drives, flash drives, and digital cameras.

video card (video adapter) An expansion card that's installed inside a system unit to translate binary data (the *1*s and *0*s the computer uses) into the images viewed on the monitor.

video graphics array (VGA) port A port to which a cathode ray tube monitor connects.

volatile storage Temporary storage, such as in random access memory. When the power is off, the data in volatile storage is cleared out.

warm boot The process of restarting the system while it's powered on.

webcam A small camera that sits on top of a computer monitor (connected to the computer by a cable) or that's built into a laptop computer and is usually used to transfer live video.

Understanding and Assessing Hardware: Evaluating Your System

Understanding and Assessing Hardware: Evaluating Your System

Evaluating Key Subsystems

Your Ideal Computing Device

OBJECTIVE

1. What kind of computing device is best for me?

Evaluating the CPU Subsystem

OBJECTIVE

2. What does the CPU do, and how can I evaluate its performance?

Sound Byte: Using Windows to Evaluate CPU Performance

Evaluating the Memory Subsystem

OBJECTIVES

3. How does memory work in my computer?
4. How do I evaluate how much memory I need?

Sound Byte: Memory Hierarchy Interactive

Active Helpdesk: Evaluating Your CPU and RAM

Sound Byte: Installing RAM

Evaluating the Storage Subsystem

OBJECTIVES

5. What are the computer's storage devices?
6. How do I evaluate my storage devices?

Sound Byte: Optical Media Reading and Writing Interactive

Sound Byte: Installing a Blu-ray Drive

Evaluating Other Subsystems and Making a Decision

Evaluating the Video and Audio Subsystems

OBJECTIVES

7. What components affect the quality of video on my computer?
8. How do I know if I need better video performance?
9. What components affect my computer's sound quality?

Active Helpdesk: Evaluating Computer System Components

Evaluating System Reliability and Making a Final Decision

OBJECTIVE

10. How can I improve the reliability of my system?

For all media in this chapter go to **pearsonhighered.com/techinaction** or MyITLab.

(Radius Images/Alamy; nigel james/Alamy; joppo/Fotolia; Cobalt./Fotolia; Scanrail/Fotolia; SSilver/Fotolia; Ivelin Radkov/Alamy)

HOW COOL IS THIS?

Scan here for more info

Want to create something really cool? The **Arduino microcontroller project** has fueled an abundance of DIY (do-it-yourself) electronics projects and created an energized community of do-it-yourselfers. This **small printed circuit board** is based on a microcontroller and includes everything you need: You **just plug it in and begin your DIY project**. The open-source hardware is licensed under the Creative Commons license, so schematics are freely available to be changed or re-created as you wish.

The **LilyPad variation of the Arduino**, designed by MIT engineer Leah Buechley, is often used to create wearable projects. Conductive thread runs from the Arduino output pins to LEDs, and the **finished garments are washable**. One project is this turn-signal biking jacket. The Arduino LilyPad fires up an LED turn signal on your back to **keep you visible on the roadways**.

Evaluating Key Subsystems

It can be tough to know if your computer is the best match for your needs. New technologies emerge so quickly, and it's hard to determine whether they're expensive extras or tools you need. Do you need USB 3.0 instead of USB 2.0? Doesn't it always seem like your friend's computer is faster than yours anyway? Maybe you could get more out of newer technologies, but should you upgrade the system you have or buy a new machine? In this chapter, you'll learn how to measure your system's performance and gauge your needs so that you end up with a system you love.

your ideal COMPUTING DEVICE

When is the best time to buy a new computer? There never seems to be a perfect time to buy. It seems that if you can just wait a year, computers will be faster and cost less. But is this actually true?

As it turns out, it is true. In fact, a rule of thumb often cited in the computer industry called **Moore's Law** describes the pace at which central processing units (CPUs) improve. Named for Gordon Moore, the cofounder of the CPU chip manufacturer Intel, this rule predicts that the number of transistors inside a CPU will increase so fast that CPU capacity will double about every two years. (The number of transistors on a CPU chip helps determine how fast it can process data.)

This rule of thumb has held true for over 45 years. Figure 1 shows a way to visualize this kind of exponential growth. If CPU capacity were put into terms of population growth, a group of 2,300 people at the start of CPU development would now be a country of over one billion! Moore himself has predicted that around the year 2020, CPU chips will be manufactured in a different way, thus changing or eliminating the effects of Moore's Law altogether.

In addition to the CPU becoming faster, other system components also continue to improve dramatically. For example, the capacity of memory chips such as dynamic random access memory (DRAM)—the most common form of memory found in personal computers—increases about 60% every year. Meanwhile, hard drives have been growing in storage capacity by some 50% each year.

OK, things change fast. How do I know what's best for me? Consider what kind of user you are and

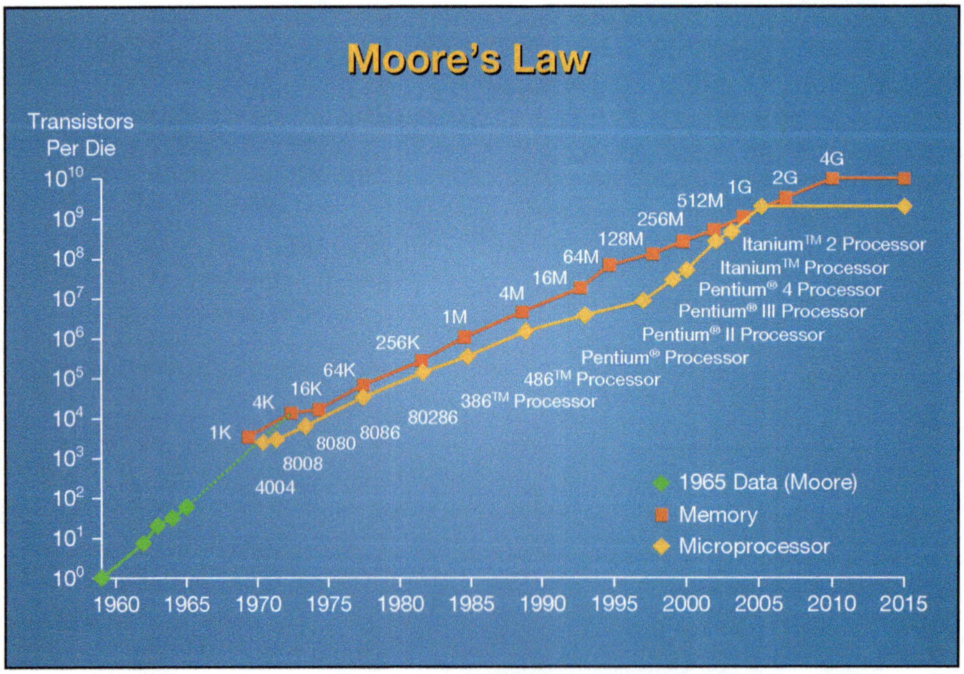

FIGURE 1 Moore's Law illustrates the amazing pace of growth in CPU capabilities. *(Courtesy of the Intel Corporation)*

FIGURE 2

What Kind of Technology User Are You?

Casual User
- Uses the computer primarily for Internet access
- Uses some software applications locally, like Microsoft Office
- Uses videos and software but does not create them

Power User
- Needs fast, powerful processing
- Needs fast storage and lots of it
- Creates videos and software programs

Mobile User
- Needs a lightweight device
- Needs a long battery life
- Is happy to sacrifice some capabilities for less weight

(ilaszlo/Shutterstock; ColorBlind Images/Iconica/Getty Images; dly/Shutterstock)

what needs you have. For example, are you a power user who wants a machine for doing video editing and high-end gaming? Are you a more casual user, mainly using a device for word processing and Internet access? Are you on the move and need to bring your computer with you everywhere? Figure 2 shows a few different types of users—which type (or types) are you?

Now ask yourself, does your current computer match your needs? As we evaluate the pieces of your system, it'll become clear whether you need a few upgrades or perhaps a new machine better suited to you.

How do I pick from all the types of devices available? A huge number of choices are on the market (see Figure 3):

- Tablets (like the iPad or Galaxy)
- Ultrabooks (like the MacBook Air)
- Netbooks (which have a screen smaller than 10 inches and a small keyboard)
- Tablet PCs (which have a touch-enabled screen and a full keyboard)
- Laptops (or notebooks)
- Desktops

The main distinction among the available options is based on your need for mobility versus your need for processing power. If you're on the move all the time and have to have the lightest solution possible, an ultrabook may be best for you. At less than 3 pounds, they're great on weight but don't include an optical drive for DVDs/Blu-rays or much storage space. Even lighter are tablets like the iPad, but they also

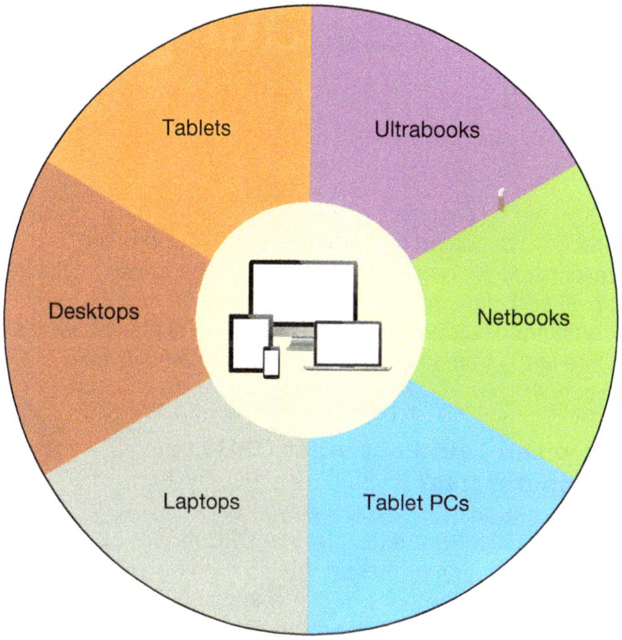

FIGURE 3 Range of Computing Devices (© tpx/Fotolia)

lack optical drives and may not be able to run all the software you need.

Why would I consider buying a desktop? Desktop systems are invariably a better value than lighter, more mobile computers. You'll find you get more computing power for your dollar, and you'll have more opportunity to upgrade parts of your system later. In addition, desktops often ship with a 24-inch or larger monitor, whereas lighter computers offer screens between 10 and 17 inches.

Desktop systems are also more reliable. Because of the vibration that a laptop experiences and the added exposure to dust, water, and temperature fluctuations that portability brings, laptops often have a shorter lifespan than desktop computers. You'll have less worry over theft or loss with a desktop, too. Manufacturers do offer extended warranty plans that cover laptop computers for accidental damage and theft; however, such plans can be costly.

How long should I plan on keeping my computing device? You should be able to count on two years, and maybe even four or five years. The answer depends in part on how easy it is to upgrade your system. Take note of the maximum amount of memory you can install in your device. Also, check whether you can upgrade your device's graphics capabilities down the road.

How can I tell if my current system is good enough? We'll begin by conducting a **system evaluation**. To do this, we'll look at your computer's subsystems, see what they do, and check how they perform during your typical workday. Then we'll compare that with what is available on the market, and the path forward for you will become clearer. Even if you're not in the market for a new computer, conducting a system evaluation will help you understand what you might want down the road.

evaluating the CPU SUBSYSTEM

Let's start by considering your system's processor, or CPU. The CPU is located on the system motherboard and is responsible for processing instructions, performing calculations, and managing the flow of information through your computer. The dominant processors on the market are the Core family from Intel, featuring the i7, i5, and i3 (see Figure 4).

How can I find out what CPU my computer has? If you have a PC, System Properties will show you the type of CPU you have installed. For example, the CPU in the computer in Figure 5 is an Intel i5 running at 2.6 GHz. AMD is another popular manufacturer of CPUs; you may have one of its processors, such as the FX-8150 or the Phenom X4. But more detailed information about your CPU, such as its number of cores and amount of cache memory, is not shown on this screen. Let's dive into that.

FIGURE 4 The Intel i5 and i7 CPU chips run many of the laptop and desktop offerings on the market today. *(David Caudery/PC Format Magazine/Future/Getty Images)*

How the CPU Works

How does the CPU actually work? The CPU is composed of two units: the *control unit* and the *arithmetic logic unit (ALU)*. The control unit coordinates the activities of all the other computer components. The ALU is responsible for performing all the arithmetic calculations (addition, subtraction, multiplication, and division). It also makes logic and comparison decisions, such as comparing items, to determine if one is greater than, less than, or equal to another.

FIGURE 5 The System Properties window identifies your computer's CPU as well as its speed. This computer has an Intel i5 running at 2.6 GHz.

>*To access your system settings, right-click the* ***Start*** *button. From the menu that displays, choose* ***System***.

Every time the CPU performs a program instruction, it goes through the same series of steps:

1. It *fetches* the required piece of data or instruction from random access memory (RAM), the temporary storage location for all the data and instructions the computer needs while it's running.
2. It *decodes* the instruction into something the computer can understand.
3. It *executes* the instruction.
4. It *stores* the result to RAM before fetching the next instruction.

This process is called a **machine cycle**.

CPU Factors

What makes one CPU different from another? You pay more for a computer with an Intel i7 than one with an i5 because of its increased processing power. A CPU's processing power is determined by the following:

- Its *clock speed*
- Whether it has multiple *cores*
- Its amount of *cache memory*

How does a CPU with a higher clock speed help me? The **clock speed** of a CPU dictates how many instructions the CPU can process each second. It is measured in gigahertz (GHz), or billions of steps per second. The faster the clock speed, the more quickly the next instruction is processed. CPUs currently have clock speeds between 2.1 and 4 GHz. There is a huge difference between a computer with a 2.1 GHz CPU and one with a 4 GHz CPU.

Some users push their hardware to perform faster, **overclocking** their processor. Overclocking means that you run the CPU at a faster speed than the manufacturer recommends. It produces more heat, meaning a shorter lifetime for the CPU, and usually voids any warranty, but in gaming systems, you'll see this done quite often.

How does a multi-core CPU help me? A **core** on a CPU contains the parts of the CPU required for processing. As shown in Figure 6a, with multiple-core technology, two or more complete processors live on the same chip, enabling the independent execution of two sets of instructions at the same time. If you had a clone of yourself sitting next to you working, you could get twice as much done: That is the idea of multi-core processing. With multi-core processing, applications that are always running behind the scenes, such as virus protection software and your operating system (OS), can have their own dedicated processor, freeing the other processors to run other applications more efficiently. This results in faster processing and smoother multitasking.

CPUs began to execute more than one instruction at a time when **hyperthreading** was introduced in 2002. Hyperthreading provides quicker processing of information by enabling a new set of instructions to start executing *before the previous set has finished*. As shown in Figure 6b, hyperthreading allows two different programs to be processed at one time, but they're sharing the computing resources of the chip.

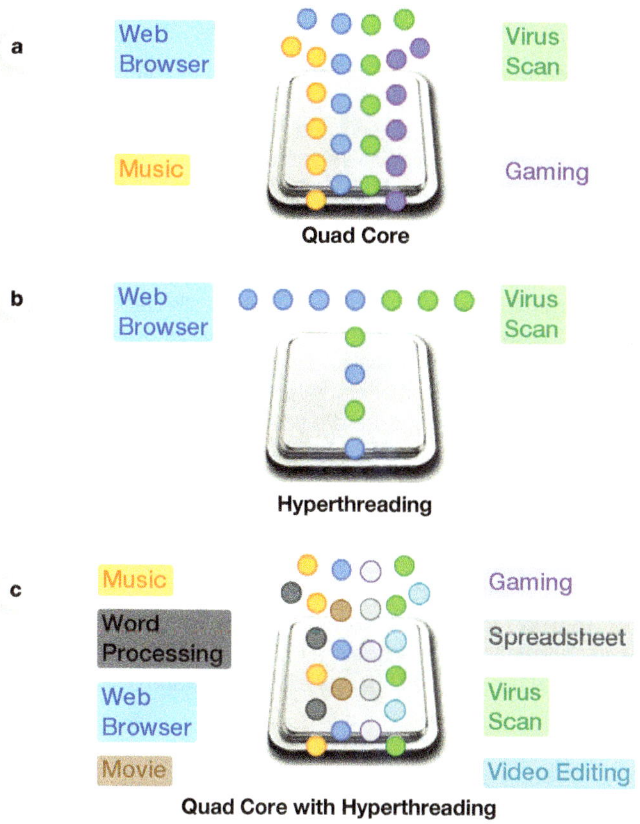

FIGURE 6 (a) Intel Quad Core processors have four cores that are able to run four programs simultaneously. (b) Hyperthreading allows work on two processes to happen in one core at the same time. (c) So, a four-core hyperthreaded processor can be working on eight programs at one time.

All of the Intel Core processors have multiple cores *and* hyperthreading (see Figure 6c). The Intel i7-990X has six cores, each one using hyperthreading, so it simulates having 12 processors!

How does more cache memory help me? The CPU's **cache memory** is a form of RAM that gets data to the CPU for processing much faster than bringing the data in from the computer's RAM. There are three levels of cache memory, defined by their proximity to the CPU:

- *Level 1 cache* is a block of memory built on the CPU chip itself for storage of data or commands that have just been used. That gets the data to the CPU blindingly fast!
- *Level 2 cache* is located on the CPU chip but is slightly farther away and so takes somewhat longer to access than Level 1 cache. It contains more storage area than Level 1 cache.
- *Level 3 cache* is slower for the CPU to reach but is larger in size than Level 2 cache.

The more expensive the CPU, the more cache memory it will have.

So how do I shop for a CPU? You'll often see models of the same computer with just a different CPU varying in cost by $200 or more. Is the price difference worth it? It's hard to know because so many factors influence CPU performance. Picking the best CPU for the kind of work you do is easier if you research some performance benchmarks. **CPU benchmarks** are measurements used to compare performance between processors. Benchmarks are generated by running software programs specifically designed to push the limits of CPU performance. Articles are often published comparing CPUs, or complete systems, based on their benchmark performance. Investigate a few, using sites like **cpubenchmark.net**, before you select the chip that's best for you.

Measuring the CPU

How can I tell whether my current CPU is meeting my needs? One way to determine whether your CPU is right for you is to watch how busy it is as you work. You can do this by checking out your **CPU usage**—the percentage of time your CPU is working.

Your computer's OS has utilities that measure CPU usage. These are incredibly useful, both for considering whether you should upgrade and for investigating if your computer's performance suddenly seems to drop off for no apparent reason.

On Windows systems, Task Manager lets you access this data (see Figure 7). The **CPU usage graph** records your CPU usage for the past minute. (Note that if you have multiple cores and hyperthreading, you'll see only one physical processor listed, but it will show that you have several virtual processors.) Of course, there will be periodic peaks of high CPU usage, but if your CPU usage levels are greater than 90% during most of your work session, a faster CPU will contribute a great deal to your system's performance.

To walk through using the Task Manager, check out the Try This and watch the "Using Windows to Evaluate CPU Performance" Sound Byte. Mac OS X has a similar utility named Activity Monitor, which is located in the Utilities folder in the Applications subfolder.

How often do I have to be watching the CPU load? Keep in mind that the workload your CPU experiences depends on how many programs are running at one time. Even though the CPU may meet the specs for each program separately, how you use your machine during a

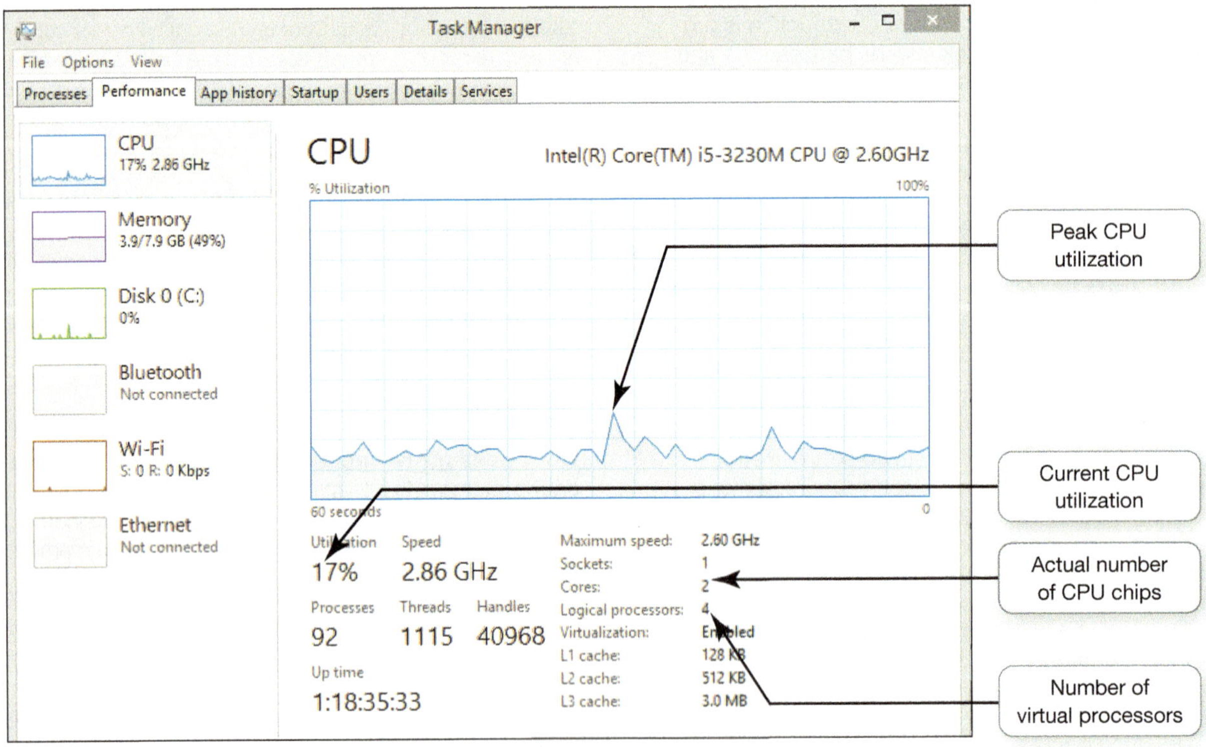

FIGURE 7 The Performance tab of the Windows Task Manager utility shows you how busy your CPU is.

>*To access the Performance tab, right-click the* ***Start*** *button. From the menu, select* ***Task Manager****, and then click the* ***Performance*** *tab.*

BITS&BYTES

The Haswell Boost

The amount of power a CPU requires is very important to designers looking to extend the battery life of an ultrabook or tablet. Intel's newest generation of the Core CPU line, its fourth-generation processors, nicknamed "Haswell," gives systems up to a 50% boost in battery life. Since Haswell-based computers also see about a 40% increase in graphics performance, look for the fourth-generation Intel CPU for a system that is fast and can make it through the day on a single charge.

typical day may tax the CPU. If you're having slow response times or decide to measure CPU performance as a check, open the Task Manager and leave it open for a full day. Check in at points when you have a lot of open windows and when you have a lot of networking or disk-usage demand.

So a better CPU means a better performing system? Your CPU affects only the *processing* portion of the system performance, not how quickly data can move to or from the CPU. Your system's *overall* performance depends on many factors, including the amount of RAM installed as well as hard drive speed. Your selection of CPU may not offer significant improvements to your system's performance if there is a bottleneck in processing because of insufficient RAM or hard drive performance, so you need to make sure the system is designed in a balanced way. Figure 8 lists factors to consider as you decide which specific CPU is right for you. ■

SOUND BYTE
Using Windows to Evaluate CPU Performance

In this Sound Byte, you'll learn how to use the utilities provided by Windows to evaluate your CPU's performance. You'll also learn about shareware utilities (software that you can install and try before you purchase it) that expand on the capabilities the Task Manager utility provides.

FIGURE 8

Evaluating the CPU

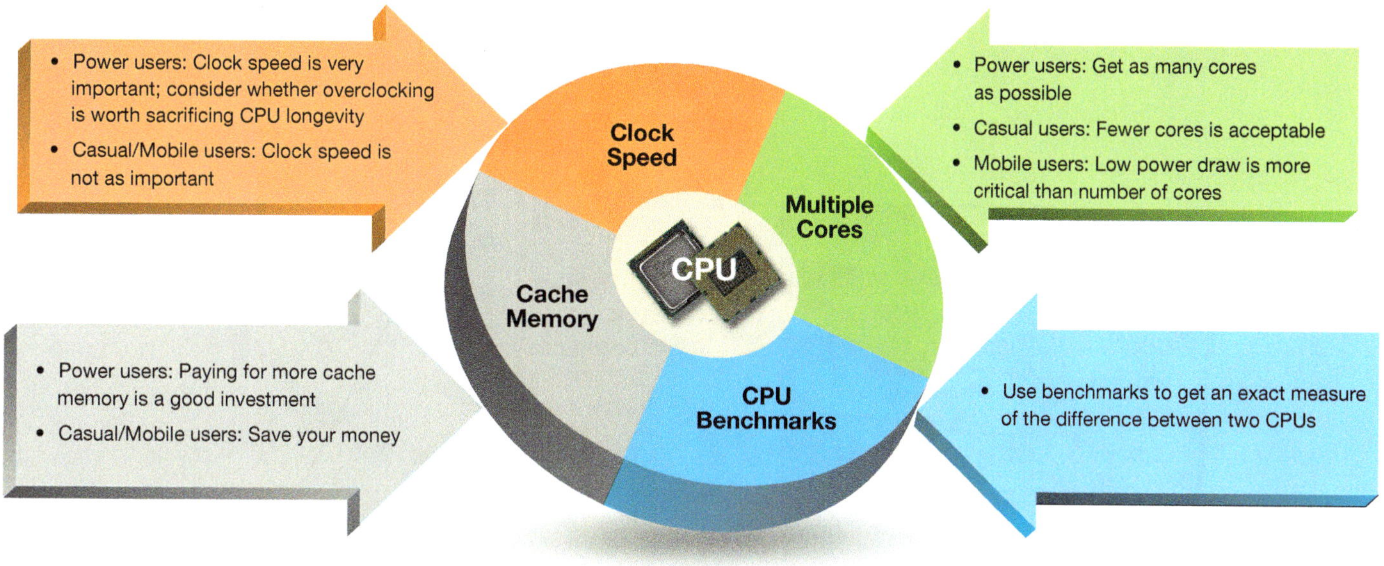

evaluating the MEMORY SUBSYSTEM

Random access memory (RAM) is your computer's temporary storage space. Although we refer to RAM as a form of storage, it really is the computer's short-term memory. It remembers everything that the computer needs in order to process data into information, such as data that has been entered and software instructions, but only when the computer is on. RAM is an example of **volatile storage**. When the power is off, the data stored in RAM is cleared out. This is why, in addition to RAM, systems always include **nonvolatile storage** devices for permanent storage of instructions and data. Read-only memory (ROM), for example, holds the critical start-up instructions. Hard drives provide the largest nonvolatile storage capacity in the computer system.

Why not use a hard drive to store the data and instructions? It's about one million times faster for the CPU to retrieve a piece of data from RAM than from a mechanical hard drive. The time it takes the CPU to grab data from RAM is measured in nanoseconds (billionths of seconds), whereas pulling data from a fast mechanical hard drive takes an average of 10 milliseconds (ms), or thousandths of seconds.

Figure 9 shows the various types of memory and storage distributed throughout your system: memory that is actually part of the CPU (such as CPU registers and cache), RAM, virtual memory, optical drives, and SSD and mechanical hard drives. Each of these has its own tradeoff of speed versus price. Because the fastest memory is so much more expensive, systems are designed with much less of it. This principle is influential in the design of a balanced computer system and can have a tremendous impact on system performance.

The RAM in Your System

Are there different types of RAM? Yes, but in most current systems, the type of RAM used is double data rate 3 (DDR3) memory modules, available in several different speeds (1066 MHz, 1333 MHz, 1600 MHz). The higher the speed, the better the performance. DDR5 (double data rate 5) memory, which has an even faster data transfer rate, is seen in high-performance video graphics cards.

RAM appears in the system on **memory modules** (or **memory cards**), small circuit boards that hold a series of RAM chips and fit into special slots on the motherboard. Most memory modules in today's systems are packaged as a *dual inline memory module (DIMM)*, a small circuit board that holds several memory chips (see Figure 10).

How can I tell how much RAM is installed in my computer? The amount of RAM actually sitting on memory

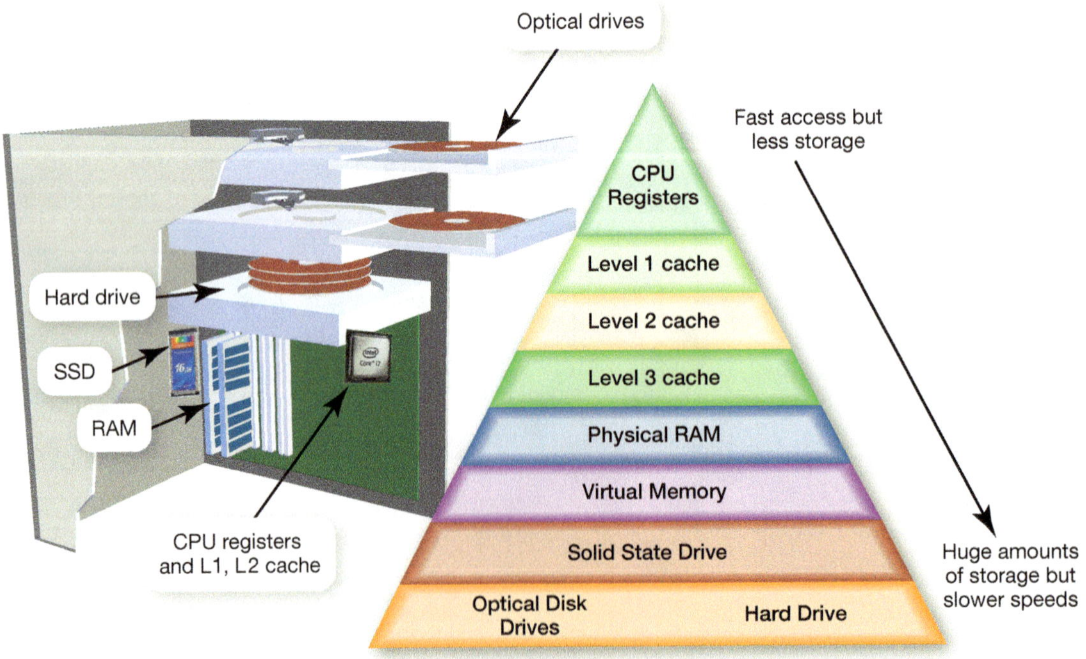

FIGURE 9 A computer system's memory has many different levels, ranging from the small amounts in the CPU to the much slower but more plentiful storage of a mechanical hard drive.

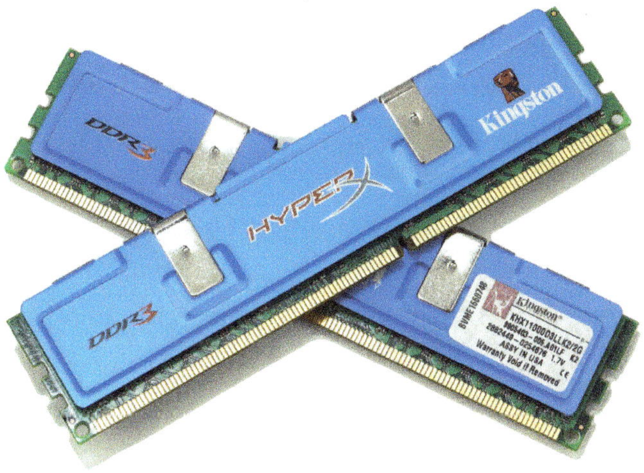

FIGURE 10 A DIMM memory module holds a series of RAM chips. *(Hugh Threlfall/Alamy)*

modules in your computer is your computer's **physical memory**. The easiest way to see how much RAM you have is to look in the System Properties window. (On a Mac, choose the Apple menu and then About This Mac.) This is the same tab you looked in to determine your system's CPU type and speed, and is shown in Figure 5. RAM capacity is measured in gigabytes (GB), and most machines sold today have at least 4 GB of RAM.

> SOUND BYTE
> **Memory Hierarchy Interactive**
> In this Sound Byte, you'll learn about the different types of memory used in a computer system.

How can I tell how my RAM is being used? To see exactly how your RAM is being used, open the Resource Monitor and click on the Memory tab (see Figure 11). The Resource Monitor gives additional details on CPU, disk, network, and memory usage inside your system, and you can use it to see how you're using all the RAM you paid for!

Windows uses a memory-management technique known as **SuperFetch**. SuperFetch monitors the applications you use the most and preloads them into your system memory so that they'll be ready to be used when you want them. For example, if you have Microsoft Word running, Windows stores as much of the information related to Word in RAM as it can, which speeds up how fast your application responds. This is because pulling information from RAM is much faster than pulling it from the hard drive. You can watch this process at work using the Resource Monitor. Figure 11 shows how the 8 GB of installed RAM is being used:

- 1.5 GB is running programs.
- 2.15 GB is holding cached data and files ready for quick access.
- 4.4 GB is currently unused.

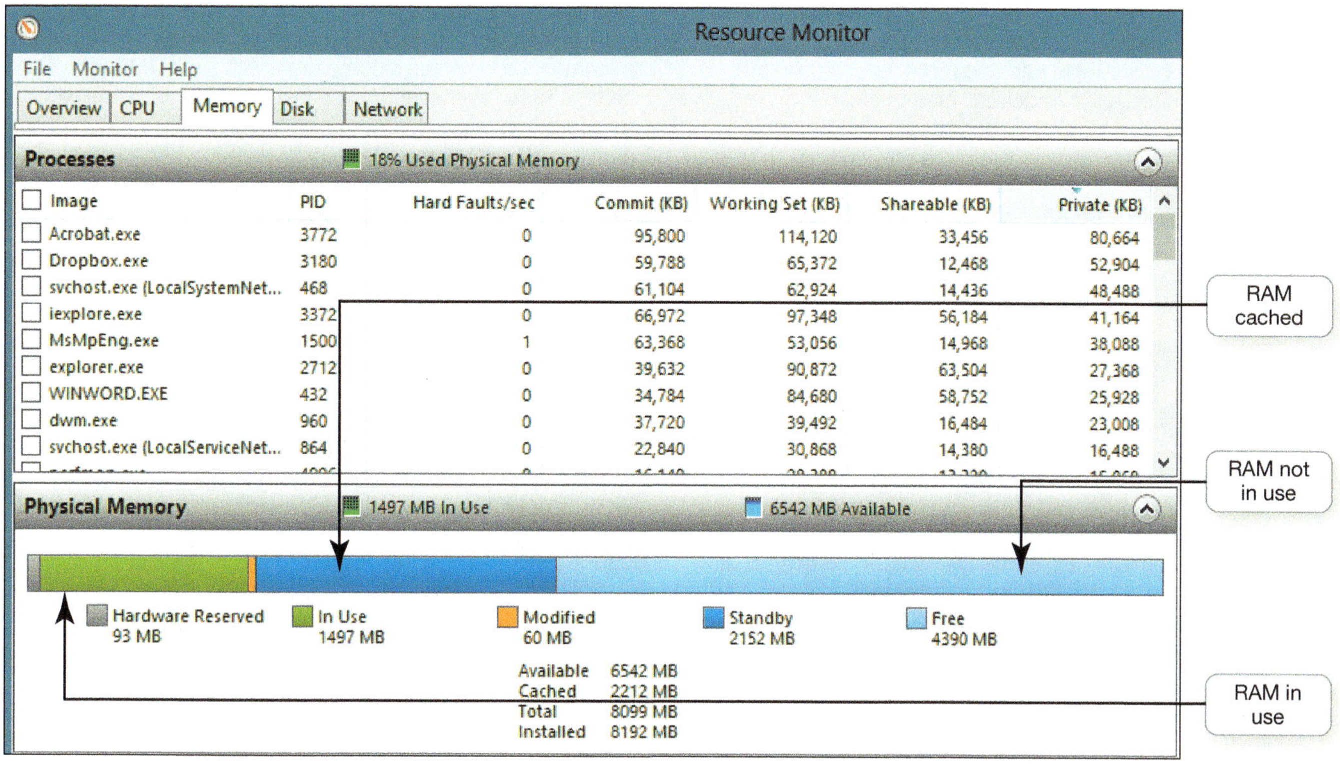

FIGURE 11 The Resource Monitor's Memory tab shows a detailed breakdown of how the computer is using memory.

*>To access the Resource Monitor, in the Task Manager, click the **Performance** tab, click **Open Resource Monitor**, and then click the **Memory** tab.*

ACTIVE HELPDESK
Evaluating Your CPU and RAM

In this Active Helpdesk call, you'll play the role of a helpdesk staffer, fielding calls about what the CPU does and how to evaluate its performance. You'll also field calls about how memory works and how to evaluate how much memory a computer needs.

SOUND BYTE
Installing RAM

In this Sound Byte, you'll learn how to select the appropriate type of memory to purchase, how to order memory online, and how to install it yourself. As you'll discover, the procedure is a simple one and can add great performance benefits to your system.

How much RAM do I need? At a minimum, your system needs enough RAM to run the OS. Running the 64-bit version of Windows 8.1 requires a minimum of 2 GB of RAM. However, because you run more applications at one time than just the OS, you'll want to have more RAM than just what's needed for the OS. For example, Figure 12 shows how much RAM is recommended for the OS, a web browser, and some software.

It's a good idea to have more than the minimum amount of RAM you need now so you can use more programs in the future. Remember, too, that "required" means these are the *minimum values* recommended by manufacturers; having more RAM often helps programs run more efficiently. New systems today ship with at least 4 GB of RAM, and high-end systems can come with 24 GB. The rule of thumb: When buying a new computer, buy as much RAM as you can afford.

FIGURE 12

Sample RAM Allocation

APPLICATION	RAM RECOMMENDED
Windows 8.1 (64 bit)	2 GB
Microsoft Office Professional 2013	2 GB
Internet Explorer 11	2 GB
iTunes 11	1 GB
Adobe Photoshop Elements 11	2 GB
Total RAM recommended to run all programs simultaneously	**9 GB**

Adding RAM

Is there a limit to how much RAM I can add to my computer? The motherboard is designed with a specific number of slots into which the memory cards fit, and each slot has a limit on the amount of RAM it can hold. To determine your specific system limits, check the system manufacturer's website.

In addition, the OS running on your machine imposes its own RAM limit. For example, the maximum amount of RAM for the 32-bit version of Windows 8.1 is 4 GB, whereas the maximum memory you can install using the 64-bit version of Windows 8.1 Pro is 192 GB.

Is it difficult or expensive to add RAM? Adding RAM is fairly easy (see Figure 13). Be sure that you purchase a memory module that's compatible with your computer. Also be sure to follow the installation instructions that come with the RAM module. Typically, you simply line up the notches and gently push the memory module in place.

RAM is a relatively inexpensive system upgrade. The cost of RAM does fluctuate in the marketplace as much as 400% over time, though, so if you're considering adding RAM, you should watch the prices of memory in online and print advertisements. ■

FIGURE 13 Adding RAM to a computer is quite simple and relatively inexpensive. On a laptop, you often gain access through a panel on the bottom. *(Editorial Image, LLC/Alamy; Editorial Image, LLC/Alamy)*

evaluating the STORAGE SUBSYSTEM

Remember, there are two ways data is stored on your computer: temporary storage and permanent storage. RAM is a form of temporary (or volatile) storage. The information residing in RAM is not stored permanently. It's critical to have the means to store data and software applications permanently.

Fortunately, several storage options exist. Storage devices include internal hard drives, SSDs, optical drives, and external hard drives. When you turn off your computer, the data that has been written to these devices will be available the next time the machine is powered on. These devices therefore provide *nonvolatile* storage.

Mechanical Hard Drives

What makes the hard drive such a popular storage device? With storage capacities exceeding 4 terabytes (TB), a mechanical **hard drive** has the largest capacity of any storage device. And because it offers the most storage per dollar, the hard drive is also a more economical device than other options.

Today, most desktop system units are designed to support more than one internal hard drive. The Apple Mac Pro has room for four hard drives, and the Thermaltake Level 10 can support six hard drives. Each one simply slides into place when you want to add more storage.

How is data stored on a hard drive? A hard drive is composed of several coated, round, thin plates of metal stacked on a spindle. Each plate is called a **platter**. When data is saved to a hard drive platter, a pattern of magnetized spots is created on the iron oxide coating of each platter. When the spots are aligned in one direction, they represent a *1*; when they're aligned in the other direction, they represent a *0*. These *0*s and *1*s are *bits* (or *binary digits*) and are the smallest pieces of data that computers can understand. When data stored on the hard drive platter is retrieved (or read), your computer translates these patterns of magnetized spots into the data you have saved.

How quickly does a hard drive find information? The hard drive's **access time**, the time it takes a storage device to locate its stored data and make it available for processing, is faster than optical drives. Mechanical hard drive access times are measured in milliseconds (ms), meaning thousandths of seconds. For large-capacity drives, access times of approximately 12 to 13 milliseconds are typical. That's less than one-hundredth of a second. For comparison, a DVD drive can take over 150 milliseconds to access data.

Solid-State Drives

Do mechanical hard drives have the fastest access times? A **solid-state drive (SSD)** uses electronic memory and has no mechanical motors or moving parts. Having no mechanical motors allows SSDs to offer incredibly fast access times, reaching data in only a tenth of a millisecond (0.1 ms). That's about 100 times faster than mechanical hard drives (see Figure 14)! SSDs also have a great advantage when booting up since a mechanical hard drive has to wait for motors to bring the plates up to the final rotation speed. The start-up time of SSDs is so fast, in fact, that most desktop and laptop systems offer an option to use at least one SSD. This "system drive" may only be 20 GB large, but it holds the operating system and means the wake-up time for the system will be very fast. In addition, SSDs run with no noise, generate very little heat, and require very little power, making them a popular option in ultrabooks.

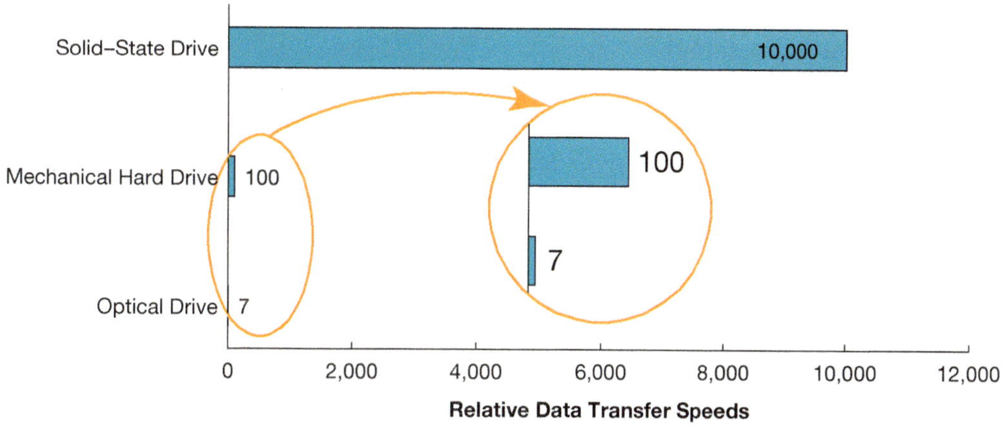

FIGURE 14 Relative Data Transfer Speeds for Nonvolatile Storage Options

DIG DEEPER How a Hard Drive Works

The thin metal platters that make up a hard drive are covered with a special magnetic coating that enables the data to be recorded onto one or both sides of the platter. Hard drive manufacturers prepare the disks to hold data through a process called *low-level formatting*. In this process, concentric circles, each called a **track**, and pie-shaped wedges, each called a **sector**, are created in the magnetized surface of each platter, setting up a gridlike pattern that identifies file locations on the hard drive. A separate process called *high-level formatting* establishes the catalog that the computer uses to keep track of where each file is located on the hard drive.

Hard drive platters spin at a high rate of speed, some as fast as 15,000 revolutions per minute (rpm). Sitting between the platters are special "arms" that contain read/write heads (see Figure 15). A **read/write head** moves from the outer edge of the spinning platter to the center, as frequently as 50 times per second, to retrieve (read) and record (write) the magnetic data to and from the hard drive platter. As noted earlier, the average total time it takes for the read/write head to locate the data on the platter and return it to the CPU for processing is called its *access time*. A new hard drive should have an average access time of approximately 12 ms.

Access time is mostly the sum of two factors—seek time and latency:

1. The time it takes for the read/write heads to move over the surface of the disk, moving to the correct track, is called the **seek time**. (Sometimes people incorrectly refer to this as access time.)
2. Once the read/write head locates the correct track, it may need to wait for the correct sector to spin to the read/write head. This waiting time is called **latency** (or **rotational delay**).

The faster the platters spin (or the faster the rpm), the less time you'll have to wait for your data to be accessed. Currently, most hard drives for home systems spin at 7,200 rpm.

The read/write heads don't touch the platters of the hard drive; rather, they float above them on a thin cushion of air at a height of 0.5 microinches. As a matter of comparison, a human hair is 2,000 microinches thick and a particle of dust is larger than a human hair. Therefore, it's critical to keep your hard drive free from all dust and dirt because even the smallest particle could find its way between the read/write head and the disk platter, causing a **head crash**—a stoppage of the hard drive that often results in data loss.

SSDs free you from worry about head crashes at all. The memory inside an SSD is constructed with electronic transistors, meaning there are no platters, no motors, and no read/write arms. Instead, a series of cells are constructed in the silicon wafers. If high voltage is applied, electrons move in and you have one state. Reverse the voltage and the electrons flow in another direction, marking the cell as storing a different value. The limiting factor for an SSD's lifespan is how many times data can be written to a cell. But the current generation of SSDs is proving to have very strong performance over time. Intel, one manufacturer of SSDs, says its drives will last five years when being written to heavily (20 GB per day).

Capacities for hard drives in personal computers can exceed 4,000 GB (4 TB). Increasing the amount of data stored in a hard drive is achieved either by adding more platters or by increasing the amount of data stored on each platter. How tightly the tracks are placed next to each other, how tightly spaced the sectors are, and how closely the bits of data are placed affect the measurement of the amount of data that can be stored in a specific area of a hard drive platter. Modern technology continues to increase the standards on all three levels, enabling massive quantities of data to be stored in small places.

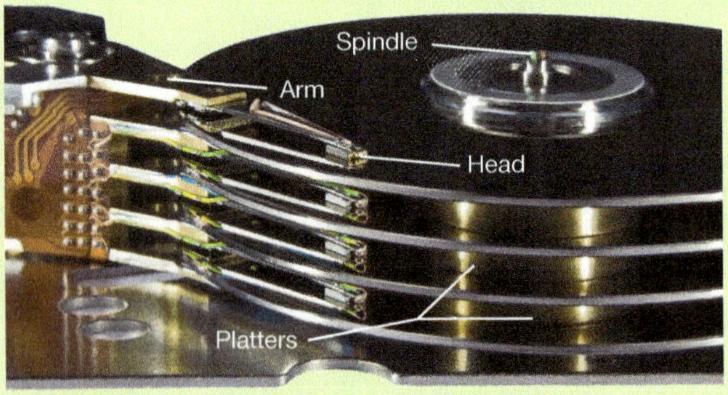

FIGURE 15 The hard drive is a stack of platters enclosed in a sealed case. Special arms fit between each platter. The read/write heads at the end of each arm read data from and save data to the platters. *(skaljac/Shutterstock)*

> **SOUND BYTE**
> **Optical Media Reading and Writing Interactive**
> In this Sound Byte, you'll learn about the process of storing and retrieving data from CD-RW, DVD, and Blu-ray discs.

Storage capacities for SSDs now range up to 2 TB, but such a large SSD is very expensive. Systems now often offer an SSD of 128 GB or 256 GB and then a mechanical hard drive, or two, to provide TBs of inexpensive slower storage space.

Optical Drives

How do optical drives work? Optical drives are disc drives that use a laser to store and read data. Data is saved to a compact disc (CD), digital video disc (DVD), or Blu-ray disc (BD) (called **optical media**) within established tracks and sectors, just like on a hard drive. But optical discs store data as tiny pits that are burned into the disc by a high-speed laser. These pits are extremely small, less than 1 micron (a millionth of a meter).

Figure 16 shows how data is read from a disc by a laser beam, with the pits and nonpits (called *lands*) translating into the *1*s and *0*s of the binary code that computers understand. CDs and DVDs use a red laser to read and write data. Blu-ray discs get their name because they are read with a blue laser light, which has a shorter wavelength and can focus more tightly and pack more information on a disc. Blu-ray drives are the fastest optical devices on the market and deliver the high-definition quality video that larger displays and monitors demand.

Why can I store data on some optical discs but not others? All forms of optical media come in three formats:

1. *Prerecorded* discs are read-only (ROM), meaning you can't save any data onto them.
2. *Recordable* (R) formats allow you to write data to them, but only once.
3. *Rewriteable* (RW) discs let you write and rewrite data to them many times.

Should I bother having an optical disc drive? Traditionally, optical media delivered music and movies, but these are now available through streaming services. Likewise, in the past, software was often installed from a DVD, but now you buy almost all software online. Therefore, many lightweight systems have stopped including optical drives. For example, netbooks and ultrabooks are so thin and lightweight they often leave out an optical drive but may include a slot for an SD memory card to allow you to transfer files. You can buy

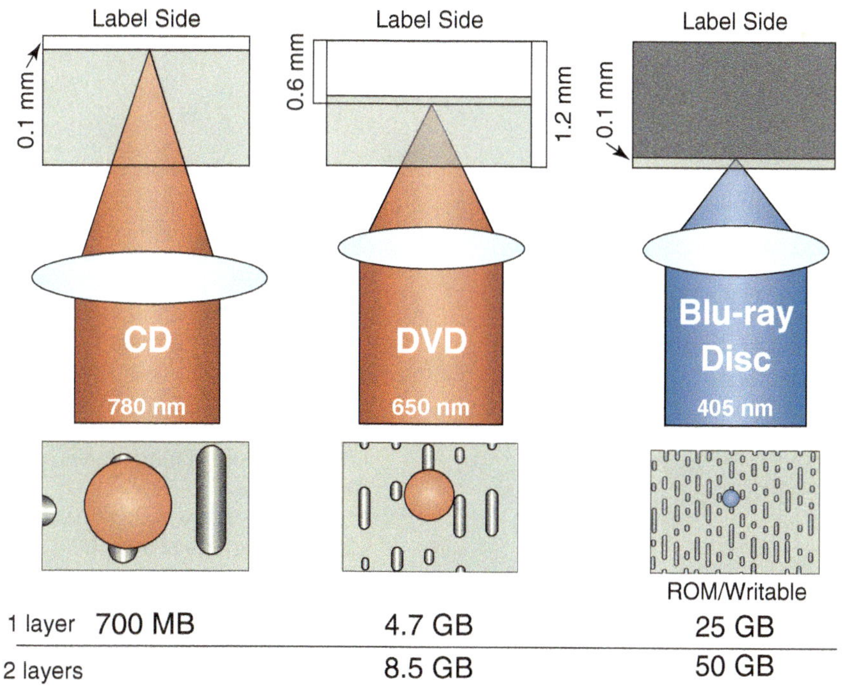

FIGURE 16 Blu-ray lasers have a shorter wavelength and so can store a much higher density of information than CDs and DVDs.

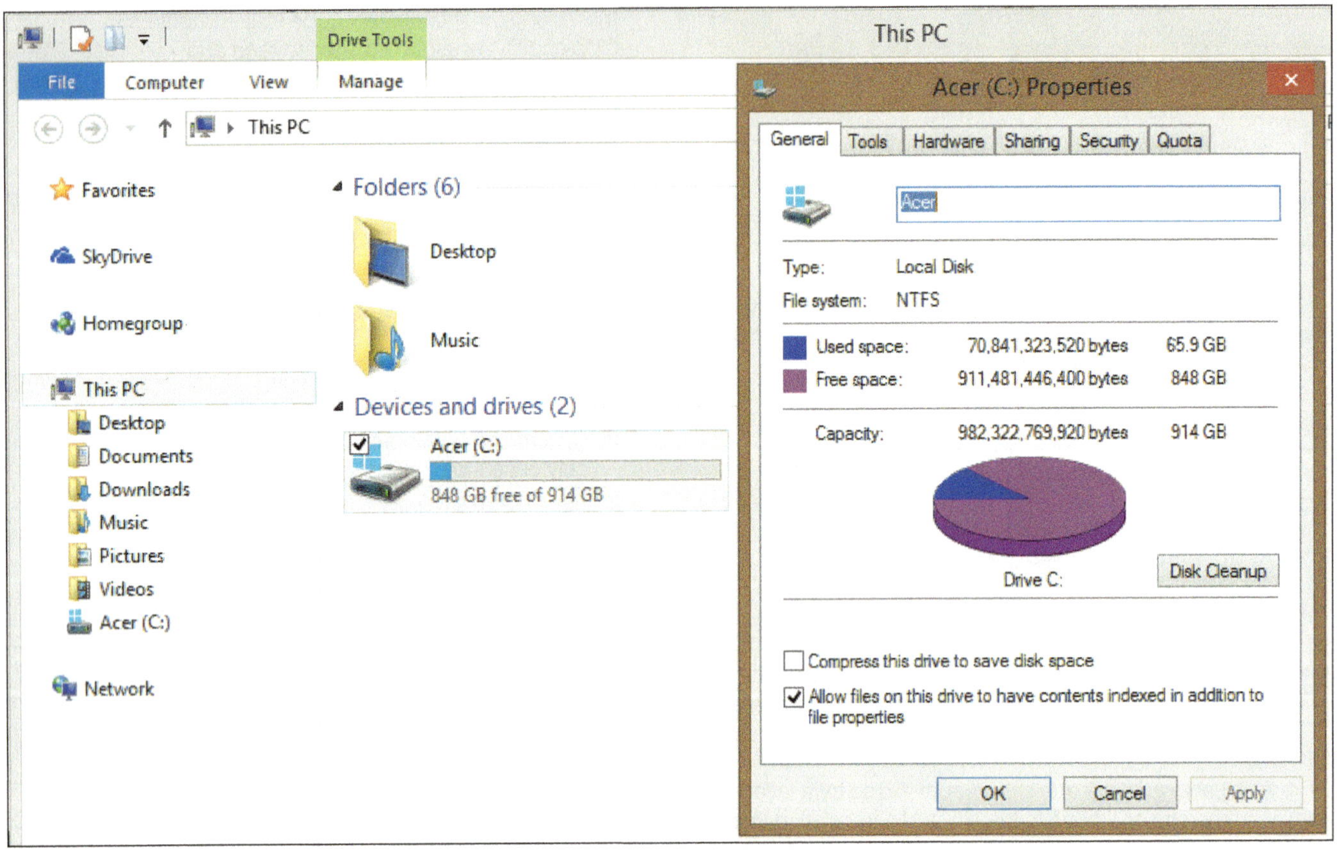

FIGURE 17 In Windows, the free and used capacity of each device in the computer system is shown in the Computer window. The General tab of the Properties dialog box gives you more-detailed information.

>To view the Computer window, launch File Explorer (previously called Windows Explorer), and then click ***This PC****. To view the pie chart, right-click the* ***C drive****, and select* ***Properties****.*

external optical drives, but if you have a need for optical drives, you're probably better off purchasing a laptop computer; these have optical drives.

Your Storage Capacity and Needs

How do I know how much storage capacity I have? Typically, hard drive capacity is measured in gigabytes (GB) or terabytes (1 TB = 1,000 GB). Windows displays the hard drives, their capacity, and usage information, as shown in Figure 17. To get a slightly more detailed view, select a drive and then right-click and choose Properties.

How much storage do I need? You need enough space to store the following:

- The OS
- The software applications you use, such as Microsoft Office, music players, and games
- Your data files
- Your digital music library, photos, videos of television shows and movies, and so on

Figure 18 shows an example of storage calculation. If you plan to have a system backup on the same drive, be sure to budget for that room as well. However, note that if you're going to store your data files online instead of on your computer, you may not need much hard drive space. For example, if you stream all the movies you watch from Netflix, keep all your data files in Microsoft OneDrive, and use online software like Google Docs to edit, you may need very little hard drive space. Most ultrabooks like the Dell XPS 13 or the Apple MacBook Air are configured with 128-GB drives. In fact, many Chromebooks have only a 16-GB drive.

Also note that you don't need an internal hard drive that has all the storage space you need. You can also add an external hard drive to your system, many of which use a USB port to connect. If you're looking to buy an external hard drive, the USB 3.0 standard is about 10 times faster than USB 2.0, so if your system supports USB 3.0, that's the better choice.

Is it better to have one huge drive or several smaller drives? It depends on what's important to you: speed or security. If you purchase two smaller drives, you can

FIGURE 18

Sample Hard Drive Space Requirements

APPLICATION/DATA	HARD DRIVE SPACE REQUIRED	HEAVY CLOUD STORAGE USER
Windows 8 (64 bit)	20 GB	20 GB
Microsoft Office 2013 Professional	3.5 GB	3.5 GB
Adobe Photoshop Elements 11	4 GB	4 GB
Adobe Premiere Pro CC	10 GB	10 GB
Video library of movies	80 GB (about 40 HD movies)	Streamed through online services
Music library	50 GB (about 7,000 songs)	Stored in cloud (iCloud or Amazon Cloud Drive)
Photographs	5 GB	Stored in iCloud or Dropbox
Total storage in use	**172.5 GB**	**37.5 GB**
Full backup	172.5 GB	Done to cloud using Carbonite
Total required	**345 GB**	**37.5 GB**

combine them using RAID technology. **RAID (redundant array of independent disks)** is a set of strategies for using more than one drive in a system (see Figure 19). RAID 0 and RAID 1 are the most popular options for consumer machines.

- When you run two hard drives in **RAID 0**, the time it takes to write a file is cut in half. If disk performance is very important—for example, when you're doing video editing or sound recording—using two files in RAID 0 could be important. RAID 0 is faster because every time data is written to a hard drive, it's spread across the two physical drives (see Figure 19a). The write begins on the first drive, and while the system is waiting for that write to be completed, the system jumps ahead and begins to write the next block of data to the second drive. This makes writing information to disk almost twice as fast as using just one

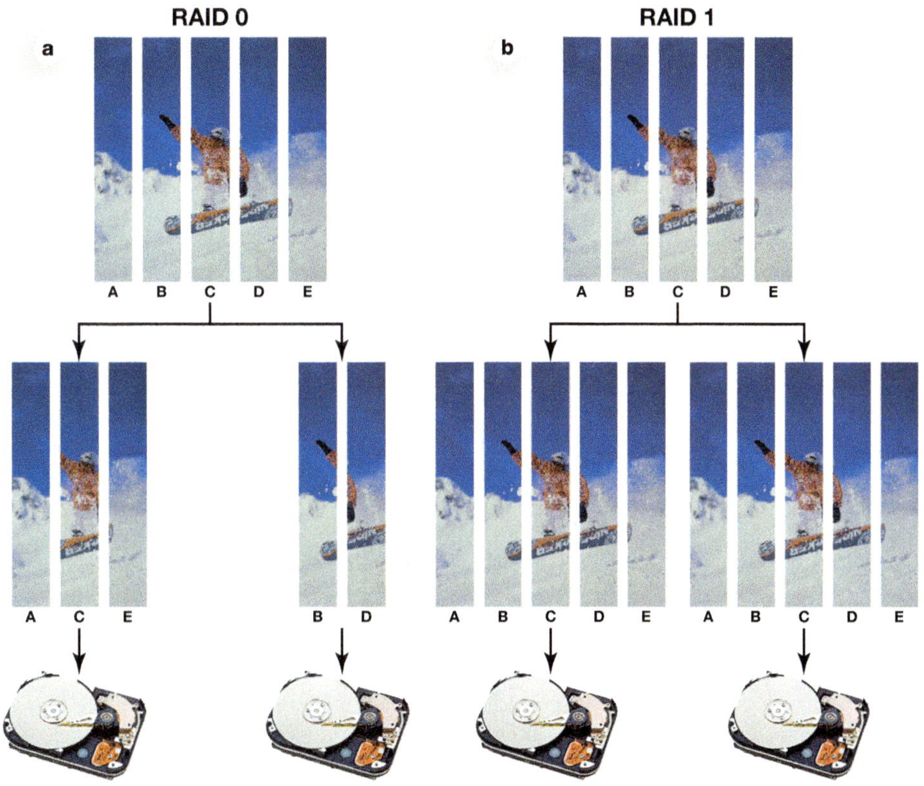

FIGURE 19 (a) A RAID 0 configuration speeds up file read/write time. (b) A RAID 1 configuration gives you an instant backup. *(World Pictures/Alamy; Ragnarock/Shutterstock)*

BITS&BYTES

How Much Storage to Buy?

No matter what kind of device you purchase, you'll have to decide how much storage you're willing to pay for. Does your Nexus 7 need 16 GB? 32 GB? Should the SSD drive in your ultrabook be 128 GB? 256 GB? 512 GB? When you make your decision, keep in mind two factors:

1. Whether you can add storage later using an SD card. If you can have a few SD cards to store music or photos, that will be a cheaper option.
2. How much usable storage is available in the device. For example, a 128-GB drive often provides much less available storage space after the operating system, the manufacturer software, and backup storage space are accounted for.

hard drive. The downside is that if either of these disks fail, you lose all your data because part of each file is on each drive. So RAID 0 is for those most concerned with performance.

> SOUND BYTE
> **Installing a Blu-ray Drive**
> In this Sound Byte, you'll learn how to install a Blu-ray drive in your computer.

- If you're really paranoid about losing data, you should consider having two drives in RAID 1. In a **RAID 1** configuration, all the data written to one drive is instantly perfectly mirrored and written to a second drive (see Figure 19b). This provides you with a perfect, instant-by-instant backup of all your work. It also means that if you buy two 1-TB drives, you only have room to store 1 TB of data because the second 1-TB drive is being used as the "mirror."

RAID 0 and RAID 1 configurations are available on many desktop systems and are even beginning to appear on laptop computers.

So how do my storage devices measure up? Figure 20 summarizes the factors you should consider in evaluating your storage subsystem. ■

> **Before moving on to Part 2:**
> - Watch Replay Video 1 .
> - Then check your understanding of what you've learned so far.

FIGURE 20

Evaluating Storage

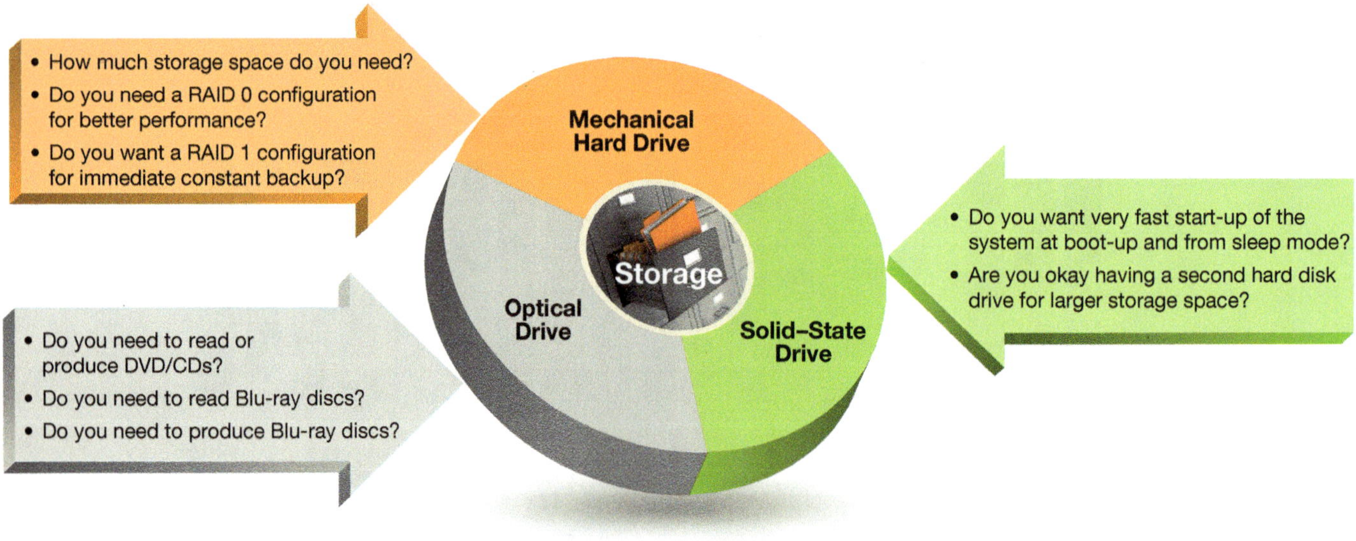

(Maxim_Kazmin/Fotolia)

check your understanding//

For a quick review to see what you've learned so far, answer the following questions. Visit **pearsonhighered.com/techinaction** to check your answers.

multiple choice

1. Which statement about ultrabook computers is FALSE?
   - **a.** Ultrabooks have the fastest optical drives.
   - **b.** Ultrabooks are equipped with SSD drives for fast start-up.
   - **c.** Ultrabooks typically weigh less than 3 pounds.
   - **d.** Ultrabooks do not offer HDMI video output ports.
2. SSDs are classified as what type of storage?
   - **a.** volatile
   - **b.** nonvolatile
   - **c.** video
   - **d.** cache
3. When would you want to consider RAID 1 technology?
   - **a.** When you need the fastest solution for writing data
   - **b.** When you need an instant backup of your work
   - **c.** If you think that SSDs are too expensive
   - **d.** When you only want to have one hard disk drive
4. CPU benchmarks are used to
   - **a.** compare system performance.
   - **b.** compare processor performance.
   - **c.** compare memory performance.
   - **d.** compare storage system performance.
5. SuperFetch is a memory-management technique that
   - **a.** determines the type of RAM your system requires.
   - **b.** makes the boot-up time for the system very quick.
   - **c.** preloads the applications you use most into system memory.
   - **d.** defragments the hard drive to increase performance.

true–false

_____ **1.** A quad core CPU with hyperthreading has eight virtual CPUs.

_____ **2.** SSD hard drives are primarily used for backup of data.

critical thinking

1. **Types of Storage**

   You can select between optical drives, portable drives, and SSD drives. There are a wide range of options. How will you decide the proper balance for your own computing needs?
2. **Emerging Technologies**

   Touch screens are now available in a range of sizes, from smartphones to iPads to larger products like the Microsoft PixelSense. Windows 8 has a redesigned interface for support of touch screens. What other new technologies will become part of our collective experience? How will these technologies and devices change entertainment and how people interact with information? What future technologies would be on your wish list?

Continue »

TRY THIS

Measure Your System Performance

Using the Windows Task Manager and the Resource Monitor can provide you with a lot of useful information about your computer system. Let's make sure you can use these Windows tools to keep an eye on your system performance.

Step 1 Hold the Windows key and hit X. From the pop-up, select **Task Manager**. Click the **Performance** tab.

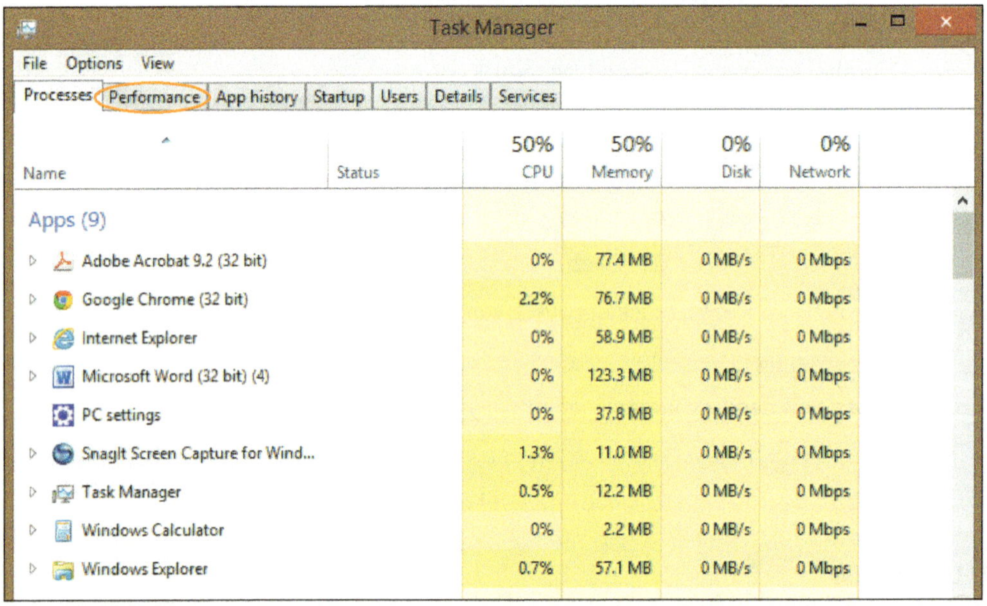

Step 2 If you leave this window open while you work, you can pop in and check the history of how your CPU, disk, memory, and network are performing. Let's start by looking at **CPU** utilization.

This computer is only occasionally going over 50%, so the system isn't limited by CPU speed.

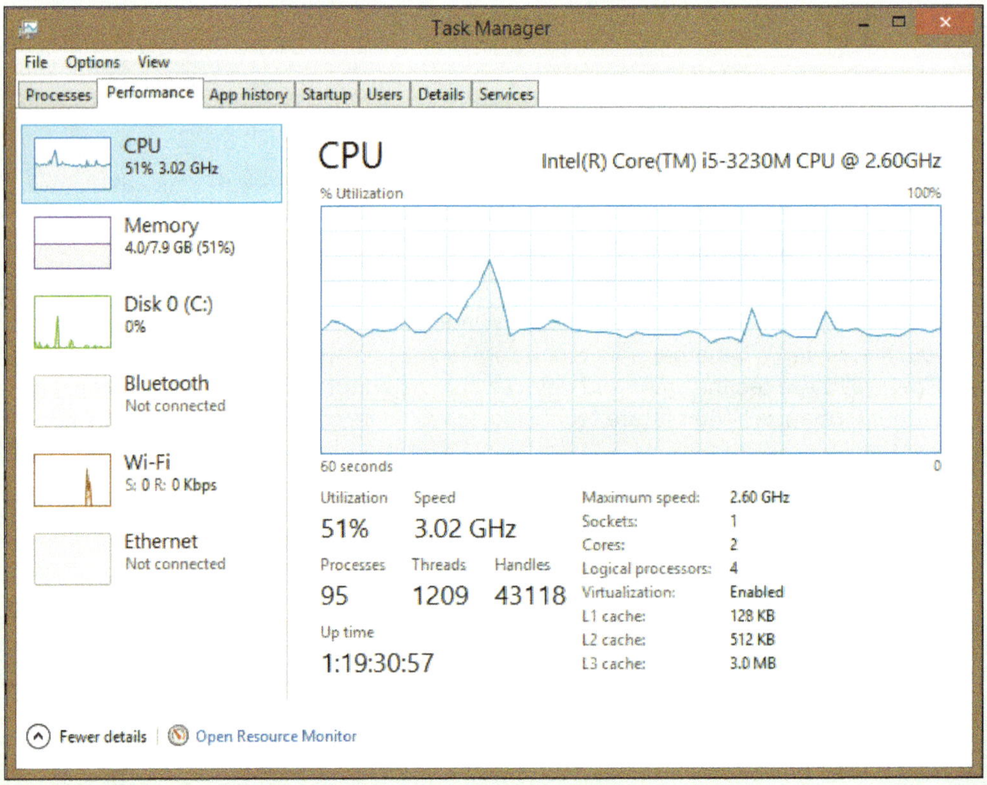

Step 3 What about memory usage? Clicking on **Memory** in the left panel shows that we have 8 GB of memory installed in this computer. This computer is running Windows 8 and has the following applications open: Word, Excel, IE 11, Chrome Browser, Adobe Acrobat, and several Windows systems utilities.

Notice that memory usage is consistent at about 4 GB. Windows 8.1 is good at allocating memory to programs on an as-needed basis and keeping programs from taking up large amounts of memory when they are idle. We have plenty of available memory so this system isn't limited by memory capacity.

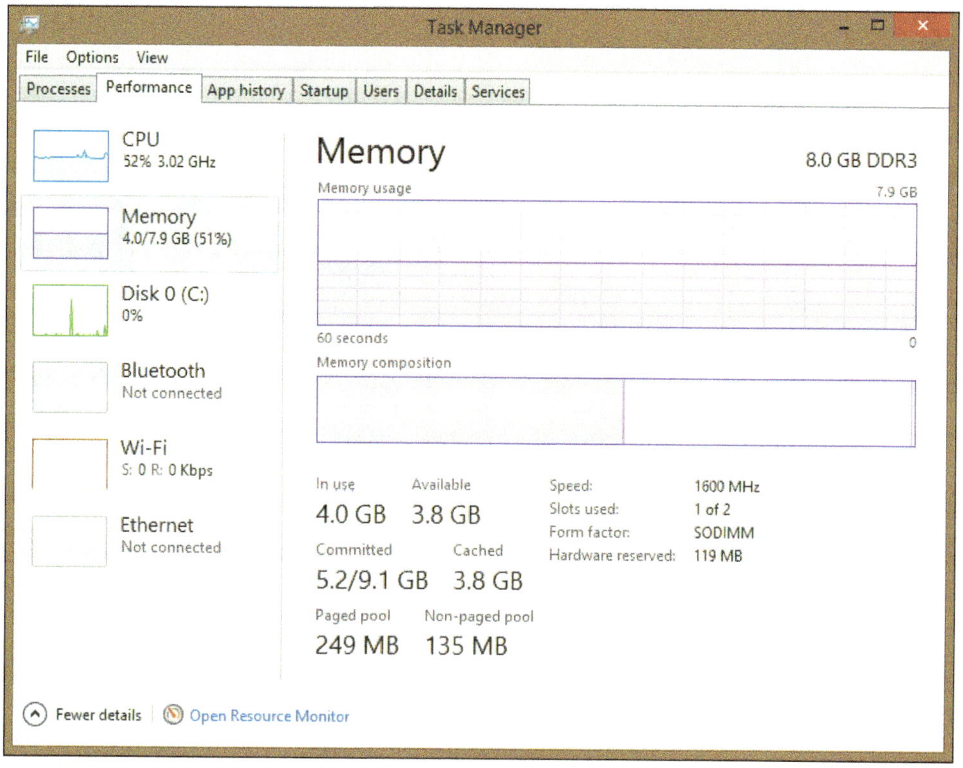

Step 4 What about disk usage? Clicking on **Disk** in the left panel shows that we have one disk drive, a 1 TB internal hard drive. The lower graph shows the history of data moving back and forth to the disk, the disk transfer rate. The larger upper graph shows how active the disk is—what percentage of time it is reading and writing. If that is consistently high, upgrading to a faster, larger disk will have a big performance impact.

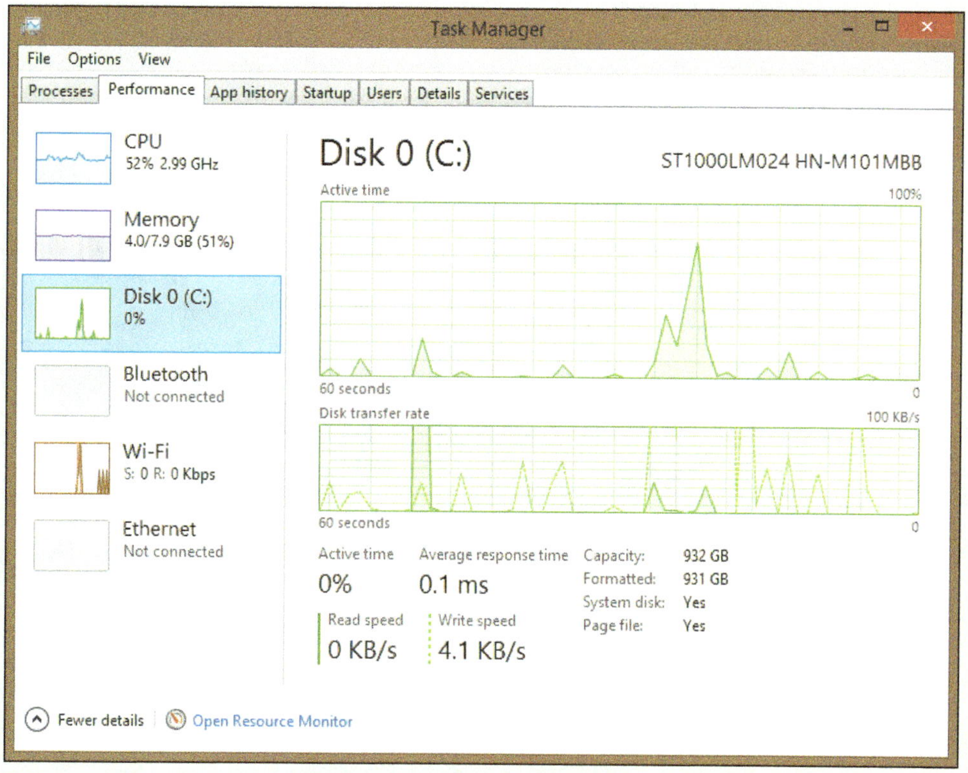

Evaluating Other Subsystems and Making a Decision

The audio and video subsystems of your computer affect much of your enjoyment of the machine. Let's evaluate those subsystems and consider what state-of-the-art audio/video would add to your computing experience. Then let's consider how to make sure your system is reliable—nothing interferes with enjoying technology like a misbehaving computer!

evaluating the VIDEO SUBSYSTEM

How video is displayed depends on two components: your video card and your monitor. If you're considering using your computer to display complex graphics, edit high-definition videos, or play graphics-rich games with a lot of fast action, you may want to consider upgrading your video subsystem.

Video Cards

What exactly is a video card? A **video card** (or **video adapter**) is an expansion card that's installed inside the system unit to translate binary data into the images you view on your monitor. Modern video cards like the ones shown in Figures 21 and 22 let you connect video equipment using a number of different ports:

- *DVI ports* for digital LCD monitors
- *HDMI ports* for high-definition TVs, Blu-ray players, or gaming consoles
- *DisplayPort adapters,* a newer style port that can connect to digital monitors or projectors

How much memory does my video card need? All video systems include their own RAM, called **video memory**. Several standards of video memory are available, including graphics double data rate 3 (GDDR3) memory and the newer **graphics double data rate 5 (GDDR5)** memory.

The amount of video memory on your video card makes a big impact on the resolution the system can support and on how smoothly and quickly it can render video. Most new laptop computers come with video cards equipped with a minimum of 1 GB of video memory. For the serious gamer, 2 GB or more is essential, and cards with 3 GB are available. These high-end video cards allow games to generate smoother animations and more-sophisticated shading and texture.

How can I tell how much memory my video card has? You'll find information about your system's video card in the Advanced Settings of the Screen Resolution dialog box.

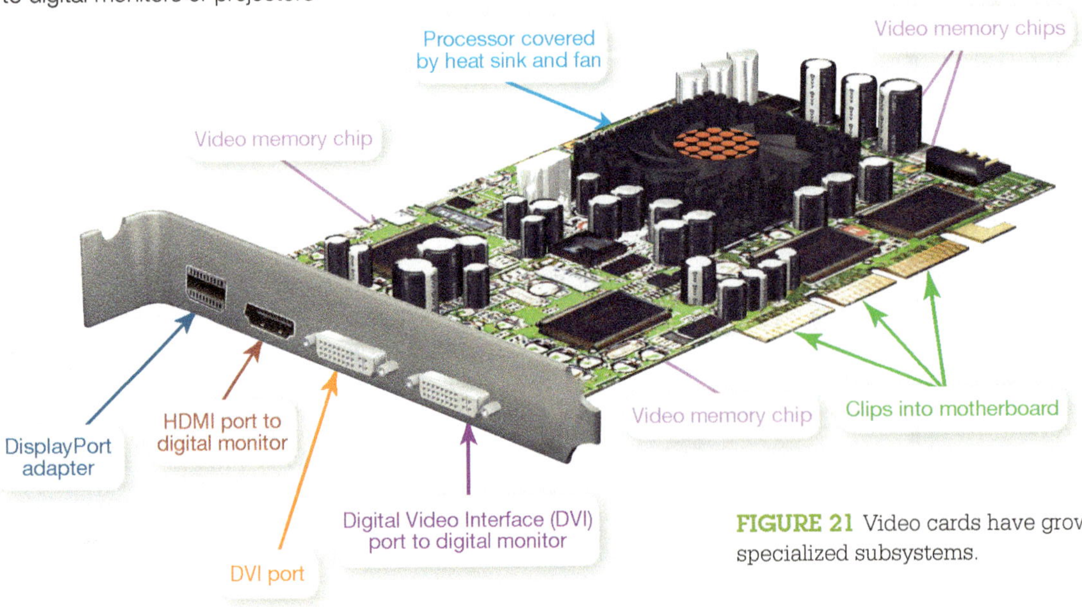

FIGURE 21 Video cards have grown to be highly specialized subsystems.

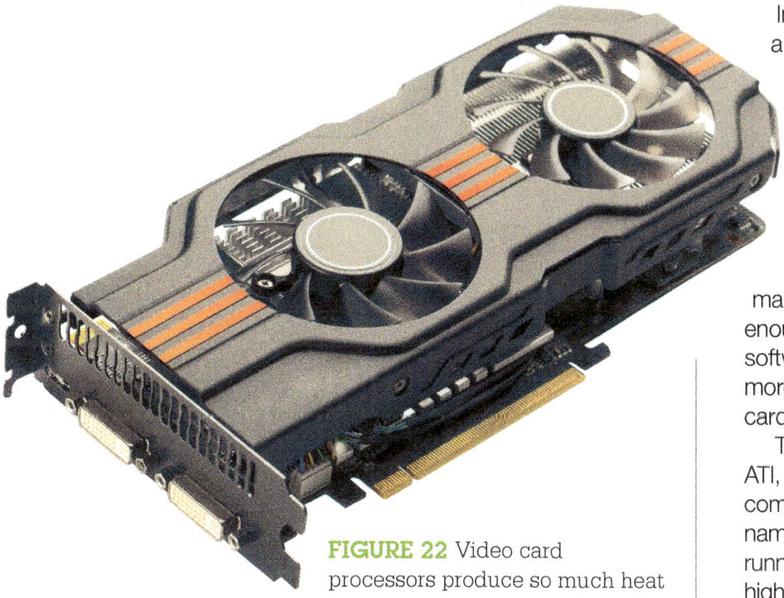

FIGURE 22 Video card processors produce so much heat that video cards have their own fan—or two. *(nikkytok/Fotolia)*

To get to the Screen Resolution dialog box, right-click on your desktop and select Screen Resolution. In the Screen Resolution dialog box, click the Advanced settings link. A window will appear that shows you the type of video card installed in your system, as well as its memory information.

How does the CPU handle intensive video calculations? Because displaying graphics demands a lot of computational work from the CPU, video cards come with their own **graphics processing unit (GPU)**. The GPU is a separate processing chip specialized to handle 3-D graphics and image and video processing with incredible efficiency and speed. When the CPU is asked to process graphics, it redirects those tasks to the GPU, significantly speeding up graphics processing. Figure 23 shows how the CPU can run much more efficiently when a GPU does all the graphics computations.

In addition, special lighting effects can be achieved with a modern GPU. Designers can change the type of light, the texture, and the color of objects based on complex interactions. Some GPU designs incorporate dedicated hardware to allow high-definition movies to be decoded or special physics engines to model water, gravity, and rigid body movements.

Why do some people use more than one video card in the same system? For users who are primarily doing text-based work, one video card is certainly enough. Computer gamers and users of high-end visualization software, however, often take advantage of the ability to install more than one video card at a time. Two or even three video cards can be used in one system.

The two major video chip set manufacturers, Nvidia and ATI, have each developed their own standards supporting the combining of multiple video cards. For Nvidia, this standard is named SLI; for ATI, it is called CrossFire. When the system is running at very high video resolutions, such as 1920 x 1200 or higher, multiple video cards working together provide the ultimate in performance. If you're buying a new system and might be interested in employing multiple video cards, be sure to check whether the motherboard supports SLI or CrossFire.

Can I run a few monitors from one video card? Working with multiple monitors is useful if you often have more than one application running at a time (see Figure 24) or even if you just want to expand your gaming experience. Some video cards can support up to six monitors from a single card.

> ACTIVE HELPDESK
> **Evaluating Computer System Components**
>
> In this Active Helpdesk call, you'll play the role of a helpdesk staffer, fielding calls about the computer's storage, video, and audio devices and how to evaluate whether they match your needs as well as how to improve the reliability of your system.

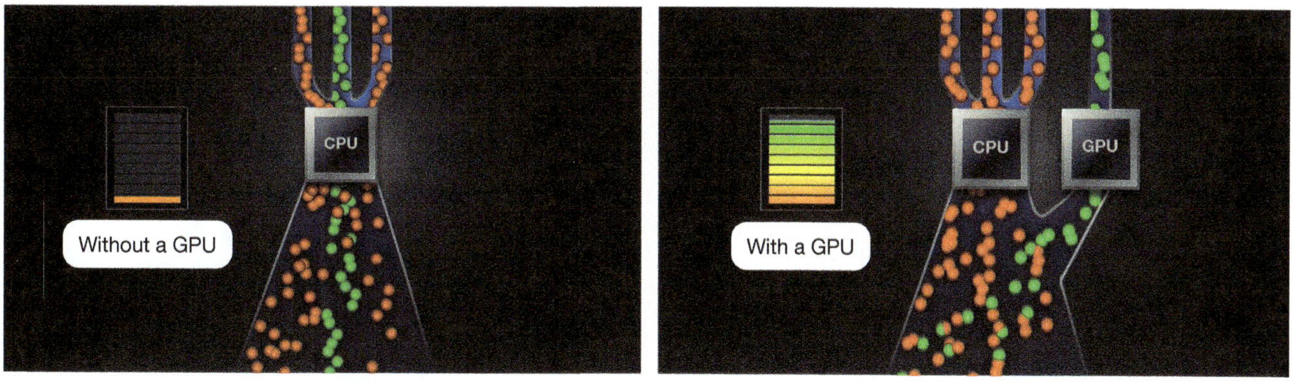

Without a GPU | **With a GPU**

FIGURE 23 The GPU is specialized to handle processing of photos, videos, and video game images. It frees up the CPU to work on other system demands.

FIGURE 24 AMD Radeon technology supports six monitors, which can be combined in any way. *(© satopon / Fotolia)*

The AMD Radeon graphics card, for example, lets you merge all six monitors to work as one screen or to combine them into any subset—for example, displaying a movie on two combined screens, Excel on one monitor, Word on another, and a browser spread across the final two.

Can I have a 3-D experience from a computer monitor? 3-D panels are available for desktop monitors and for some laptops. Using the 3-D wireless vision glasses included with the panels, the glasses make existing games or 3-D movies display in stereoscopic 3-D.

How do I know if I'm putting too much demand on my video card? If your monitor takes a while to refresh when you're editing photos or playing a graphics-rich game, then the video card could be short on memory or the GPU is being taxed beyond its capacity. You can evaluate this precisely using the software that came with your card. For example, AMD Overdrive software monitors the GPU usage level, the current temperature, and the fan speed.

Review the considerations listed in Figure 25 to see if it might be time to upgrade your video card. On a desktop computer, replacing a video card is fairly simple: Just insert the new video card in the correct expansion slot on the motherboard. The video card in a laptop is more difficult to upgrade since the display and keyboard usually have to be removed to replace the video card. Note that some very basic laptop systems have video adapters integrated into the motherboard, so these video cards can't be upgraded. ■

BITS&BYTES

Where's the Free TV?

Most major networks are streaming content for free so that you can catch episodes of most TV series on the go. Subscription channels like HBO and Showtime all have free streaming of content. If you have HBO at home, you can watch any show from the HBO GO website. If you're interested in more international viewing, head to Squid TV and select broadcasts from around the world. If you're looking for homemade shows, sites like Justin.tv and Ustream are filled with live and archived video webcasts. And if you want to make TV instead of just watching, you can webcast your own show from the Ustream webapp using your webcam or smartphone video camera.

FIGURE 25

Evaluating the Video Card

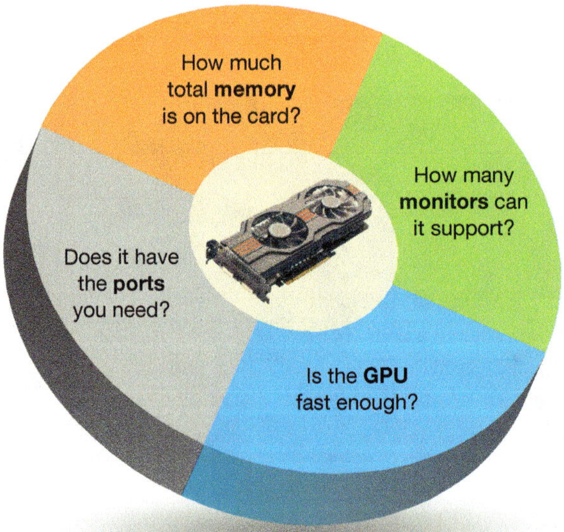

trends in IT

Thunderbolt: The New Standard for Data Transfer

Faster is always better, and the newest input/output standard, Thunderbolt, is faster than anything seen before. And speed isn't its only advantage.

Intel used fiber optics—the transmission of digital data through pure glass cable as thin as human hair—to develop the new input/output technology named Thunderbolt. Thunderbolt supports blazingly fast transfer rates of 10 Gb/s, zooming past even the theoretical limit of the new USB 3.0, which is 4.8 Gb/s. How fast is that? Intel says that Thunderbolt could transfer a full-length HD movie in under 30 seconds or in just 10 minutes copy a library of music that would take a solid year to play through. And Thunderbolt can supply much more power to devices than the USB standard allows. It also has a very slim connector design, allowing laptop designers to make their systems even thinner (see Figure 26).

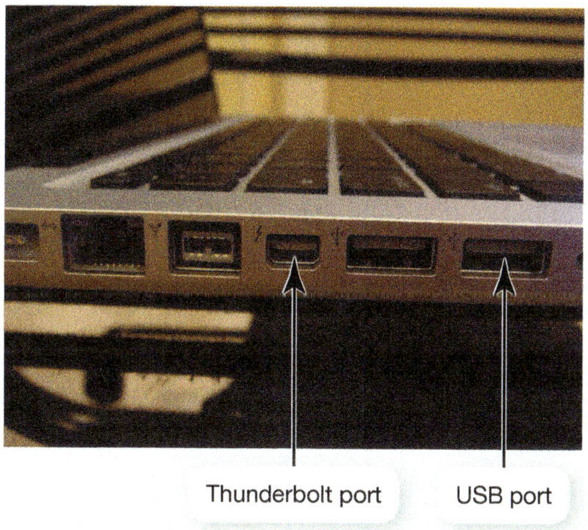

FIGURE 26 Thunderbolt ports are very thin, allowing for new design options. *(Kendall Martin)*

But one of the greatest hopes that comes with Thunderbolt is that the technology will be able to replace a number of different ports, cleaning up the cluttered design we see now on the sides of laptops and the backs of desktop units. Apple has introduced Thunderbolt ports on its full line of systems. A Thunderbolt port looks like a single thin port that supports both the video standard DisplayPort and the bus standard PCI Express (see Figure 27). So Thunderbolt can connect monitors to computers using VGA, DisplayPort, DVI, or HDMI and can connect systems to external hard drives that use USB, FireWire, or eSATA. One Thunderbolt port can support several devices because the cables can be daisy-chained (connected one after another in a serial fashion), so having just one Thunderbolt port on a laptop allows you to connect up to six different peripherals to your system.

Thunderbolt technology also gives you a two-for-one deal, because each connector can support two separate channels to send and receive data, each one still operating at the full 10 Gb/s bandwidth.

What will this mean to laptop designers? Some speculate we'll see the heavy, heat-producing video cards currently integrated into gaming laptops become external graphics boxes. An incredibly thin, light laptop design would let you be wonderfully mobile all day, and then when you come home, you'd attach one cable. It would run from your Thunderbolt port to your 60-inch HDTV and then continue on to a separate graphics processor box. That same laptop would then be running a huge high-definition monitor with a high-resolution graphics and physics engine.

Apple is not the only company that uses the Intel technology. Hard-drive companies like LaCie and Western Digital, as well as audio/video processing companies like Avid and Apogee, now offer Thunderbolt products. And the USB community may need to put up a bit of a fight to keep their standard around. But the allure of incredible speed, great versatility, and small, thin packaging is going to make the Thunderbolt technology a trend to watch.

Could Thunderbolt make USB a thing of the past?

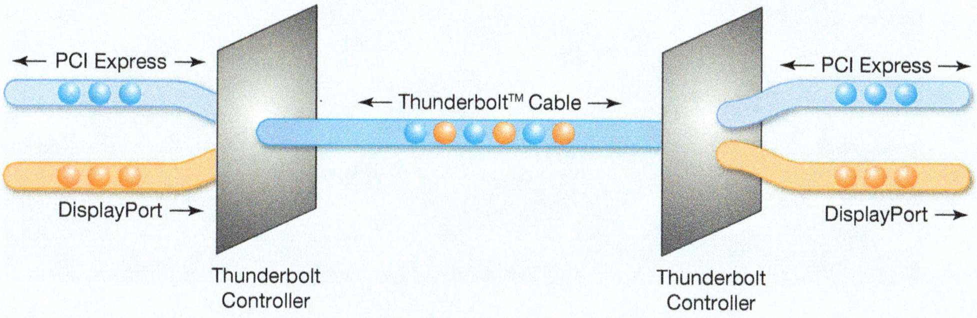

FIGURE 27 Thunderbolt can carry two channels of information on the same connector.

evaluating the AUDIO SUBSYSTEM

For many users, a computer's preinstalled speakers and sound card are adequate. However, if you often use your computer to play games, music, and video, you may want to upgrade your speakers or your sound card.

What does the sound card do? Like a video card, a **sound card** is an expansion card that attaches to the motherboard inside your system unit. A sound card enables the computer to drive the speaker system. Most desktop systems have a separate sound card, although low-end computers often have integrated the job of managing sound onto the motherboard itself. You can upgrade laptop sound cards using an ExpressCard solution, like the Creative Sound Blaster X-Fi.

What does a basic sound card do for me? Many computers ship with a **3-D sound card**. 3-D sound technology is better at convincing the human ear that sound is omnidirectional, meaning that you can't tell from which direction the sound is coming. This tends to produce a fuller, richer sound than stereo sound. However, 3-D sound is not surround sound.

What is surround sound, then? **Surround sound** is a type of audio processing that makes the listener experience sound as if it were coming from all directions by using multiple speakers. The current surround-sound standard is from Dolby. There are many formats available, including Dolby Digital EX and Dolby Digital Plus for high-definition audio. Dolby TrueHD is the newest standard. It features high-definition and lossless technology, which means that no information is lost in the compression process.

To create surround sound, another standard, Dolby Digital 7.1, takes digital sound from a medium (such as a Blu-ray disc) and reproduces it in eight channels. Seven channels cover the listening field with placement to the left front, right front, left rear, right rear, and center of the audio stage, as well as two extra speakers to the side, as shown in Figure 28. The eighth channel holds extremely low-frequency (LFE) sound data and is sent to a subwoofer, which can be placed anywhere in the room.

The name 7.1 surround indicates that there are seven speakers reproducing the full audio spectrum and one speaker handling just lower frequency bass sounds. There is also a 5.1 surround-sound standard, which has a total of six speakers—one subwoofer, a center speaker, and four speakers for right/left in the front and the back. If you have a larger space or want precise location of sounds, use the newer 7.1 system.

To set up surround-sound on your computer, you need two things:

1. A set of surround-sound speakers and, for the greatest surround-sound experience,
2. A sound card that is Dolby Digital compatible

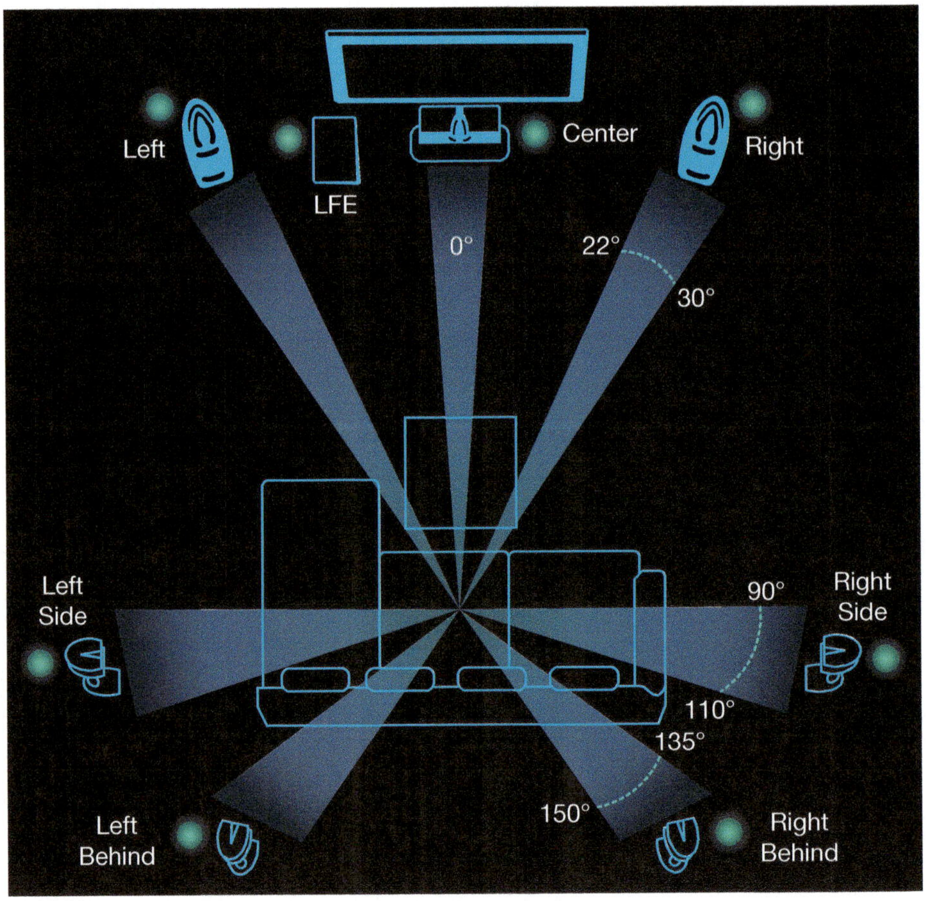

FIGURE 28 Dolby Digital 7.1 surround sound gives you a better quality audio output.

(simon5586/Fotolia; aleksangel/Fotolia; Maksym Yemelyanov/Fotolia; Sashkin/Fotolia; Mariusz Blach/Fotolia; AbsentAnna/Fotolia; M-Audio)

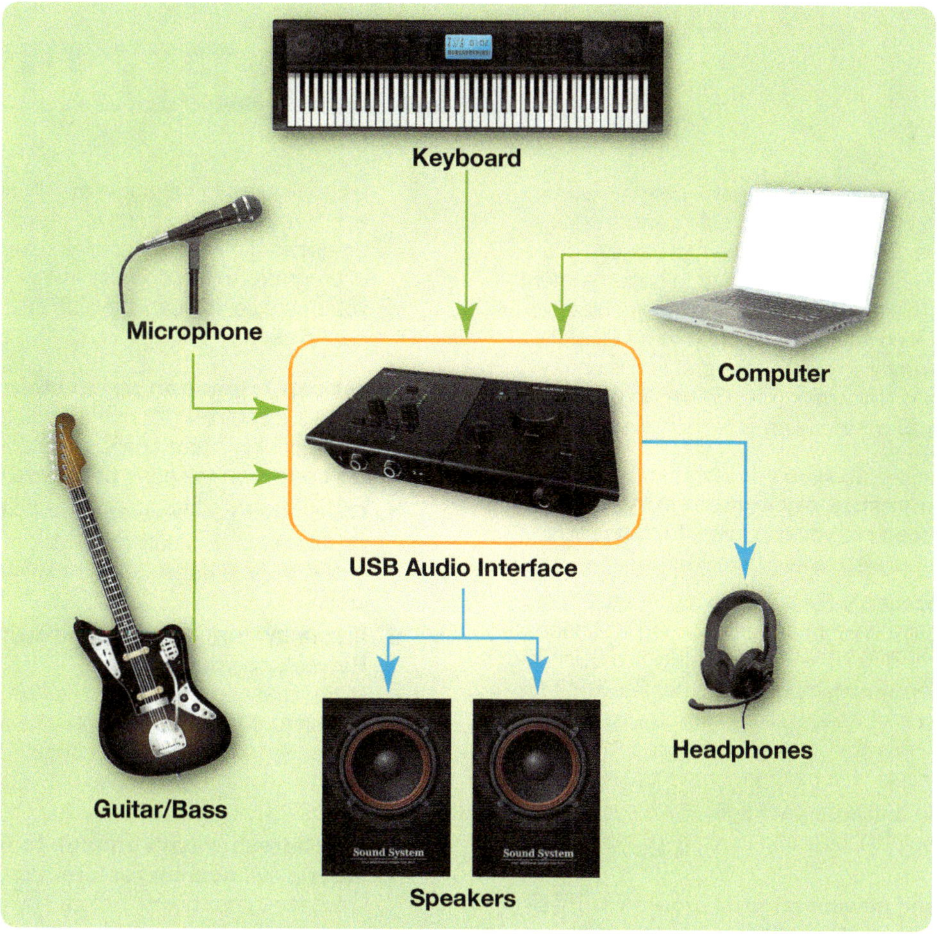

FIGURE 29 Sample Home Recording Studio Setup

Does it matter what kind of speakers my laptop has? The limited size for speakers in a laptop and the added weight of circuitry to drive them means most people use headphones or ear buds for great audio instead of speakers. However, some laptops have built-in higher-quality speakers, like the Alienware line featuring Klipsch speakers and the HP series offering Beats speakers.

What setup do I need if I want to use my computer for recording my band? You can connect MIDI instruments, high-quality microphones, and recording equipment to your computer through an **audio MIDI interface** box. MIDI is an electronics standard that allows different kinds of electronic instruments to communicate with each other and with computers. The audio interface box attaches to your computer through a USB port and adds jacks for connecting guitars and microphones. You can edit and mix tracks through many different software packages, like Cakewalk or GarageBand. Figure 29 shows a simple home recording studio setup.

Figure 30 lists the factors to consider when deciding whether your audio subsystem meets your needs. ■

FIGURE 30

Evaluating the Audio Subsystem

evaluating system RELIABILITY

Many computer users decide to buy a new system because they're experiencing problems such as slow performance, freezes, and crashes. Over time, even normal use can cause your computer to build up excess files and to become internally disorganized. This excess, clutter, and disorganization can lead to deteriorating performance or system failure. If you think your system is unreliable, see if the problem is one you can fix before you buy a new machine. Proper upkeep and maintenance also may postpone an expensive system upgrade or replacement.

What can I do to ensure my system stays reliable? Here are several procedures you can follow to ensure your system performs reliably (see also Figure 31):

- **Clear out unnecessary files.** Temporary Internet files can accumulate quickly on your hard drive, taking up unnecessary space. Running the Disk Cleanup utility is a quick and easy way to ensure your temporary Internet files don't take up precious hard drive space. Likewise, you should delete any unnecessary files from your hard drive regularly because they can make your hard drive run more slowly.
- **Install a reliable antivirus package.** Make sure it's set to update itself automatically and to run a full system scan frequently.
- **Run spyware and adware removal programs.** These often detect and remove different pests and should be used in addition to your regular antivirus package.
- **Run the Disk Defragmenter utility on your hard drive.** When your hard drive becomes fragmented, its storage capacity is negatively affected. When you defragment (defrag) your hard drive, files are reorganized, making the hard drive work more efficiently. But remember that this only makes sense for mechanical drives. With no motors, there is no need to defrag an SSD drive.
- **Automate the key utilities.** The utilities that need to be run more than once, like Disk Cleanup, Disk Defragmenter, and the antivirus, adware, and spyware programs, can be configured to run automatically at any time interval you want. You can use Windows Task Scheduler or third-party programs like Norton Security Suite to set up a sequence of programs to run one after the other every evening while you sleep, so you can wake up each day to a reliable, secure system.

What can I do when my system crashes? Computer systems are complex. It's not unusual to have your system stop responding occasionally. If rebooting the computer doesn't help, you'll need to begin troubleshooting:

1. **Check that you have enough RAM.** You learned how to do this in the "Evaluating the Memory Subsystem" section earlier in this chapter. Systems with insufficient RAM often crash.
2. **If your system isn't responding, try doing a Windows Refresh on your system.** This Windows 8 utility removes all the changes you've made to the system and brings it back to the state it came to you from the factory. It removes all the applications from third-party vendors, but it won't remove personal files like your music, documents, or videos.
3. **If a Refresh wasn't enough to fix the problem, consider a full system restore.** Windows 8 automatically creates restore points before any major change to the system takes place, such as when you install a new program or change a device driver. You can also click on System and Security and manually create a restore point at any time. You can then select any restore point and bring your system back to the state it was in at that point. Open the Control Panel, click on System, and then select System Protection to learn more about System Restore.

   For Mac systems, the Mac OS X Time Machine, shown in Figure 32, provides automatic backup and enables you to look through and restore (if necessary) files, folders, libraries, or the entire system.

FIGURE 31

Utilities to Keep Your System Reliable

TO AVOID THIS PROBLEM	USE THIS TOOL	
Your hard drive is running low on space, making it run slowly	Disk Cleanup utility	
Your system is slowing down; browsers or other programs are behaving strangely	Antivirus software Spyware and adware removal software	
Files are spread across many spots on the hard drive, making the hard drive run slowly	Disk Defragmenter utility	
System not responding	Windows Refresh	

FIGURE 32 Mac's Time Machine keeps copies of files, folders, and libraries and can restore your system back to any previous point in time. *(Courtesy of Apple, Inc.)*

4. **If you see an error code in Windows, visit the Microsoft Knowledge Base (support.microsoft.com).** This online resource helps users resolve problems with Microsoft products. For example, it can help you determine what an error code indicates and how you may be able to solve the problem.
5. **Search Google.** If you don't find a satisfactory answer in the Knowledge Base, try copying the entire error message into Google and searching the larger community for solutions.

Can my software affect system reliability? Having the latest version of software makes your system much more reliable. You should upgrade or update your OS, browser software, and application software as often as new patches (or updates) are reported for resolving errors. Sometimes these errors are performance related; sometimes they're potential system security breaches.

If you're having a software problem that can be replicated, use the Steps Recorder to capture the exact steps that lead to it. In Windows 8.1, display the Charms bar, select Search, then type "ste" in the search box. Now run the Steps Recorder and go through the exact actions that create the problem you're having. At any particular step, you can click the Add Comment button and add a comment about any part of the screen. The Steps Recorder then produces a documented report, complete with images of your screen and descriptions of each mouse movement you made. You can then e-mail this report to customer support to help technicians resolve the problem.

How do I know whether updates are available for my software? You can configure Windows so that it automatically checks for, downloads, and installs any available updates for itself, Internet Explorer, and other Microsoft applications such as Microsoft Office. From the Windows Control Panel, open System and Security and then Windows Update. Click Change Settings.

Many other applications now also include the ability to check for updates. Check under the Help menu of the product, and you'll often find a Check for Updates command.

What if none of this helps? Is buying a new system my only option? If your system is still unreliable after these changes, consider upgrading your OS to the latest version. There are often substantial increases in reliability with a major release of a new OS. However, upgrading the OS may require hardware upgrades such as additional RAM, an updated graphics processor, and even a larger hard drive. When you launch the Windows 8 upgrade from the web, it determines whether your hardware, applications, and devices will work with the new OS. ■

making a final DECISION

Now that you've evaluated your computer system, you need to shift to questions of *value*. How closely does your system come to meeting your needs? How much would it cost to upgrade your current system to match what you'd ideally like your computer to do, not only today but also a few years from now? How much would it cost to purchase a new system that meets these specifications?

To know whether upgrading or buying a new system would have better value for you, you need to price both scenarios. Conduct a thorough system evaluation (Figure 33) to gather the data to help you decide. Purchasing a new system is an important investment of your resources, and you want to make a well-reasoned, well-supported decision.

Getting Rid of Your Old Computer

What should I do with my old computer? Before you get rid of your computer, be sure to consider what benefit you might obtain by having two systems. Would you have a use for the older system? Would you be able to donate it?

FIGURE 33

Key Items in System Evaluation

CPU

- What is your CPU usage level?

RAM

- Do you have at least 4 GB?

Storage

- Do you need an SSD start-up drive?
- Do you have a fast-access mechanical drive for large storage space?
- Do you need RAID 0 or RAID 1 storage drives for extra-fast performance or mirroring?

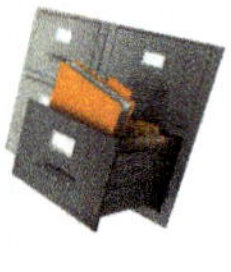

Video

- Do you have enough graphics memory?
- Is your GPU powerful enough?
- Do you have HDMI ports?
- How many monitors do you need to run simultaneously?

Audio

- Do you have 7.1 or 5.1 surround sound?

Also, before you decide to throw it away, consider the environmental impact (Figure 34). Mercury in LCD screens, cadmium in batteries and circuit boards, and flame retardants in plastic housings all are toxic. An alarming, emerging trend is that discarded machines are beginning to create an e-waste crisis.

So how can I recycle my old computer? Instead of throwing your computer away, you may be able to donate it to a nonprofit organization. Here are a few ways to do this:

- Many manufacturers, such as Dell, offer recycling programs and have formed alliances with nonprofit organizations to help distribute your old technology to those who need it.
- Sites like Computers with Causes (**computerswithcauses.org**) organize donations of both working and nonworking computers, printers, and mice.
- You can also take your computer to an authorized computer-recycling center in your area. The Telecommunications Industry Association provides an e-cycling information site you can use to find a local e-cycling center (**ecyclingcentral.com**).

For companies that need to retire large quantities of computers, the risk of creating an environmental hazard is serious. Firms like GigaBiter (**gigabiter.com**) offer a solution. GigaBiter eliminates security and environmental risks associated with electronic destruction by first delaminating the hard drive and then breaking down the computer e-waste into recyclable products. The result of the final step is a sand-like substance that is 100% recyclable.

Can I donate a computer safely, without worrying about my personal data? Before donating or recycling a computer, make sure you carefully remove all data from your hard drive. Built into Windows 8 is an option to help with this, Remove everything and reinstall Windows. It removes all user-installed applications and all of your personal data, and resets your PC settings back to the default values.

Becoming a victim of identity theft is a serious risk. Credit card numbers, bank information, Social Security numbers, tax records, passwords, and personal identification numbers (PINs) are just some of the types of sensitive information that we casually record to our computers' hard drives. Just deleting files that contain proprietary personal information is not protection enough. Likewise, reformatting or erasing your hard drive does not totally remove data, as was proved by two MIT graduate students. They bought more than 150 used hard drives from various sources. Although some of the hard drives had been reformatted or damaged so that the data was supposedly nonrecoverable, the two students were able to retrieve medical records, financial information, pornography, personal e-mails, and more than 5,000 credit card numbers!

ethics in IT Free Hardware for All

The open source software movement has flourished over the past decade. In response to increasing prices and the limitations placed on commercially available software, programmers began to donate time to design, develop, and support software systems. These products, like Gimp (a photo-editing tool), were then made freely available.

In the world of hardware, a similar but different approach called the open source hardware movement has flourished. Because hardware projects require materials and tools to assemble, products distributed as open source are not free in terms of cost, but they are free from any restrictions on how you modify them. Inexpensive hardware devices now span the range from the Digispark, a $9 microcontroller the size of a quarter, to the $35 Raspberry Pi, a full Linux-based computer the size of a credit card. Sample open source hardware projects include video game systems, audio equipment, and 3-D printers.

Is open hardware good for the world? Does it undermine the intellectual property of others who want to create hardware resources and sell them for a profit? What is the impact on developing countries if they have immediate access to hardware designs instead of being required to purchase these items from a for-profit company? Follow the future of open source hardware by keeping an eye on conferences like the Open Hardware Summit (**openhardwaresummit.org**), developer and supplier sites like littleBits (**littlebits.cc**), and homebrew blogs like Procrastineering (**procrastineering.blogspot.com**).

FIGURE 34 An electronics garbage dump can cause environmental concerns, like the leaching of lead and mercury into the ground. *(Minnesota Public Radio, Tim Post/AP Photo)*

The U.S. Department of Defense suggests a seven-layer overwrite for a "secure erase." This means that you fill your hard drive seven times over with a random series of *1*s and *0*s. Fortunately, several programs exist for doing this. For PCs running Windows, look for utility programs like File Shredder or Eraser. Wipe is available for Linux, and ShredIt X can be used for Mac OS X. These programs provide secure hard drive erasures, either of specific files on your hard drive or of the entire hard drive. ■

Before moving on to the Chapter Review:

- **Watch Replay Video 2**.
- Then check your understanding of what you've learned so far.

check your understanding//

For a quick review to see what you've learned so far, answer the following questions. Visit **pearsonhighered.com/techinaction** to check your answers.

multiple choice

1. To document a problem you are having, you can use
   - **a.** Disk Cleanup.
   - **b.** Steps Recorder.
   - **c.** PC Decrapifier.
   - **d.** Resource Monitor.
2. Which is NOT a type of video port?
   - **a.** HDMI
   - **b.** DVI
   - **c.** USB 3.0
   - **d.** DisplayPort
3. When a computer is no longer useful, it can be
   - **a.** securely donated.
   - **b.** recycled.
   - **c.** turned into a sand-like substance.
   - **d.** all of the above.
4. To improve video performance, modern computers have a _______ in addition to the CPU.
   - **a.** GPU
   - **b.** VPU
   - **c.** DPU
   - **d.** APU
5. The faster data transfer port for computers today is the _______ port
   - **a.** USB 3.0
   - **b.** HDMI
   - **c.** Thunderbolt
   - **d.** DisplayPort

true–false

_____ **1.** Windows Refresh is a utility to transfer files to a new system.

_____ **2.** GDDR5 memory is often used in external hard drives.

critical thinking

1. The Early Adopter

We're all aware of the technology price curve: When first introduced, products have the highest prices and the most instability. As these products settle into the market, they become more reliable and the prices fall, sometimes very quickly. People who make those first-release purchases are called *early adopters*. What are the advantages to being an early adopter? What are the disadvantages? How do you decide at what point you should step into the technology price curve for any given product?

2. A Green Machine

Review the impacts on the environment of your computer during its entire lifecycle. How do the production, transportation, and use of the computer affect the increase of greenhouse gas emissions? How does the selection of materials and packaging impact the environment? What restricted substances (like lead, mercury, cadmium, and PVC) are found in your machine? Could substitute materials be used? How would the ultimate "green machine" be designed?

Continue

Chapter Review

summary//

Your Ideal Computing Device

1. What kind of computer is best for me?

- Review the types of computer devices available and consider what your needs are for weight, screen size, and processing power.
- Evaluate your computer system so you have clear data on what you currently have. Then you can compare it with what is on the market and make a decision to upgrade or purchase a new device.

Evaluating the CPU Subsystem

2. What does the CPU do, and how can I evaluate its performance?

- You can find out what processor you have using the System Properties window.
- The CPU works by running a series of four steps: fetch, decode, execute, and store.
- CPUs are compared based on their clock speed, the number of cores they have, and their amount of cache memory.
- CPU benchmarks help you compare the overall performance of different CPUs.
- The CPU performance can be measured and recorded using the CPU usage graph of the Resource Monitor.

Evaluating the Memory Subsystem

3. How does memory work in my computer?

- RAM is used to hold instructions and data because the CPU can access RAM much faster than it can access the hard drive.
- Memory modules are small circuit boards that hold a series of RAM chips in your system.

4. How do I evaluate how much memory I need?

- The System Properties window shows how much physical memory you have installed.
- The Resource Monitor shows how the installed RAM is being used by your system.
- You can easily install RAM in your system, though each system has a limit on how much RAM it can hold.

Evaluating the Storage Subsystem

5. What are the computer's storage devices?

- Data is stored on mechanical hard drives, solid-state drives, and optical drives.
- There is a wide range of difference in access times and cost between different storage solutions, so most systems have a combination of types.

6. How do I evaluate my storage devices?

- The Properties dialog box in File Explorer (previously called Windows Explorer) displays information on the amount of storage available in your system.
- Compute the amount of storage you need for the software and data files you want to keep locally.
- Decide how many drives you want, what type each should be, and how you will configure them. RAID 0 is an option for combining drives for optimal performance. RAID 1 is an option for combining drives for immediate backup.

Evaluating the Video and Audio Subsystems

7. What components affect the quality of video on my computer?

- The video card is key to video quality. Be aware of how much video memory is installed and what kind of GPU is used on the card.
- Some users install multiple video cards for high-end graphics performance.
- With only one card, you can run multiple monitors.

8. How do I know if I need better video performance?

- If you see long refresh times, you may want an upgraded video card. The software that comes with the card can run performance testing to give you specific data on how the card is doing.

9. What components affect my computer's sound quality?

- The sound card and speakers control the sound quality in your system.
- If you want surround sound, you may want to invest in a new sound card and additional speakers.

Evaluating System Reliability and Making a Final Decision

10. How can I improve the reliability of my system?

- To make sure your system stays reliable, clear out unnecessary files, run antivirus software, run spyware and adware removal programs, run the Disk Defragmenter on mechanical hard drives, and use the Task Scheduler to automate these tasks.
- If your system is crashing often, check that you have enough RAM. Then consider doing a system refresh or even a full system restore.
- Keep your software updated. Use the Steps Recorder to capture problems as they happen and report them to the manufacturer.

Be sure to check out the companion website for additional materials to help you review and learn, including a Tech Bytes Weekly newsletter—
pearsonhighered.com/techinaction
And don't forget the Replay Videos .

key terms//

3-D sound card
access time
audio MIDI interface
cache memory
clock speed
core
CPU benchmarks
CPU usage
CPU usage graph
graphics double data rate 5 (GDDR5)
graphics processing unit (GPU)
hard drive
head crash
hyperthreading
latency (rotational delay)
machine cycle
memory module (memory card)
Moore's Law
nonvolatile storage
optical drive
optical media
overclocking
physical memory
platter
random access memory (RAM)
read/write head
redundant array of independent disks (RAID)
RAID 0
RAID 1
sector
seek time
solid-state drive (SSD)
sound card
SuperFetch
surround sound
system evaluation
track
video card (video adapter)
video memory
volatile storage

making the transition to . . . next semester//

1. **Go Small or Stay Home**

   Manufacturers are releasing a number of systems that are trying to capitalize on size—or the lack of size! Explore some of the small form factor (SFF) computers appearing on the market.

   a. Research the Falcon Northwest FragBox and Tiki (**falcon-nw.com**).

   b. Compare that system with the Apple Mac mini and the Apple Mac Pro (**apple.com**).

   Why are these SFF computers appearing? What role do you see these systems fulfilling? What kind of performance and hardware would you recommend for such a system?

2. **How Does Your System Measure Up?**

   A number of tools are available to measure your system's performance. Explore the following tools and use one to gather data on your current system's performance.

   a. Windows 8 Resource Monitor: Use the Resource Monitor to collect data on CPU utilization and memory usage over a typical school day.

   b. Benchmarking suites: Examine a sample of consumer benchmarking programs like PassMark's PerformanceTest, Primate Lab's Geekbench, and Maxon's Cinebench. Which subsystems do each of these products evaluate?

3. **Storage on the Go**

   You will want to keep an archive of all your academic work so you can develop the best possible e-portfolio at graduation. Which type of portable hard drive is best suited to your needs? What size? Do you need built-in WiFi? Can the drive stream media content? Do you think you could store everything you produce in your academic career in a single cloud storage account?

making the transition to . . . the workplace//

1. **Video Connections**

   You have a position in a pharmaceutical research firm. Your group does simulations of protein folding to predict if a new drug will be effective. You collaborate daily with a team in India using videoconferencing. Now you've found out you also have the responsibility of creating a series of training videos to teach the Indian team how to use the newest release of software. What video and processing hardware would your workstation need to tackle this? Specify the video card performance and the CPU and memory requirements this project would have.

2. **Let Me Tell You My Problem**

   You may be responsible for helping others solve various computer problems. Test out the Steps Recorder in Windows to see how the program can help you help them. From the Charms bar, search for "psr." Run the program and click Start Record. Then just click between different applications, visit the Control Panel, and add a comment. Save the file to your desktop and close the Steps Recorder. View the annotated report. How could you use the Steps Recorder to describe a problem or to gather information?

team time//

Many Different Devices for Many Different Needs

Problem

Even within one discipline, there are needs for a variety of types of computing solutions. Consider the Communications Department in a large university. Because it's an interdisciplinary area, there are some groups involved in video production, some groups producing digital music, and some groups creating scripts and screenplays. The department as a whole needs to decide on a complete computing strategy.

Process

1. Split the class into teams.
2. Select one segment of the Communications Department that your team will represent: video production, digital music, or scripting. The video production team requires its labs to be able to support the recording, editing, and final production and distribution of digital video. The digital music group wants to establish a collegiate recording studio (after the model of the Drexel University recording label, Mad Dragon Records, at **maddragonmusic.com**). The scripting group needs to support a collaborative community of writers and voice-over actors.
3. Analyze the computing needs of that segment, with particular focus on how it needs to outfit its computer labs.
4. Price the systems you would recommend and explain how they will be used. What decisions have you made in order to guarantee they will still be useful in three years?
5. Write a report that summarizes your findings. Document the resources you used and generate as much enthusiasm as you can for your recommendations.

Conclusion

The range of available computing solutions has never been so broad. It can be a cause of confusion for those not educated in technology. But with a firm understanding of the basic subsystems of computers, it is precisely this pace of change that is exciting. Being able to evaluate a computer system and match it to the current needs of its users is an important skill.

ethics project//

Benchmarking

In this exercise, you'll research and then role-play a complicated ethical situation. The role you play might not match your own personal beliefs; regardless, your research and use of logic will enable you to represent the view assigned. An arbitrator will watch and comment on both sides of the arguments, and together, the team will agree on an ethical solution.

Problem

We've seen that for complex systems like computers, performance often is determined not by comparing the specifications of individual parts but by using benchmarks, software suites that test a full area of performance. There are benchmarks for battery life, for CPU performance, and for video performance. The results of these tests become a major force in marketing and selling the product.

There have been a number of claims of unethical conduct in the area of benchmarking. Companies have been accused of using out-of-date testing software to skew their results. Some companies have manipulated the settings on the machine to artificially raise their score (for example, turning off the display and wireless network before testing for battery life). Some companies have a pattern of making sure the systems sent out to magazines and other evaluators have better-performing components than you might get off the shelf in your own new system.

Where is the line between gaining a competitive edge and lying when it comes to hardware assessment?

Research Areas to Consider

- SysMark2002
- BAPCo
- MobileMark
- 2009 Nobel Prize for Physics

Process

1. Divide the class into teams.
2. Research the areas cited above from the perspective of either an Intel engineer working on a new CPU, an AMD engineer working on a competing CPU, or a benchmark designer.
3. Team members should write a summary that provides factual documentation for the positions and views their character takes around the issue of equitable testing of hardware. Then, team members should create an outline to use during the role-playing event.
4. Team members should arrange a mutually convenient time to meet for the exchange, using a virtual meeting tool or by meeting in person.
5. Team members should present their case to the class or submit a PowerPoint presentation for review by the rest of the class, along with the summary and resolution they developed.

Conclusion

As technology becomes ever more prevalent and integrated into our lives, more and more ethical dilemmas will present themselves. Being able to understand and evaluate both sides of the argument, while responding in a personally or socially ethical manner, will be an important skill.

Glossary

3-D sound card An expansion card that enables a computer to produce omnidirectional or three-dimensional sounds.

access time The time it takes a storage device to locate its stored data.

audio MIDI interface Interface technology that allows a user to connect guitars and microphones to their computer.

cache memory Small blocks of memory, located directly on and next to the central processing unit (CPU) chip, that act as holding places for recently or frequently used instructions or data that the CPU accesses the most. When these instructions or data are stored in cache memory, the CPU can more quickly retrieve them than if it had to access the instructions or data from random access memory (RAM).

clock speed The steady and constant pace at which a computer goes through machine cycles, measured in hertz (Hz).

core A complete processing section from a central processing unit, embedded into one physical chip.

CPU benchmarks Measurements used to compare performance between processors.

CPU usage The percentage of time the central processing unit (CPU) is working.

CPU usage graph Records your central processing unit (CPU) usage for the past several seconds.

graphics double data rate 5 (GDDR5) A standard of video memory.

graphics processing unit (GPU) A specialized logic chip that's dedicated to quickly displaying and calculating visual data such as shadows, textures, and luminosity.

hard disk drive (HDD) The computer's nonvolatile, primary storage device for permanent storage of software and documents.

head crash Impact of the read/write head against the magnetic platter of the hard drive; often results in data loss.

hyperthreading A technology that permits quicker processing of information by enabling a new set of instructions to start executing before the previous set has finished.

latency (rotational delay) The process that occurs after the read/write head of the hard drive locates the correct track and then waits for the correct sector to spin to the read/write head.

machine cycle The series of steps a central processing unit goes through when it performs a program instruction.

memory module (memory card) A small circuit board that holds a series of random access memory (RAM) chips.

Moore's Law A prediction, named after Gordon Moore, the co-founder of Intel; states that the number of transistors on a central processing unit chip will double every two years.

nonvolatile storage Permanent storage, as in read-only memory (ROM).

optical drive A hardware device that uses lasers or light to read from, and even write to, CDs, DVDs, or Blu-ray discs.

optical media Portable storage devices, such as CDs, DVDs, and Blu-ray discs, that use a laser to read and write data.

overclocking Running the central processing unit at a speed faster than the manufacturer recommends.

physical memory The amount of random access memory (RAM) that's installed in a computer.

platter A thin, round, metallic storage plate stacked onto the hard drive spindle.
RAID 0 The strategy of running two hard drives in one system, cutting in half the time it takes to write a file.

random access memory (RAM) The computer's temporary storage space or short-term memory. It's located in a set of chips on the system unit's motherboard, and its capacity is measured in megabytes or gigabytes.

read/write head The mechanism that retrieves (reads) and records (writes) the magnetic data to and from a data disk.

redundant array of independent disks (RAID) A set of strategies for using more than one drive in a system.

RAID 1 The strategy of mirroring all the data written on one hard drive to a second hard drive, providing an instant backup of all data.

sector A section of a hard drive platter, wedge-shaped from the center of the platter to the edge.

seek time The time it takes for the hard drive's read/write heads to move over the surface of the disk to the correct track.

solid-state drive (SSD) A storage device that uses the same kind of memory that flash drives use but that can reach data in only a tenth of the time a flash drive requires.

sound card An expansion card that attaches to the motherboard inside the system unit and that enables the computer to produce sounds by providing a connection for the speakers and microphone.

SuperFetch A memory-management technique used by Windows 7. Monitors the applications you use the most and preloads them into your system memory so that they'll be ready to go.

surround sound A type of audio processing that makes the listener experience sound as if it were coming from all directions.

system evaluation The process of looking at a computer's subsystems, what they do, and how they perform to determine whether the computer system has the right hardware components to do what the user ultimately wants it to do.

track A concentric circle that serves as a storage area on a hard drive platter.

video card (video adapter) An expansion card that's installed inside a system unit to translate binary data (the *1*s and *0*s the computer uses) into the images viewed on the monitor.

video memory Random access memory that's included as part of a video card.

volatile storage Temporary storage, such as in random access memory. When the power is off, the data in volatile storage is cleared out.

Using the Internet: Making the Most of the Web's Resources

Using the Internet: Making the Most of the Web's Resources

Working and Playing on the Web

The Internet and How It Works

OBJECTIVES

1. What is the origin of the Internet?
2. How does data travel on the Internet?

Communicating and Collaborating on the Web

OBJECTIVES

3. How can I communicate and collaborate using Web 2.0 technologies?
4. How can I communicate using e-mail and instant messaging?

Sound Byte: Blogging

Web Entertainment

OBJECTIVE

5. What multimedia files are found on the web, and what software is needed to access those files?

Conducting Business over the Internet: E-Commerce

OBJECTIVE

6. What is e-commerce, and what online safeguards are available?

Active Helpdesk: Doing Business Online

Using the Web Effectively

Accessing and Moving Around the Web

OBJECTIVES

7. What is a web browser, and what are a URL and its parts?
8. How can I use hyperlinks and other tools to get around the web?

Sound Byte: Welcome to the Web

Searching the Web Effectively

OBJECTIVE

9. How do I search the Internet effectively, and how can I evaluate websites?

Active Helpdesk: Using Subject Directories and Search Engines

Active Helpdesk: Getting Around the Web

Sound Byte: Finding Information on the Web

For all media in this chapter go to **pearsonhighered.com/techinaction** or **MyITLab.**

HOW COOL IS THIS?

Have you ever wanted to **share your computer screen** with someone but couldn't because you didn't know how or didn't have the right software? Now you can share your computer screen with anyone on **any device via the web** with one click, hassle-free, with **Screenleap** (**screenleap.com**).

All you need to do is **click a link that generates a code**, then send the code to whomever you want to share your screen with; they will be able to view your screen immediately from their web browser on their smartphone, tablet, or PC. You can share your screen publicly, or privately to only a select few. There is also an extension to initiate sharing directly from your Gmail account. Using this technology may help you to **better communicate** with classmates or your professors when seeking or offering help. A **free account** will give you two hours of sharing time per day. So, share your screen with someone today with Screenleap! *(by-studio/fotolia; Courtesy of Google, Inc.)*

Scan here for more info

Working and Playing on the Web

You most likely know at least a little bit about how to use the web's resources to communicate and collaborate with others, how to work with multimedia files, and how business is conducted over the web. In this section, we'll explore these and other topics. But first, let's start with a brief lesson on the history of the Internet.

the internet and how IT WORKS

It's hard to imagine life without the **Internet**, the largest computer network in the world. The Internet is actually a network of networks that connects billions of computer users globally, but its beginnings were much more modest.

The Origin of the Internet

Why was the Internet created? The concept of the Internet was developed in the late 1950s while the United States was in the midst of the Cold War with the Soviet Union (see Figure 1). At that time, the U.S. Department of Defense needed a computer network that wouldn't be disrupted easily in the event of an attack.

At the same time, researchers for the Department of Defense were trying to get different computers to work with each other using a common communications method that all computers could use. The Internet was created to respond to these two concerns: establishing a *secure* form of

FIGURE 1 How the Internet Began.

1958 — The **Advanced Research Projects Agency (ARPA)** is established for the US Department of Defense. This agency creates the ARPANET—the beginnings of the Internet.

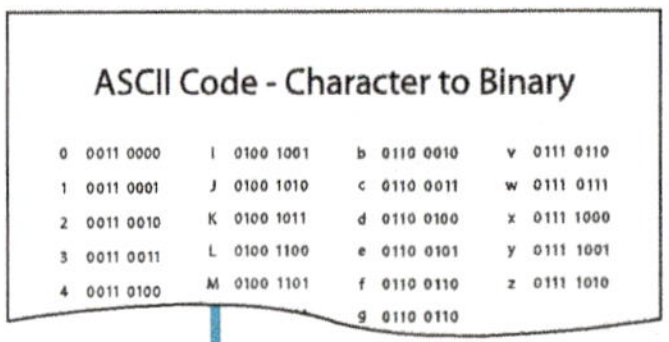

1963 — **ASCII code** is developed as the standard for computers from different manufacturers to exchange data.

1969 — Researchers at UCLA **send the first message via a networked computer system** to researchers at Stanford University.

1964 — A **new network scheme** is developed with multiple paths so if one communication path was destroyed (from a potential Soviet Union attack), the rest of the network would still be able to communicate.

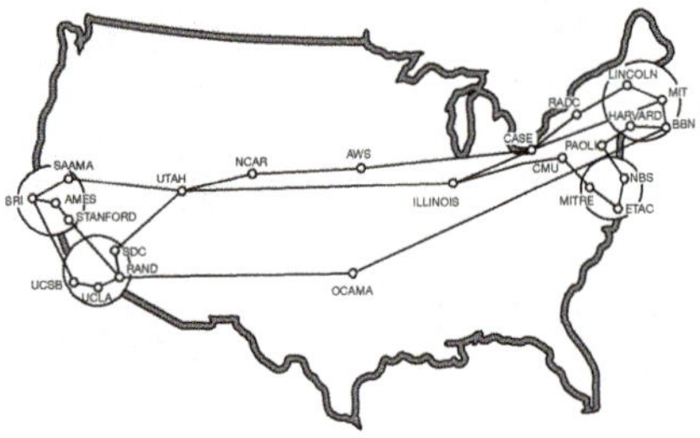

communications and creating a means by which *all* computers could communicate.

Who invented the Internet? The modern Internet evolved from an early U.S. government-funded "internetworking" project called the Advanced Research Projects Agency Network (ARPANET). ARPANET began as a four-node network involving UCLA, Stanford Research Institute, the University of California at Santa Barbara, and the University of Utah in Salt Lake City. The first real communication occurred in 1969 between the computer at Stanford and the computer at UCLA. Although the system crashed after the third letter of "Login" was transmitted, it was the beginning of a revolution. Many people participated in the creation of the ARPANET, but two men, Vinton Cerf and Robert Kahn, are generally acknowledged as the "fathers" of the Internet. These men earned this honor because in the 1970s they were primarily responsible for developing the communications protocols (standards) still in use on the Internet today.

So are the web and the Internet the same thing? Because the **World Wide Web** (**WWW** or the **web**) is what we use the most, we sometimes think of the Internet and the web as being interchangeable. However, the web is only a subset of the Internet, dedicated to broadcasting HTML pages; it is the means by which we access information over the Internet. The web is based on the Hypertext Transfer Protocol (HTTP), which is why you see an *http://* at the beginning of web addresses. What distinguishes the web from the rest of the Internet is its use of the following:

- Common communications protocols that enable computers to talk to each other and display information in compatible formats
- Special links that enable users to navigate from one place to another on the web

Who created the web? The web began in 1991. It was based on a protocol developed by Tim Berners-Lee, a physicist at the European Organization for Nuclear Research (CERN), who wanted a method for linking his research documents so that other researchers could access them. In conjunction with Robert Cailliau, Berners-Lee developed the basic architecture of the web and created the first **web browser**, software that lets you display and interact with text and other media on the web. The original browser could handle only text. Then, in 1993, the Mosaic browser, which could display graphics as well as text, was released. The once-popular Netscape Navigator browser evolved from Mosaic and heralded the beginning of the web's monumental growth.

How the Internet Works

How does the Internet work? All computers and other devices such as tablets and smartphones that are connected to the Internet create a network of networks. These

1973

Vincent Cerf and Bob Kahn develop a set of communication rules–the **TCP/IP protocol**–that allow different types of computers to communicate.

1991

Tim Berners-Lee developed and made public **HTTP protocol and the World Wide Web**. WWW is a subset of the Internet that is connected via hypertext (text containing hyperlinks to other documents and media).

1972

Ray Tomlinson writes a program to send **e-mail** over the ARPANET and develops the "user@host" convention.

1978

By 1978, there were 111 hosts on ARPANET.

1992

By 1992, there were 1 million hosts on ARPANET.

Internet Domains (1989–1997)

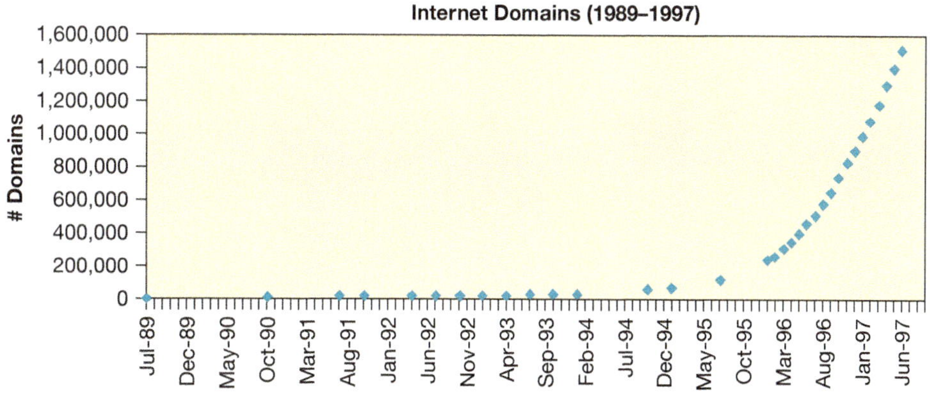

(Cristi180884/Shutterstock; Izmogood/Shutterstock; Matthias Pahl/Shutterstock; Alphaspirit/Shutterstock)

BITS&BYTES

Ever Heard of the Internet2?

Although the Internet2 may sound like a new and separate network meant to replace the Internet, this is not the case. The Internet2 is actually a consortium of U.S. leaders in education, research, industry, and government that seeks to expand the possibilities of the existing Internet by developing new technologies and applications and then deploying them to the public. These experimental technologies require a faster and more efficient Internet, so the researchers use separate data lines that support extremely high-speed communications—up to 8.8 terabits per second (Tbps). In fact, many of the Internet's current technologies are possible because of the research done by the Internet2 consortium.

Internet-connected devices communicate with each other in turns, just as we do when we ask a question or reply with an answer. Thus, a computer (or other device) connected to the Internet acts in one of two ways: Either it's a **client**, a computer that asks for data, or it's a **server**, a computer that receives the request and returns the data to the client. Because the Internet uses clients and servers, it's referred to as a **client/server network**.

When a client computer puts out a request for information from the server computer, the request travels along transmission lines. These transmission lines are similar to our highway system of roads, with some roads having different speed limits. The transmission lines with the fastest speeds are referred to as **Internet backbones**.

How do computers talk to each other? Suppose you want to order something from Amazon.com. Figure 2 illustrates what happens when you type **www.amazon.com** into your web browser and when Amazon's home page displays on your computer monitor. As you can see, the data request from your computer (the client computer) is sent via Internet communication pathways to a server computer. The server computer (in this case, Amazon's server) processes the request and returns the requested data to your client computer via Internet communication pathways. The data reply most likely takes a different route than did the data request. The web browser on your client computer interprets the data and displays it on its monitor.

How does the data get sent to the correct computer? Each time you connect to the Internet, your computer is assigned a unique identification number. This number, called an **Internet Protocol (IP) address**, is a set of four groups of numbers separated by periods, such as 123.45.245.91, and is commonly referred to as a *dotted quad* or *dotted decimal*. IP addresses are the means by which computers connected to the Internet identify each other. Similarly, each website is assigned a unique IP address. However, because the numbers that make up IP addresses are difficult for people to remember, websites are given text versions of their IP addresses. So, Amazon's website has an IP address of 72.21.211.176 and a name of **www.amazon.com**. When you type "www.amazon.com" into your browser, your computer (with its unique IP address) looks for Amazon's IP address (72.21.211.176). Data is exchanged between Amazon's server computer and your computer using these unique IP addresses. ■

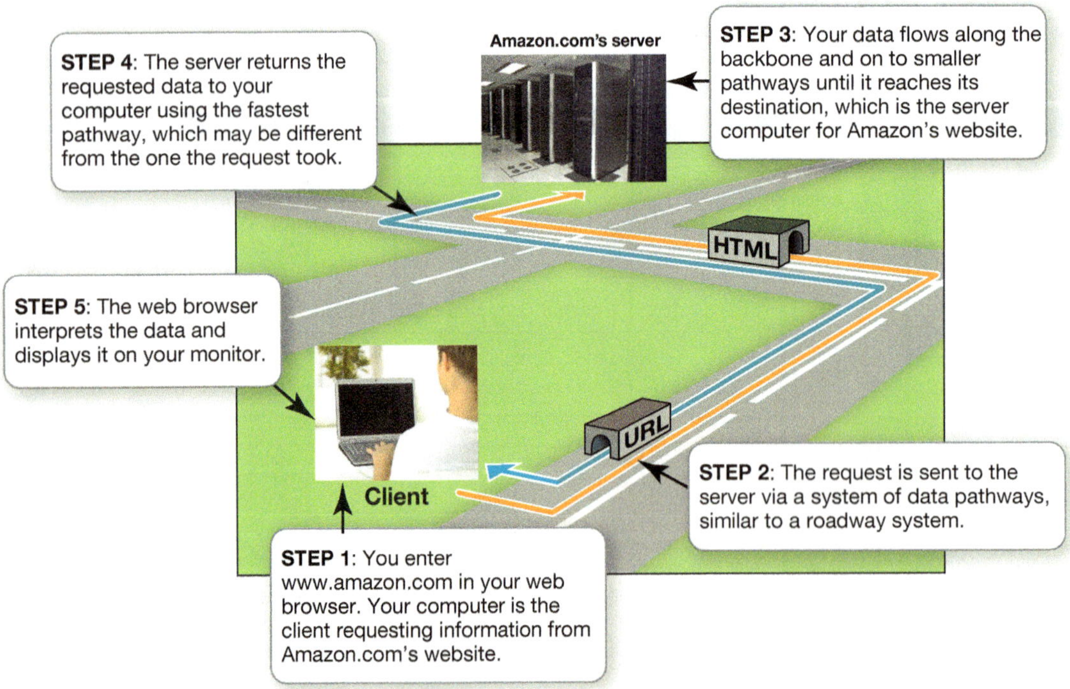

FIGURE 2 How the Internet's Client/Server Model Works. *(Leo Lintang/Fotolia; Edhar/Shutterstock)*

communicating and collaborating ON THE WEB

Over time, our use of the web has evolved from passively browsing web pages that were created for us to actively creating our own web content and sharing and collaborating on it with others. This new collaborative, user-created web content has been dubbed **Web 2.0**. Web 2.0 can be classified as the *social web,* in which the user is also a participant. Before Web 2.0 technologies were in place, we were unable to collaborate with others through web applications such as Google Docs, to rate and recommend products or services with Yelp, to tag a friend on social networks such as Facebook, or to share a video on YouTube or a favorite image on Pinterest. These new means of Web 2.0 communication are collectively called *social media* and include social networking, blogs, wikis, podcasts, and webcasts. Although **e-mail** (short for **electronic mail**) still remains the most widely used form of communication on the Internet, social media has truly changed how we communicate.

Social Networking

Who hasn't heard of Facebook or social networking? As you probably know, **social networking** refers to using the web to communicate and share information among your friends and others. Social networking services such as Facebook and Twitter have become widely popular because they provide fun ways for users to communicate with their friends through wall posts, chats, tagged images, and tweets. Other social networking sites, such as YouTube, Flickr, and Pinterest, provide ways for users to show friends their favorite videos or images that they have taken themselves or have found on the web.

How is social networking used in business? In the business community, professionals often engage in in-person networking to locate and fill open job positions as well as to find clients. Today, networking also happens online. Professional, business-oriented online networks such as LinkedIn are helpful for members seeking potential clients, business opportunities, jobs, or job candidates. Like a true business network, these sites can help you meet other professionals through the people you already know. In addition, businesses use social networking for marketing and communicating directly with their customers. For example, companies may post special deals and offers on their Facebook page or solicit responses from followers that may help with product development or future marketing campaigns.

Figure 3 shows the various sites that are considered Web 2.0 social networking sites. As you can see, there is more to social networking than just Facebook and Twitter.

What are some dos and don'ts of social networking? When social networking sites first became popular, there was concern over privacy issues, especially for school-aged children who put personal information on their pages without considering the possibility of that information being misused by a stalker or identity thief. Although those concerns still exist, many of the most popular social networking sites have improved their privacy policies, thereby reducing, but not eliminating, such concerns. Still, users must be cautious about the type of content they post on these sites. Consider these precautions as you use social networking sites:

- Keep your personal information personal. The year you were born, your physical address, and the routines of your life (sports games, practices, work schedules) should not be broadcast to the general public.
- Know who your friends are, and know who can see the information you post. Review your privacy settings periodically, as sites change and update their privacy practices frequently.
- Do not post information such as your favorite teacher or your first pet's name because these are often used as security questions to verify your identity.
- Use caution when posting images, and know what images others are posting of you. Although privacy settings may offer some comfort, some images may be available for view through search engines and may not require site registration to be seen. Online images may become public property and subject to reproduction, and you might not want some—or any—of those images to be distributed.

Many employers and colleges use social networks as a means of gaining information about potential applicants before granting an interview or extending admission or a job offer. In fact, there have been instances of people being fired from their jobs and being expelled from school for using social media, such as Facebook, Twitter, and blogs, in a questionable way. Generally, questionable content on social media includes negative discussion about the poster's job, employer, or colleagues or inappropriate content about the poster. The responsibility for your content rests with you. Even though you may have strong privacy settings, you can't control what those who you allow to see your content do with it. Therefore, treat all information posted on the web as public, and avoid posting damaging words and pictures. Bottom line: Make sure your profile, images, and site content project an image that accurately represents you.

E-Mail

Why do I need e-mail? Despite the increasing popularity of social networking, e-mail is still the primary means of communication over the Internet. E-mail is a written message sent or received over the Internet. E-mail is the primary method of electronic communication worldwide because it's fast and convenient. And because it's *asynchronous*, users do not need to be communicating at the same time. They can send and

FIGURE 3

Types of Social Networking Sites

	DESCRIPTION	SUGGESTED URLS
Social Exchange Networks	Allow users to connect with others, provide status updates	**facebook.com** **twitter.com**
Create Your Own Social Networks	Allow users to create their own social network around a common topic; groups can be public or private	**ning.com** **mixxt.net**
Business-Related Social Networks	Allow users to seek potential clients, business opportunities, jobs, or job candidates	**linkedin.com**
Media Sharing Networks	Allow users to share pictures and videos	**youtube.com** **flickr.com** **picassa.google.com**
Information Sharing Networks	Allow users to share information	**delicious.com** **wikipedia.org** **slideshare.net**
Information Recommendations and Filtering (Bookmarking) Networks	Allow users to post their opinion of a product, service, news, or web item for others to see and use	**reddit.com** **digg.com**

(Kevin Britland/Alamy; M4OS Photos/Alamy; © Anil Kumar / Alamy; Mixxt; Kristoffer Tripplaar/Alamy; PhotoEdit/Alamy; © PSL Images / Alamy M4OS Photos/Alamy; Web Pix/Alamy; PhotoEdit/Alamy;SlideShare, Inc.; M4OS Photos/Alamy; NetPics/Alamy)

respond to messages at their own convenience. E-mail is also convenient for exchanging and collaborating on documents via attachments.

How private is e-mail? Although e-mail is a more private exchange of information than public social networking sites, e-mails really are not private. Consider the following:

- Because e-mails can be printed or forwarded to others, you never know who may read your e-mail.
- Most e-mail content is not protected, so you should never use e-mail to send personal or sensitive information such as bank account or Social Security numbers. Doing so could lead to identity theft.
- Employers have access to e-mail sent from the workplace, so use caution when putting negative or controversial content in e-mail.
- Even after you've deleted a message, it doesn't really vanish. Many Internet service providers and companies archive e-mail, which can be accessed or subpoenaed in the event of a lawsuit or investigation.

What are some tips on e-mail etiquette? When you write a casual e-mail to friends, you obviously don't need to follow any specific e-mail guidelines (except to remember that your e-mail may be forwarded). But when you send e-mail for professional reasons, you should use proper e-mail etiquette. The following are a few guidelines (also see Figure 4):

- Be concise and to the point.
- Use the spell-checker and proofread your e-mail before sending it.
- Avoid using abbreviations such as *u*, *r*, *LOL*, and *BTW*.
- Include a meaningful subject line to help recipients prioritize and organize e-mails.
- Add a signature line that includes your contact information.
- Include only those people on the e-mail who truly need to receive it.

Following such guidelines maintains professionalism, increases efficiency, and might even help protect a company from lawsuits.

Are there different types of e-mail systems? There are two different types of e-mail systems:

1. **Web-based e-mail**, such as Yahoo! mail or Gmail, is managed with your web browser and allows you to access your e-mail from the web.
2. An **e-mail client** requires a program, such as Microsoft Outlook, to be installed on your computer. When you open the program, your e-mail is downloaded to your computer.

The primary difference between the two is access. Web-based e-mail allows you to access e-mail from any Internet-connected device, but you can't see your e-mail when you're offline. With an e-mail client, you view your e-mail on the computer on which the e-mail client software has been installed, but you can then view and manage your e-mail while you're offline. Both systems can be used together for the "best of both worlds." You can have a Gmail account, for example, so that you can read your e-mail from any computer connected to the

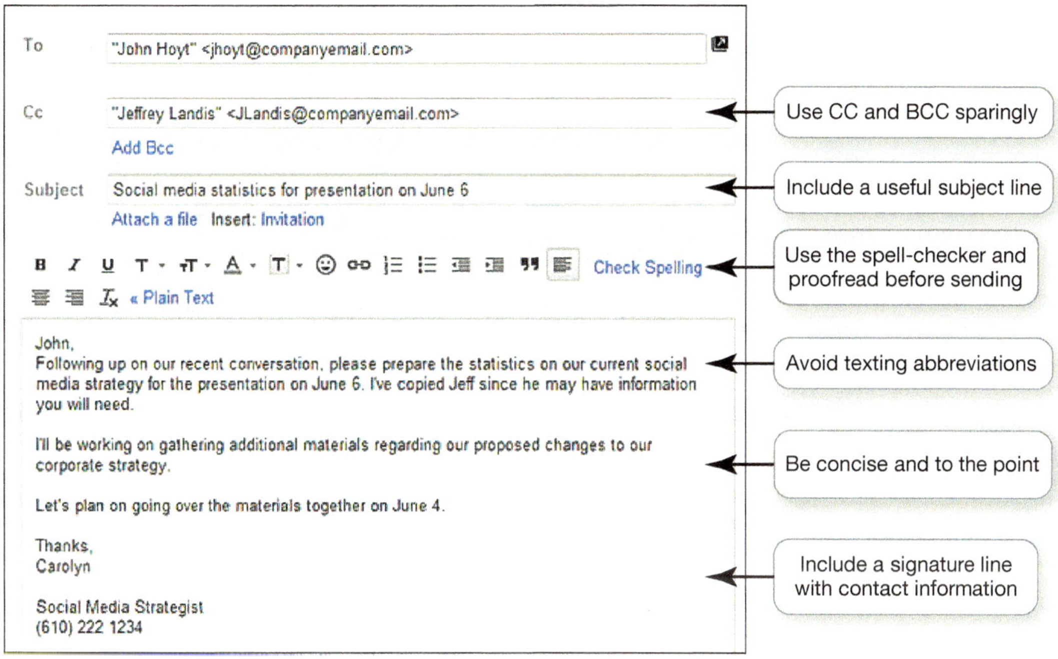

FIGURE 4 Using simple guidelines of e-mail etiquette can promote a professional image and make your message more effective.

Internet, and you can also have Outlook installed on your primary computer and set up the program to display your Gmail account (see Figure 5).

Instant Messaging

Is instant messaging just for friends? You've most likely used **instant messaging (IM)** services—programs that let you communicate in real time over the Internet. Although IM is most often used for conversations between friends, many businesses use IM as a means of instant communication between co-workers. Some IM systems provide mechanisms to hold conversations with more than one person, either through simultaneous individual conversations or with group chats. And some programs even let you conduct video chats using a webcam.

AIM, Google Chat, Windows Messenger, and Yahoo! Messenger are proprietary IM services, meaning you can IM or chat only with those who share the same IM service and are on your contact or buddy list. Another option is to chat with those you've "friended" on Facebook through Facebook's chat option. There are also universal chat services such as Trillian and Digsby that you install on your computer and that allow you to chat with users of all popular IMs, regardless of the service they use.

Wikis

What are wikis? You've no doubt heard of Wikipedia (**wikipedia.org**), the popular collaborative online encyclopedia. Wikipedia is one example of a **wiki**, a web application that allows users to add, remove, or edit its content. Wiki content such as that found on Wikipedia is created collaboratively by multiple users, resulting in an emergent "common" opinion rather than the opinion of an individual writer. Because of wiki technology, Wikipedia's content can be updated continually.

BITS&BYTES

Outlook.com

With the release of Office 2013, Microsoft introduced Outlook.com, a free web-based e-mail service that is linked to your desktop Outlook data and can pull additional contact information from Facebook, Twitter, and LinkedIn as well as your calendar. Outlook.com is a combination of Hotmail and Windows Live (which no longer exist). All you need in order to access the web-based e-mail is a Windows account—which you already may have if you have access to OneDrive, Xbox Live, or have a current Hotmail or Windows Live account. Outlook.com offers a clean, ad-free inbox, with additional features borrowed from the installed version of Outlook that can simplify using e-mail. If you already have another web-based e-mail account (such as Gmail) and you don't want to switch your e-mail address, you can still enjoy the features of Outlook.com; just plug in your Gmail e-mail address, and it syncs automatically.

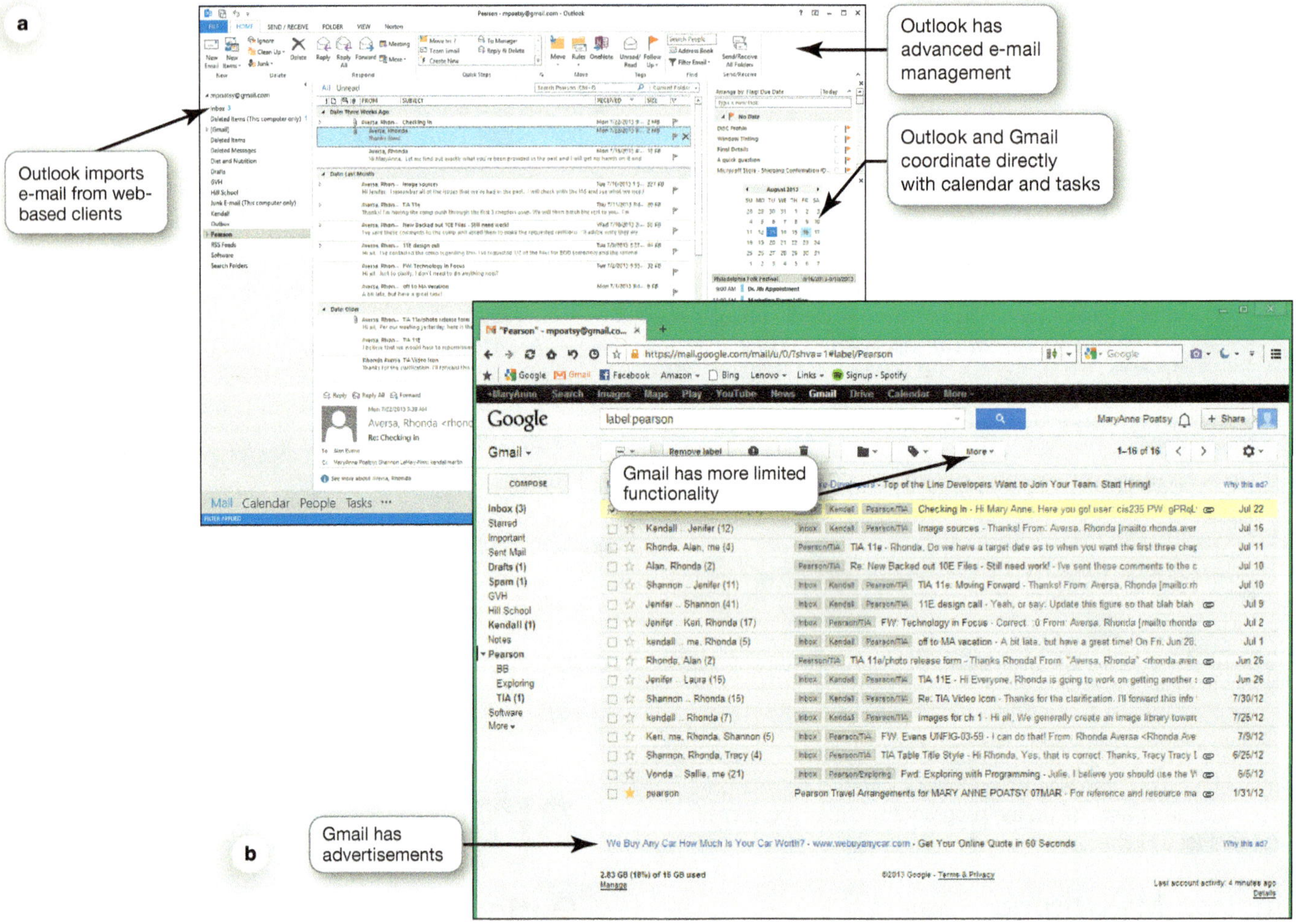

FIGURE 5 (a) Client-Based and (b) Web-Based E-mail Systems *((b)Courtesy of Google, Inc.)*

What else are wikis used for? Wikis are not just used to create Wikipedia; they're also useful tools for business collaboration. Rather than needing to pass documents back and forth via e-mail and possibly losing track of which version is the most recent, wikis allow all who have access to the wiki page to post their ideas and modify the content of the current version of a single document (see Figure 6). Wikis provide the extra benefit of users being able to access, review, and even revert back to past versions at any time.

Some web-based document products, such as Google Docs (**docs.google.com**), have wiki-like features to promote similar online collaboration, and specific wiki software, such as Wikispaces (**wikispaces.com**) and MediaWiki (**mediawiki.org**), is available that you can download for free. The Wikimedia Foundation, which hosts Wikipedia, also hosts other collaborative projects, such as Wikibooks (textbooks), Wikiversity (learning tools),

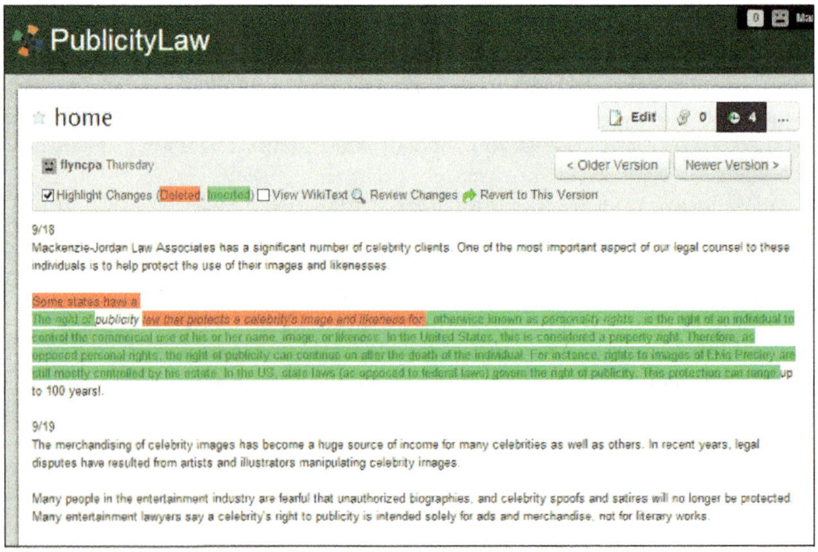

FIGURE 6 Different users can collaborate on a wiki page. A member of this wiki's group has modified the original text. Text that the person deleted appears in red, while inserted text appears in green. *(Courtesy of Wikipedia)*

and Wikisource (a document library). These wiki-type collaborative efforts apply to a variety of other useful applications. For example, wikiHow (**wikihow.org**) is an online project that uses both wikis and the collaborative process to build a large, online how-to manual.

Why isn't Wikipedia good to use as a source for a research paper? The idea behind content that is managed and edited by many users, such as that found in Wikipedia and other large public wikis, is that the group will keep the content current and valid. However, because wikis are publicly editable, they can't be trusted completely. If a user adds erroneous content, the community of users can quickly catch and correct it, but if you used Wikipedia as a source, you may have referenced erroneous content before it was corrected. To help address these concerns, Wikipedia has implemented tighter access controls, requiring users who want editing privileges to register with the site, but the risks still remain. Citizendium (**citizendium.org**), another open wiki encyclopedia, requires contributors to provide real names and sign an ethics pledge, and all postings are monitored.

Blogs

Why do people write blogs? A **blog** (short for **weblog**) is a personal log or journal posted on the web. Anyone can create a blog, and there are millions of blogs available to read, follow, and comment on. Blogs are generally written by a single author and are arranged as a listing of entries on a single page, with the most recent blog entry appearing at the top of the list. In addition, blogs are public. Blogs have searchable and organized content, making them user friendly. They're accessible from anywhere using a web browser.

Many people use blogs as a sort of personal scrapbook. Whenever the urge strikes, they report on their daily activities. Many other blogs focus on a particular topic. For example, the Movie Blog (**themovieblog.com**) contains reviews and opinions about movies, and engadget (**engadget.com**) is a blog devoted to discussing technogadgets. Many corporations, such as Walmart and Best Buy, have blogs written by employees. Technorati (**technorati.com**) and Blogcatalog (**blogcatalog.com**) are two of many blog directories that can help you find blogs that fit your interests.

Are all blogs text-based? The traditional form of a blog is primarily text-based but may also include images and audio. A **video log** (**vlog** or **video blog**) is a blog that uses video as the primary content (although it can also contain text, images, and audio). Vlogs are quickly becoming a popular means of personal expression, and many can be found by searching YouTube (**youtube.com**) and Tout (**tout.com**).

How do I create a blog? Many websites provide the tools you need to create your own blog. Two sites that offer free blog hosting are Blogger (**blogger.com**) and WordPress (**wordpress.com**). Such tools also let you add features like pictures or subpages to your blog. You can also choose to host your blog yourself so that the URL reflects your name or the name of your business. If you choose this option, you'll need your own website and a URL so people can access it.

SOUND BYTE
Blogging
In this Sound Byte, you'll see why blogs are one of today's most popular publishing mediums. You'll also learn how to create and publish your own blog.

Are there any problems with blogs? The popularity of blogs has brought about a new problem: *spam blogs* (*splogs*), which are artificially created blog sites filled with fake articles or stolen text (a tactic known as *blog scraping*). Splogs, which contain links to other sites associated with the splog's creator, have the intention of either increasing traffic to, or increasing search engine rankings for, these usually disreputable or useless websites. Although not really harmful, splogs are another unwanted form of content that continues to grow like weeds on the web.

Podcasts and Webcasts

What is a podcast? A **podcast** is a form of digital media comprised of a series of audio or video files that are distributed over the Internet. There are podcasts for radio shows, audiobooks, magazines, and even educational programs, which you can download to any device that can play audio files. What makes podcasts different from other audio files found on the web is that podcasts deliver their content using **Really Simple Syndication (RSS)**. RSS is a format that sends the latest content of the podcast series automatically to an **aggregator** such as iTunes or Feedspot. An aggregator locates all the RSS series to which you've subscribed and automatically downloads only the new content to your computer or media player. If you have several favorite websites or podcasts, rather than needing to check each site for updated content, aggregators collect all the site updates in one place. These updates or changes to the content are then delivered automatically if you subscribe to the podcast, instead of you having to search for the latest content and download it yourself.

Where can I find podcasts? Most online news and radio sites offer podcasts of their programs. Although many podcasts are news related, others offer entertaining and educational content. For example, you can access lessons on yoga, foreign language classes, or DIY tips. Many schools supply students with course content updates through podcasts, and instructors sometimes create podcasts of their lectures. Figure 7 lists some websites where you can find podcasts.

Can I create my own podcast? It's simple to create a podcast. To record the audio content all you need is a computer with a microphone, and if you want to make a video podcast, you also need a webcam or video camera. Although high-end equipment will produce more sophisticated output, you certainly can use whatever equipment you might own. You may also need additional software to edit the audio and video

FIGURE 7

Podcast Directories and Aggregators

iTunes (itunes.com)

- Software makes it easy to play, manage, and share your favorite podcasts

Podfeed (podfeed.net)

- Broad collection of podcasts

Stitcher (stitcher.com)

- Customize podcast playlists

YouTube (youtube.com)

- Good source for video blogs (vlogs)

content, depending on how professional you wish the podcast to be. After you've recorded and edited the podcast content, you need to export it to MP3 format. The free program Audacity (**audacity.sourceforge.net**) lets you both edit audio files and export them to MP3 format. All that's left is for you to create an RSS feed (tricky, but doable) and then upload the content to a site that hosts podcasts, such as iTunes, Podfeed, or Stitcher.

What's a webcast? A **webcast** is the (usually live) broadcast of audio or video content over the Internet. Unlike podcasts, which are prerecorded and made available for download, most webcasts are distributed in "real time," meaning that they're live or one-time events. Some webcasts are archived so they can be viewed at a later date. Webcasts are not updated automatically like podcasts, but some, such as Microsoft's On-Demand Webcasts, are RSS feeds.

Webcasts use continuous audio and video feeds, which let you view and download large audio and video files. Webcasts can include noninteractive content such as a simultaneous broadcast of a radio or television program, but more recent webcasts invite interactive responses from the viewing or listening audience. For example, ORLive (**orlive.com**) provides surgical webcasts that demonstrate the latest surgical innovations and techniques. Webcasts also are used in the corporate world to broadcast annual meetings and in the educational arena to transmit seminars.

Figure 8 lists the popular methods of online communication that we've discussed. ■

FIGURE 8

Methods of Online Communication

SOCIAL NETWORKING

- Web 2.0 technology
- Lets you build an online network of friends
- Lets you share media content

E-MAIL

- Most common form of online communication
- Asynchronous (not having to be done at the same time)

INSTANT MESSAGING

- Real-time exchange
- Can be used with multiple persons simultaneously
- Video/audio chats available

WIKIS

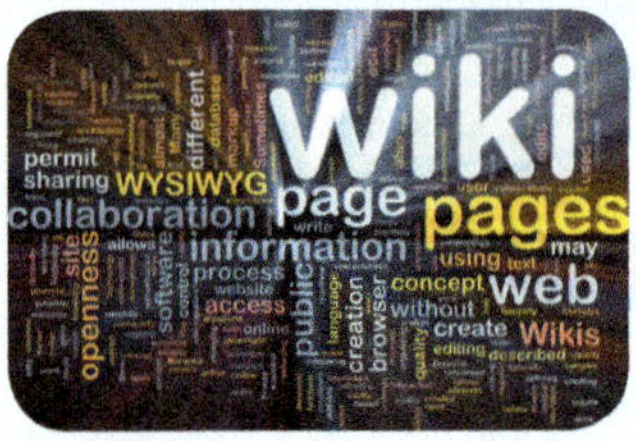

- Great collaborative tool
- Content updated by many users
- Historical content kept, so you can revert to past versions

BLOGS

- Written by a single author
- Chronologic entries
- Searchable content
- May include images, audio, and video

PODCASTS

- Audio/video files delivered via RSS
- New RSS content collected with aggregator
- Can download and view content on portable media player

WEBCASTS

- Most often live, streamed broadcasts

(Ben Legend/Fotolia; Beboy/Fotolia; LiveStock/Shutterstock; Kheng Guan Toh/Shutterstock; ayzek/Shutterstock; 3drenderedlogos com/Shutterstock; Brisbane/Shutterstock)

web ENTERTAINMENT

When you think of how you use the Internet for entertainment purposes, what comes to mind? Streaming audio and video, Internet radio, MP3s, interactive gaming, and smart TV are all favorite responses. What makes all these forms of web entertainment so popular is their multimedia content. **Multimedia** is anything that involves one or more forms of media in addition to text. It includes the following:

- *Graphics* such as drawings, charts, and photos (the most basic form of multimedia)
- *Audio files* such as the clips you hear when you visit websites, MP3 files you download, podcasts and webcasts, and live broadcasts you can listen to through Internet radio
- *Video files* ranging from simple, short video clips on sites such as YouTube (**youtube.com**) to movies and television shows on sites such as Hulu (**hulu.com**)

What is streaming media?

Streaming media is multimedia (audio and video) that is continuously fed to your browser so you avoid having to wait for the entire file to download completely before listening to or watching it. Without streaming media, you wouldn't be able to watch movies on Netflix or on demand from your cable provider, listen to live audio broadcasting, or even play some online games. Internet radio also uses streaming media to present a continuous stream of audio to its listeners. Pandora (**pandora.com**) enables you to personalize your audio stream by specifying a favorite artist, song, or composer that you want to hear. Then the service picks music with the same characteristics. In addition to Internet radio service, Spotify (**spotify.com**) lets you pick your own songs, build playlists, and share your playlists with others.

Do I need anything besides a browser to view or hear multimedia on the web? Most graphics on the web will appear in your browser without any additional software. However, to view and hear some multimedia files—for example, podcasts, YouTube videos, and audio files—you might need a **plug-in** (or **player**)—a special software component that adds a specific feature to an existing software program. Figure 9 lists the most popular plug-ins.

FIGURE 9

Popular Plug-Ins and Players and Their Uses

PLUG-IN NAME	WHERE YOU GET IT	WHAT IT DOES
Adobe Reader	adobe.com	Views and prints portable document format (PDF) files
Flash Player	adobe.com	Plays animation and movies through web browsers
QuickTime Player	apple.com	Plays MP3, animation, music, musical instrument digital interface (MIDI), audio, and video files
Shockwave Player	adobe.com	Plays interactive games, multimedia, graphics, and streaming audio and video on the web
Silverlight	microsoft.com	Similar to Flash; plays web-based animations and videos
Windows Media Player	microsoft.com	Plays MP3 and WAV music files, movies, and live audio and video on broadcasts on the web

(NetPhotos3/Alamy; NetPhotos3/Alamy; NetPhotos3/Alamy; N/A, Alamy; franck reporter/Shutterstock; Nicemonkey/Shutterstock)

BITS&BYTES

HTML5 Versus Flash

Adobe's Flash is a plug-in you're no doubt familiar with that is designed to run multimedia through web browsers. Flash has been the multimedia standard for decades and was at one time used with all browsers. However, in 2007, a controversy between Flash and HTML5 began when the Apple iPhone was introduced—and this controversy continued with the later introduction of the iPad. What was the problem? Both the iPhone and the iPad ran with an operating system that supported HTML5 rather than Flash. Flash-based YouTube videos, for example, would not play on an iPhone or an iPad.

Why would Apple choose HTML5 over Flash? HTML5—the fifth revision of the HTML standard—is open-source code, meaning the program code is available to the general public to use or modify, unlike Flash, which is owned by one company. The goal of HTML5 is to ease the handling of multimedia and graphical content on the web, to reduce or eliminate the need for plug-ins, and to become device independent. Although the major browsers support many of the new HTML5 elements, the standard itself is still a work in progress.

Because Flash had been so dominant for so long, it's taken a while for the HTML5 standard to catch on. But even Flash stalwarts such as YouTube, which was solely Flash dependent, added capability to run HTML5 video in 2011. Similarly, most Flash-dependent websites have incorporated HTML5 players or extensions. It's becoming clear that HTML5 is not going away soon. What do you think is the future for Flash?

How do I get players and plug-ins? If you purchased your computer within the past several years, most popular plug-ins probably came preinstalled on your computer. If a website requires a plug-in not installed on your computer, you are usually automatically directed to a site where you can download the plug-in free of charge. For example, to use streaming video, your browser might send you to the Adobe website, where you can download Flash Player.

Is there any way to get multimedia web content to load faster? When you're on the Internet, your browser keeps track of the sites you've visited so that it can load them faster the next time you visit them. This *cache* (temporary storage place) of the text pages, images, and video files from recently visited websites can make your web surfing more efficient, but it can also slow down your hard drive. Additionally, if you don't have your cache settings configured to check for updates to the web page, your browser may not load the most recent content. To keep your system running efficiently, consider doing the following:

- Delete your temporary Internet cache every month or so, depending on your usage.
- To ensure the most recent website content is displayed, click Refresh or press the F5 key if you revisit a site in the same browsing session.
- Clear your Internet cache manually or adjust the setting in your web browser so that it clears the cache automatically every time you exit the browser. ■

conducting business over the internet: E-COMMERCE

It's hard to believe that only a few years ago, many people were scared to buy things online. Today, there is little hesitation, and you can buy nearly anything on the web, including big-ticket items such as homes and cars. **E-commerce**—short for **electronic commerce**—is the process of conducting business online. Figure 10 shows the most common items purchased through e-commerce transactions.

Are there different types of e-commerce? There are three types of e-commerce business models:

1. **Business-to-consumer (B2C)** transactions take place between businesses and consumers. Such transactions include those between customers and completely online businesses (such as **Amazon.com**) and those between customers and stores that have both an online and a physical presence, such as Target (**target.com**). Such businesses are referred to as *click-and-brick* businesses. Some click-and-bricks allow online purchases and in-store pick-ups and returns.
2. **Business-to-business (B2B)** transactions occur when businesses buy and sell goods and services to other businesses. An example is Omaha Paper Company (**omahapaper.com**), which distributes paper products to other companies.
3. **Consumer-to-consumer (C2C)** transactions occur when consumers sell to each other through sites such as eBay (**ebay.com**), Craigslist (**craigslist.org**), and Etsy (**etsy.com**).

FIGURE 10 Top Five Online Consumer Purchases. *(© allegro/ Fotolia)*

Social commerce is a subset of e-commerce that uses social networks to assist in marketing and purchasing products. If you're on Facebook, you've no doubt noticed the many businesses that have Facebook pages asking you to "Like" them. Consumers are voicing their opinions on Facebook and other sites about products and services by providing ratings and reviews, and studies show that such peer recommendations have a major influence on buying behavior. When you see your friend on Facebook recommend a product or service, you're more likely to click through to that retailer and check out the product.

For example, after implementing the Facebook "Like" button, American Eagle noticed that Facebook-referred visitors spent 57 percent more than other online shoppers. Other peer-influenced e-commerce trends include group buying and individual customization. Groupon and LivingSocial are two popular deal-of-the-day group purchase websites that require a certain number of people to buy the discounted deal before the deal can go through. CafePress and Zazzle sell T-shirts and other items that are customized with your own graphic designs.

But e-commerce encompasses more than just shopping opportunities. Today, anything you can do inside your bank you can do online, and approximately 80 percent of U.S. households do some form of online banking. Many people use online services to check their account balances, pay bills online, and check stock and mutual fund performance. Credit card companies allow you to view, schedule, and pay your credit card bill; brokerage houses allow you to conduct investment activities online.

E-Commerce Safeguards

Just how safe are online transactions? When you buy something online, you most likely use a credit or debit card; therefore, money is exchanged directly between your credit card company and the online merchant's bank. Because online shopping eliminates a salesclerk or other human intermediary from the transaction, it can actually be safer than traditional retail shopping.

What precautions should I take when shopping online? In addition to using some basic common computing sense such as having a firewall and up-to-date antivirus

> ACTIVE HELPDESK
> **Doing Business Online**
> In this Active Helpdesk call, you'll learn about e-commerce and what e-commerce safeguards protect you when you're doing business online.

software on your computer and using strong passwords for all your online accounts, there are several important guidelines to follow to ensure your online shopping experience is a safe one (see Figure 11):

- **Look for visual indicators that the website is secure.** Check that the beginning of the URL changes from "http://" to "https://"—with the *s* standing for secure, indicating that the **secure sockets layer** protocol has been applied to manage the security of the website. Also, look for a small icon of a closed padlock in the toolbar (in both Internet Explorer and Firefox) and a green-colored address bar, indications that the site may be secure. (However, note that even if a site has these indicators, it still might not be safe. Consider the validity of the site before making a purchase.)
- **Shop at well-known, reputable sites.** If you aren't familiar with a site, investigate it with the Better Business Bureau (**bbb.org**) or at bizrate (**bizrate.com**). Make sure the company has a phone number and street address in addition to a website. You can also look for third-party verification such as that from TRUSTe or the Better Business Bureau. But let common sense prevail. Online deals that seem too good to be true are generally just that—and may be pirated software or illegal distributions.
- **Pay by credit card, not debit card.** Federal laws protect credit card users, but debit card users don't have the same level of protection. If possible, reserve one credit card for Internet purchases only; even better, use a prepaid credit card that has a small credit limit. For an extra layer of security, find out if your credit card company has a service that confirms your identity with an extra password or code that only you know to use when making an online transaction or that offers a one-time-use credit card number. Also, consider using a third-party payment processor such as PayPal or Google Wallet. PayPal also offers a security key that provides additional security to your PayPal account.
- **When you place an order, check the return policy, save a copy of the order, and make sure you receive a confirmation number.** Make sure you read and understand the fine print on warranties, return policies, and the retailer's privacy statements. If the site disappears overnight, this information may help you in filing a dispute or reporting a problem to a site such as the Better Business Bureau.
- **Avoid making online transactions when using public computers.** Public computers may have *spyware*

FIGURE 11

Online Shopping Precautions

When shopping at home, use a firewall and antivirus software for general computer protection.

Don't shop on public WiFi networks, as they may contain spyware.

Check for visual indicators such as https:// in the URL, a closed padlock icon, and a green address bar.

Look for third-party verification from TRUSTe or the Better Business Bureau symbol.

Use a credit card, not a debit card, to protect transactions, or use a third-party payer such as PayPal or Google Wallet.

Create a strong password for all online accounts (one that includes numbers and other symbols such as @).

Deals that are too good to be true are usually just that.

Read and understand the fine print on warranties, return policies, and the retailer's privacy statements.

(beboy/Shutterstock; © Roy Wylam / Alamy; photoinnovation/Shutterstock; HANDOUT/KRT/ Newscom; Maxx-Studio/Shutterstock; isak55/Shutterstock; Alhovik/Shutterstock; iConcept/ Shutterstock) installed, programs that track and log your keystrokes and can retrieve your private information. Similarly, unless you have specific protection on your own notebook computer, avoid making wireless transactions on public hotspots.

Whether you're doing business, playing games, or communicating with friends or colleagues, the Internet makes these activities more accessible. The Internet can potentially make these experiences and activities more enriched as well, although you must take precautions for the safest of experiences. ■

Before moving on to Part 2:
- **Watch Replay Video 1.**
- **Then check your understanding of what you've learned so far.**

BITS&BYTES

Making Safe Online Payments Using PayPal and Google Wallet

When people first began making online purchases, many were not comfortable buying from sites like eBay because the sites required them to give personal financial information such as credit card numbers to strangers. PayPal (**paypal.com**) resolved that issue by serving as a payment intermediary that allows anyone to pay with credit cards and bank accounts without sharing their financial information. PayPal is now a standard means of payment for many online merchants and offers buyer protection and dispute resolution services. Figure 12 shows how PayPal works.

Google Wallet (**google.com/wallet**) offers similar services to PayPal. For example, you can pay directly from your bank account with Google Wallet. However, and you can only make purchases within the United States, and Google Wallet only provides customer support through forums and e-mail. PayPal has increased its customer service considerably, so that you can chat live with PayPal representatives when additional assistance is needed.

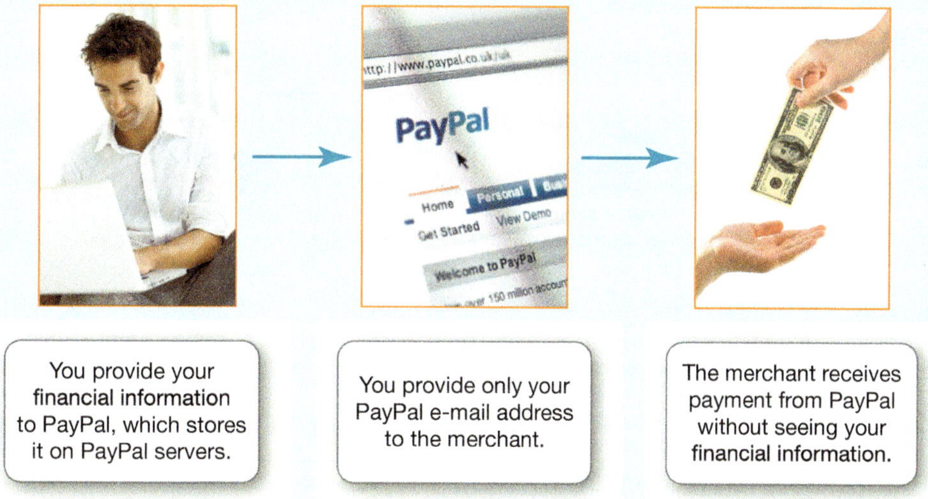

FIGURE 12 How PayPal Works. *(Yuri Arcurs/Shutterstock; AKP Photos/Alamy; happydancing/Shutterstock)*

DIG DEEPER Discovering the Semantic Web

Think about all the types of data on the web that you access manually, such as appointment times, transportation and entertainment schedules, and store locations and hours. It would seem that computers would be helpful in plugging through all this web data, but oddly, that is not the case. Web pages are designed for people to read, not for computers to manipulate. As yet, no reliable way exists for computers to process the meaning of data on a web page so that it can be used to see relationships or make decisions.

The **semantic web** (or **Web 3.0**) is an evolving extension of the web in which data is defined in such a way to make it more easily processed by computers. Right now, search engines function by recognizing keywords such as *office hours* and *dentist*, but they can't determine, for example, in which office and on what days Dr. Smith works and what his available appointment times are. By using a so-called "agent," the semantic web would enable computers to find that type of information, coordinate it with your other schedules and preferences, and then make the appointment for you.

The semantic web would also assist you in comparing products, prices, and shipping options by finding the best product option based on specified criteria and then placing the order for you. Additionally, the agent would record the financial transaction into your personal bookkeeping software and arrange for a technician to help install the software, if needed.

For the semantic web to work, businesses, services, and software would all use the same categorization structures so that similar information would share the same attributes, ensuring consistency of metadata throughout the web. The semantic web would build on this type of capability so that each website would have text and pictures (for people to read) and metadata (for computers to read) describing the information on the web (see Figure 13).

Although some of the semantic web's functionalities are beginning to emerge in technologies such as Siri in the current iPhone operating system, the majority of its functionality and implementation are still in development. The greatest challenge is recoding all the information currently available on the web into the type of metadata that computers can recognize. The very grandeur of that task means that we will not see a fully functional semantic web until sometime in the distant future. In the meantime, we can continue to benefit from each small step toward that goal.

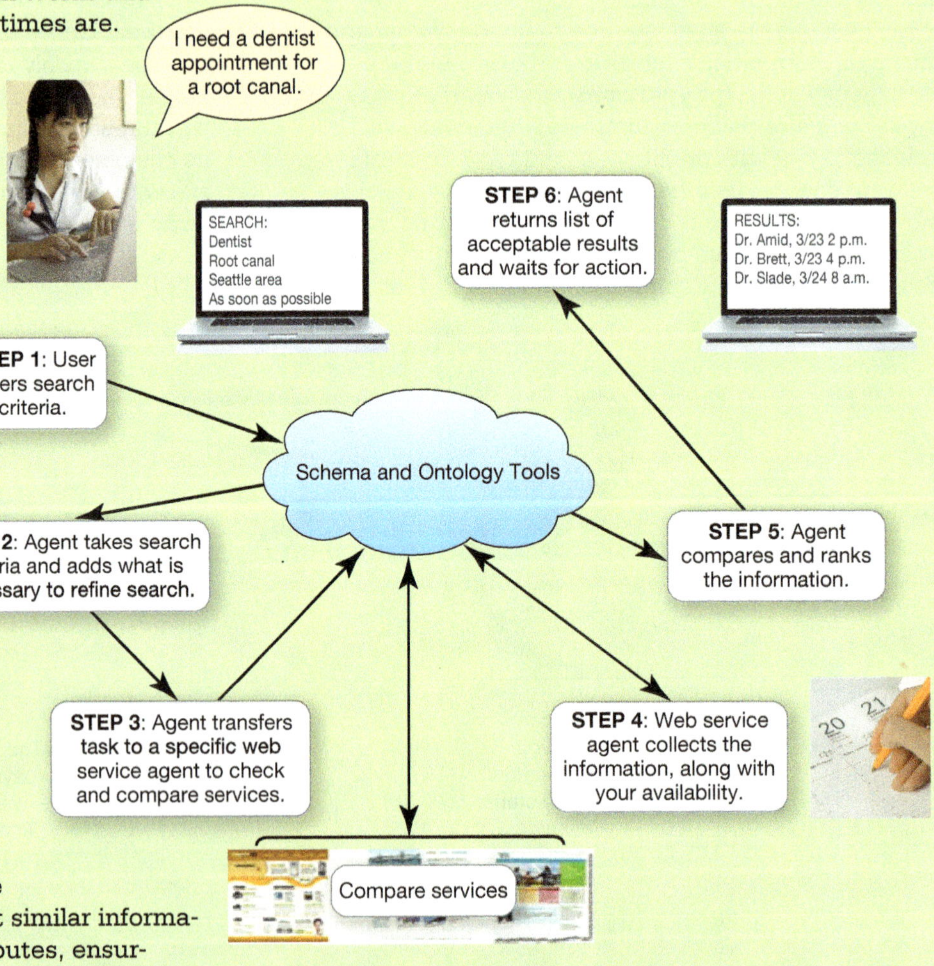

FIGURE 13 The Semantic Web. *(William Casey/Shutterstock; Tomasz Sz/Shutterstock; nattstudio/Fotolia)*

check your understanding//

For a quick review to see what you've learned so far, answer the following questions. Visit **pearsonhighered.com/techinaction** to check your answers.

multiple choice

1. Which is NOT true about the Internet?

- **a.** It is the largest computer network in the world.
- **b.** It was created to establish a secure form of military communications.
- **c.** It was developed as an additional means of commerce.
- **d.** It was designed as a means for all computers to communicate with each other.

2. What do you need if you want to read, send, and organize e-mail from *any* computer connected to the Internet?

- **a.** an e-mail client program
- **b.** an e-mail server
- **c.** an e-mail aggregator
- **d.** a web-based e-mail account

3. Which is NOT an example of Web 2.0 technology?

- **a.** e-mail
- **b.** social networking
- **c.** blogging
- **d.** wiki

4. Which of the following is NOT a characteristic of a blog?

- **a.** Blogs are used to express opinions.
- **b.** Blogs are generally written by a single author.
- **c.** Blogs are private and require password access.
- **d.** Blogs are arranged as a listing of entries.

5. Which of the following would be the correct classification for Target.com?

- **a.** B2B
- **b.** C2C
- **c.** B2C
- **d.** Click-and-brick business

true–false

_______ **1.** Deleted e-mails can be recovered—they don't really vanish.

_______ **2.** The first web browser was created by ARPANET.

critical thinking

1. Social Networking and Society

Social networking seems to have taken over our lives! Almost everyone is on Facebook and Twitter. But is this a good thing?

- **a.** What advantages and disadvantages does social networking bring to your life and to society?
- **b.** How are businesses using social networking?

2. Mobile E-Commerce Safety

The text lists several ways to ensure your online transactions are secure and to reduce the risk of things going awry as you shop and sell online. However, surveys indicate that many feel that shopping from a mobile device, such as a smartphone, presents additional risks. Do you agree there are additional risks when conducting e-commerce from a mobile device? Why or why not?

Continue »

TRY THIS

Create a OneDrive Account to Store and Share Your Files in the Cloud

You probably have your favorite ways of moving your files around. Perhaps you have a USB drive or you e-mail files to yourself, or maybe you have a portable external hard drive. With any of these solutions, there can be confusion as to which is the most current version of the file if you have worked on it on multiple devices at different times. You also run the risk of losing your USB drive or deleting the e-mail attachment by mistake. These methods also make exchanging files difficult if you want to share your files or collaborate with a group.

A simpler solution is to use a web-based or cloud storage and sharing service such as OneDrive or Dropbox. OneDrive is part of Microsoft's Office 365 suite of web apps. With 7 GB of free storage space for new users, you can store thousands of files and get to them anytime you're online. Note: Microsoft had announced changing the name of SkyDrive to OneDrive, but had not updated the website, so images still reflect SkyDrive.

Step 1 Sign in to OneDrive: Go to **onedrive.com**. Sign in to your Microsoft account. If you don't have a Microsoft account, creating one is easy. A Microsoft account will give you access to services such as OneDrive, Xbox LIVE, and **Outlook.com**.

Step 2 Create a Folder and Add Files: Once you're in OneDrive, you can create a folder and then begin to add files.

- To create a folder: Click **Create** at the top of the page, click **Folder**, and then give your new folder a name. Click the new folder to open it.
- To add a file: Click **Upload** at the top of the page, then locate the file and click **Open**. To upload more than one file, hold the **Ctrl key** while you select each file.

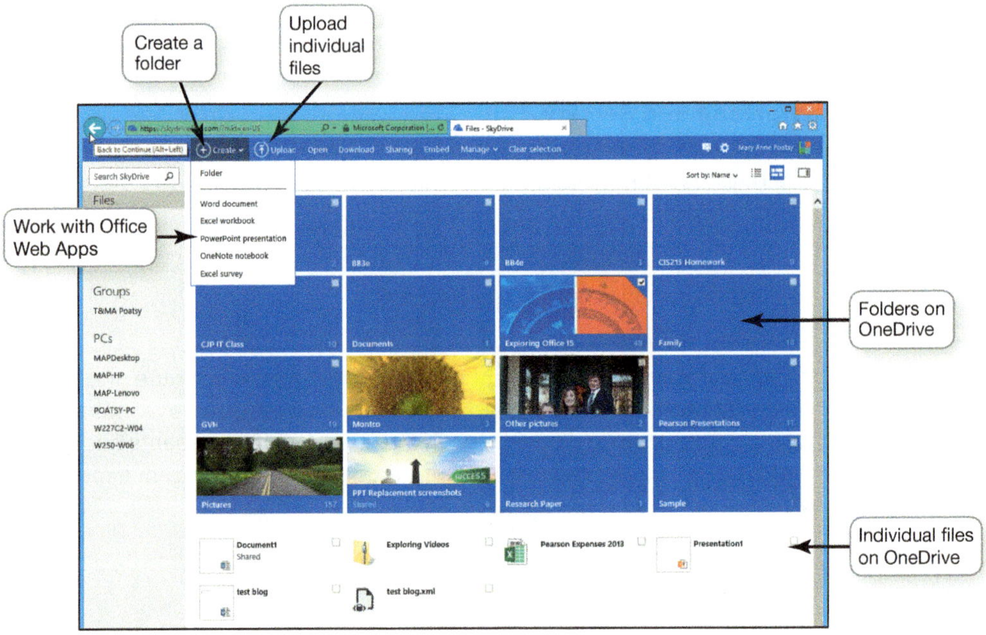

Step 3 Share a File or Folder: To share a file or folder, do the following:

- Right-click the file or folder that you want to share, and click **Sharing**.
- Fill in the e-mail form.
- Establish editing privileges by checking the **Recipients can edit** box, if desired, then click **Share**.

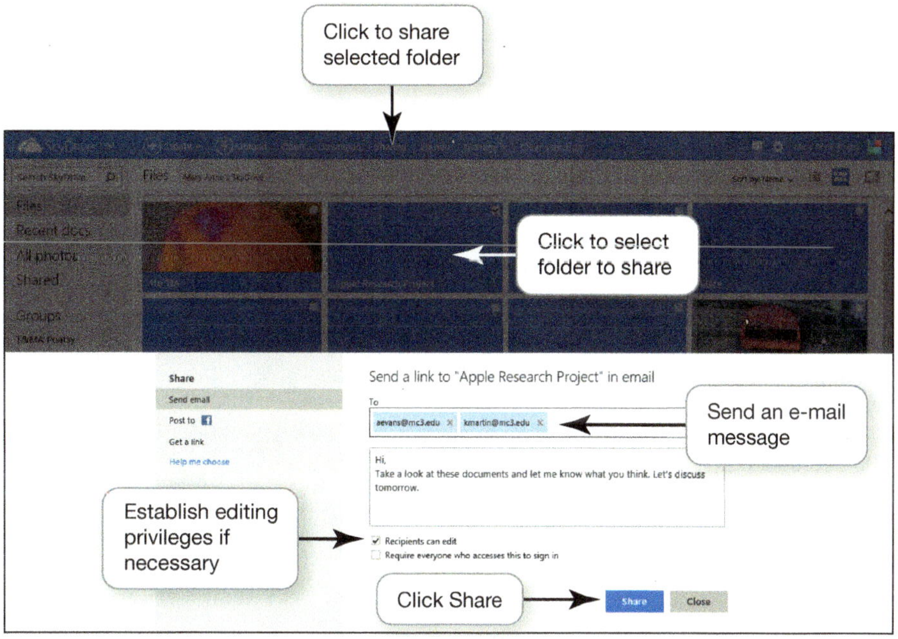

- To see what files that have been shared with you, click **Shared** in the left menu.

Step 4 Sync with Your Smartphone: If you have an iPhone, Android, or Windows Phone, you can access your documents wherever you go. You can download the OneDrive app, or you can always access OneDrive through your phone's browser at **onedrive .com**.

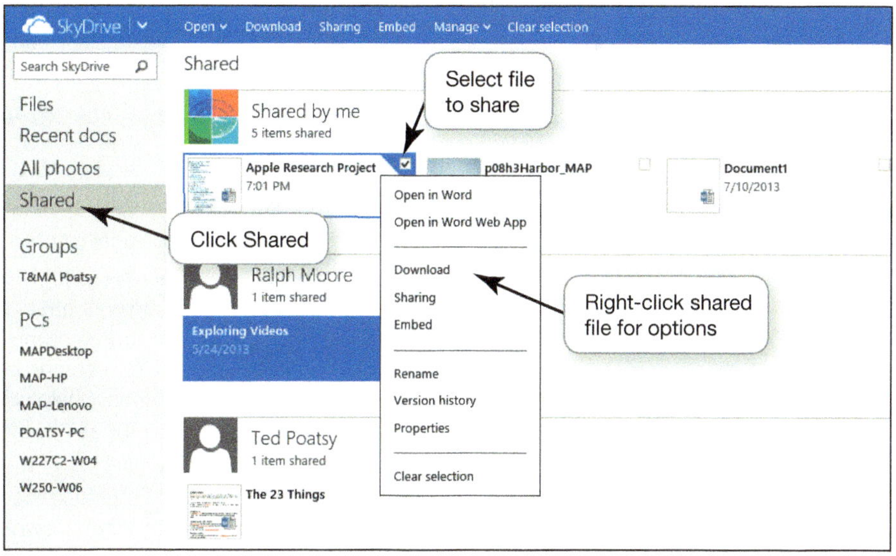

Using the Web Effectively

You no doubt know how to use the web—to buy products, send e-mail, visit Facebook, and use Google—but do you know how to use it effectively? In this section, we'll look at ways to make your online experience more enjoyable, more productive, and even more efficient.

accessing and moving AROUND THE WEB

None of the activities for which we use the web could happen without an important software application: a web browser. Recall that a browser is software that lets you locate, view, and navigate the web. Most browsers today are *graphical* browsers, meaning they can display pictures (graphics) in addition to text and other forms of multimedia such as sound and video. The most common browsers are displayed in Figure 14.

Web Browsers

What features do browsers offer? Most popular browsers share similar features that make the user experience more efficient (as shown in Figure 15). For example, most browsers include a built-in search box in which you can designate your preferred default search engine and tools for printing, page formatting, and security settings. Other features include the following:

- *Tabbed browsing:* Web pages are loaded in "tabs" within the same browser window. Rather than having to switch among web pages in several open windows, you can flip between the tabs in one window. You may also save a group of tabs as a Favorites group if there are several tabs you often open at the same time.
- *Pinned tabs:* You can "dock" tabs to the taskbar (in Internet Explorer) or minimize and save them permanently (Google Chrome and Firefox) for easier navigation of your favorite sites.
- *Tear-off tabs:* An opened tab can be dragged away from its current window so it's then opened in a new window.
- *Thumbnail previews:* Another convenient navigation tool that most browsers share is providing thumbnail previews of all open web pages in open tabs.
- *Tab isolation:* With this feature, tabs are independent of each other, so if one crashes, it does not affect the other tabs.
- *Combined search and address bar:* With this feature, you can both type a website URL or search the web from the address bar.
- *SmartScreen filter:* Most browsers offer built-in protection against phishing, malware, and other web-based threats.
- *Privacy browsing:* Privacy features (such as InPrivate Browsing in Internet Explorer) let you browse the web without retaining a history trail, temporary Internet files, cookies, or usernames and passwords. These features are especially helpful when you use public computers at college or the public library, for example.
- *Add-ons:* Add-ons are small programs that customize and increase the functionality of the browser. Examples include Video DownloadHelper that converts web videos, like those found on YouTube, to files you can save, as well as a Facebook toolbar that integrates Facebook functionality into your browser.
- *Session Restore:* Brings back all your active web pages if the browser or system shuts down unexpectedly.

(Pablo Fonseca Q./La Nacion de Costa Rica/Newscom; Lucia Lanpur/Alamy; Tommy (Louth)/Alamy; 2020WEB/Alamy)

FIGURE 14 Common Web Browsers

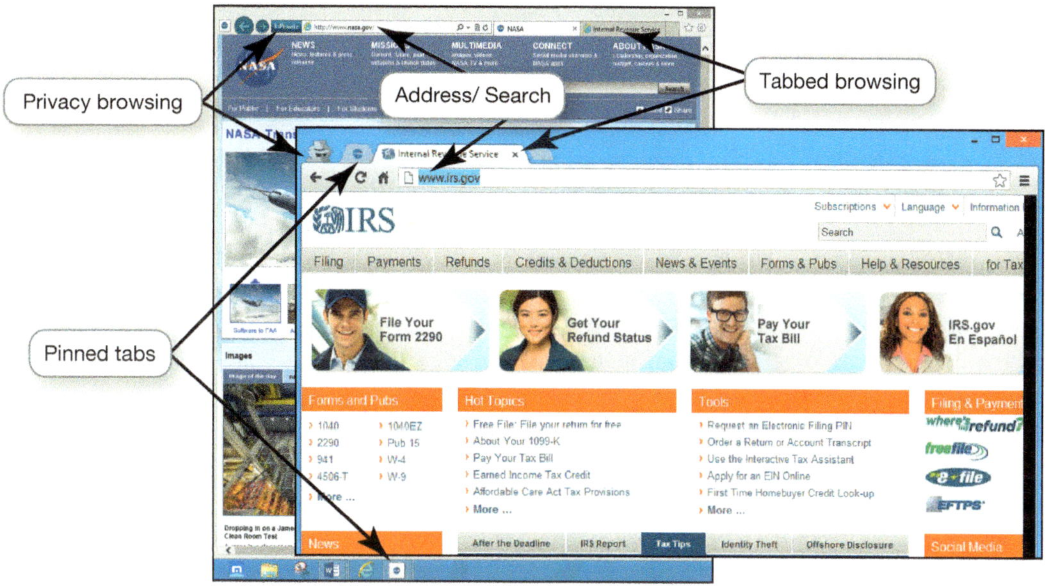

FIGURE 15 Like most of the popular web browsers, Internet Explorer and Google Chrome include tabbed and privacy browsing and an address bar that doubles as a search bar. Pinned tabs make accessing your favorite sites even easier. *(Courtesy of NASA; Courtesy of the IRS)*

BITS&BYTES

Maxthon: A Great Alternative Brower

Not well known in the United States but quite popular elsewhere globally, Maxthon is a web browser that rivals our U.S. favorites. Maxthon has the convenient features of tabbed browsing, bookmarking capabilities, thumbnails of previously viewed sites, and privacy viewing, so you'll feel quite at home rather quickly. Since Maxthon is a cloud-based browser, when you access the browser on any device, all your settings are synced. Maxthon does have some unique features, such as Maxthon's dock—a sidebar that resides in the desktop, with customizable shortcut icons to your favorite websites. In addition, Maxthon enables you to use mouse gestures so that you can match a specific mouse movement with a specific command. In addition, super drag and drop enables you to drag and drop a link, image, or highlighted text into the search box rather than typing the content; night mode adjusts the brightness of the screen; "snap" enables you to take screen grabs; and SkyNote lets you save and access notes. If you haven't already, you may enjoy taking Maxthon for a test drive.

URLs, Protocols, and Domain Names

What do all the parts of a URL mean? You gain initial access to a particular **website** by typing its unique address, or **Uniform Resource Locator** (**URL**, pronounced "you-are-ell"), in your browser. A website is comprised of many different web pages, each of which is a separate document with its own unique URL. Like a regular street address, a URL is comprised of several parts that help identify the web document it stands for (see Figure 16):

- the *protocol* (set of rules) used to retrieve the document;
- the **domain name**; and
- the *path* or subdirectory

Although every part of a URL is important information that ensures the web page you requested actually displays in your

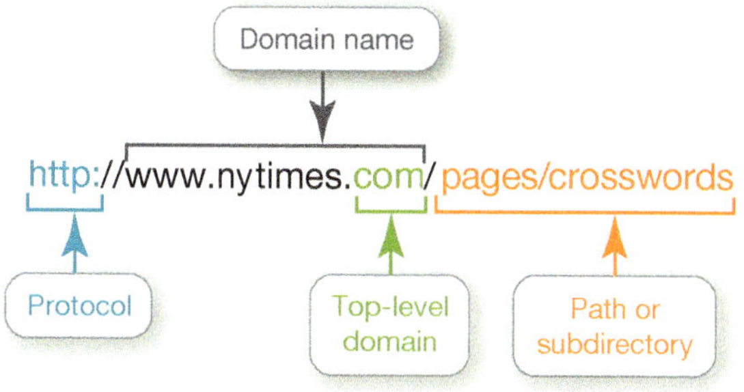

FIGURE 16 The Parts of a URL

FIGURE 17

Common Top-Level Domains and Their Authorized Users

DOMAIN NAME	WHO CAN USE IT
.biz	Businesses
.com	Originally for commercial sites, but now can be used by anyone
.edu	Degree-granting institutions
.gov	Local, state, and federal U.S. governments
.info	Information service providers
.mil	U.S. military
.net	Originally for networking organizations, but no longer restricted
.org	Organizations (often not-for-profits)

browser, you don't have to type in every part in the location or address bar of the browser. Most current browsers no longer require you to enter the http://protocol or the "www," and most don't even require the domain if it's a .com—the browser will enter those automatically.

What's the protocol? You're probably most familiar with URLs that begin with *http*, which is short for **Hypertext Transfer Protocol (HTTP)**. HTTP is the protocol that allows files to be transferred from a **web server**—a computer that hosts the website you're requesting—so that you can see it on your computer. The HTTP protocol is what the web is based on.

Is HTTP the only protocol I need to use? HTTP is the most common protocol, but it's not the only one. HTTP is part of the Internet protocol suite, a group of protocols that govern how information is exchanged on a network. Another protocol in that group is the **File Transfer Protocol (FTP)**. As its name implies, FTP was originally designed, before the HTTP protocol was developed, to transfer files from your computer to a web server. Today, FTP is often used when you have large files to upload or download. To connect to most FTP servers, you need a user ID and password. To upload and download files from FTP sites, you can use a browser or file transfer software such as WS_FTP, Fetch, or FileZilla.

BitTorrent, like FTP, is a protocol used to transfer files, though it's not part of the Internet protocol suite. To use BitTorrent, you install a software client program. It uses a *peer-to-peer networking system,* so that sharing occurs between connected computers that also have the BitTorrent client installed. BitTorrent was developed in 2001 and has been gaining popularity, especially among users who want to share music, movies, and games. Use caution, however, when accessing BitTorrent content. Because it is a peer-to-peer system, it's possible for copyrighted material to be shared illegally.

What's in a domain name? The domain name identifies the site's **host**, the location that maintains the computers that store the website files. For example, **www.berkeley.edu** is the domain name for the University of California at Berkeley website. The suffix in the domain name after the dot (such as "com" or "edu") is called the **top-level domain**. This suffix indicates the kind of organization to which the host belongs. Figure 17 lists the most frequently used top-level domains.

Each country has its own top-level domain. These are two-letter designations such as .za for South Africa and .us for the United States. A sampling of country codes is shown in Figure 18. Within a country-specific domain, further subdivisions can be made for regions or states. For instance, the .us domain contains subdomains for each state, using the two-letter abbreviation of the state. For example, the URL for Pennsylvania's website is **www.state.pa.us**.

What's the information after the domain name that I sometimes see? When the URL is the domain name, such as **www.nytimes.com**, you're requesting a site's home page. However, sometimes a forward slash and additional text follow the domain name, such as in **www.nytimes.com/pages/crosswords**. The information after each slash indicates a particular file or **path** (or **subdirectory**)

FIGURE 18

Examples of Country Codes

COUNTRY CODE	COUNTRY
.au	Australia
.ca	Canada
.jp	Japan
.uk	United Kingdom

Note: For a full listing of country codes, refer to **iana.org/domains/root/db/**.

FIGURE 19 Navigating a Web Page *(Courtesy of the U.S. Small Business Administration)*

within the website. In Figure 16, you would connect to the crossword page on the *New York Times* site.

Hyperlinks and Beyond

What's the best way to get around in a website? As its name implies, the web is a series of interconnected paths, or links. You've no doubt moved around the web by clicking on **hyperlinks**, specially coded elements that let you jump from one web page to another within the same website or to another site altogether (see Figure 19). Generally, text that operates as a hyperlink appears in a different color (often blue) and is usually underlined, but sometimes images also act as hyperlinks. When you hover your cursor over a hyperlink, the cursor changes to a hand with a finger pointing upward.

What other tools can I use to navigate a website? To move back or forward one page at a time, you can use the browser's Back and Forward buttons (see Figure 19).

To help navigate more quickly through a website, some sites provide a **breadcrumb trail**—a navigation aid that shows users the path they have taken to get to a web page, or where the page is located within the website. It usually appears at the top of a page. Figure 19 shows an example of a breadcrumb trail. "Breadcrumbs" get their name from the fairy tale "Hansel and Gretel," in which the characters drop breadcrumbs on the trail to find their way out of a forest. By clicking on earlier links in a breadcrumb trail, you can go directly to a previously visited web page without having to use the Back button to navigate back through the website.

The History list on your browser's toolbar is also a handy feature. The History list shows all the websites and pages you've visited over a certain period of time. These sites are organized according to date and can go back as far as three weeks, depending on your browsing activity. To access the History list in Internet Explorer, click the star in the upper right-hand corner of the browser window and then click the History tab.

SOUND BYTE

Welcome to the Web

In this Sound Byte, you'll visit the web in a series of guided tours of useful websites. This tour serves as an introductory guide for web newcomers but is also a great resource for more experienced users.

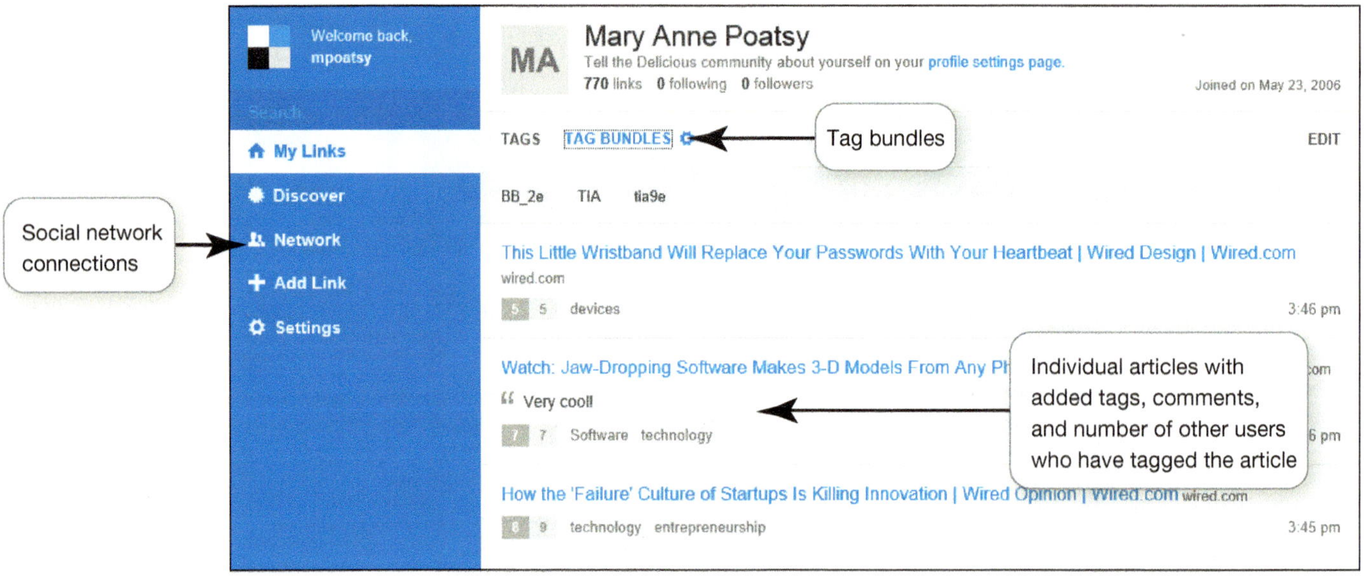

FIGURE 20 Delicious is a social bookmarking website that allows you to organize and share your favorite websites. *(AVOS Systems, Inc., www.delicious.com)*

Favorites, Live Bookmarks, and Tagging

What's the best way to mark a site so I can return to it later? If you want an easy way to return to a specific web page, you can use your browser's **Bookmarks** feature (Internet Explorer calls this feature **Favorites**). This feature places a marker of the site's URL in an easily retrievable list in your browser's toolbar. To organize the sites into categories, most browsers offer tools to create folders.

Favorites and Bookmarks are great for quickly locating those sites you use most, but they're accessible to you only when you're on your own computer. Although most browsers provide features that let you export the list of bookmarks to a file you can import to another computer or another browser, another way to access your Bookmarks and Favorites from any computer is to use MyBookmarks (**mybookmarks.com**), a free Internet service that stores your Bookmarks and Favorites online.

What are live bookmarks? Live bookmark is a feature in Firefox that adds the technology of RSS feeds to bookmarking. Safari and Internet Explorer also have built-in RSS readers, while Chrome requires that you add on an extension. Because the web is constantly changing, the site you bookmarked last week may subsequently change and add new content. Traditionally, you would notice the change only the next time you visited the site. Live bookmarks deliver content updates to you as soon as they become available using RSS, the same technology that updates blogs and podcasts that we described earlier in the chapter. Live bookmarks and RSS feeds are useful if you're interested in the most up-to-date news stories, sports scores, or stock prices.

What is tagging? Tagging, also known as **social bookmarking**, is like bookmarking your favorite website, but instead of saving it to your browser for only you to see, you're saving it to a social bookmarking site so that you can share it with others. A social bookmark or tag is a **keyword** or term that you assign to a web page, digital image, or video. A tag can be something you create to describe the digital content, or it can be a suggested term provided by the website. For example, as you were surfing the web you came across a web page with a great article on inexpensive places to go for spring break. You might tag the article with the term *vacations*. Others on the same social bookmarking site who are looking for websites about vacations may use *vacations* as the search term and find the article you tagged.

Delicious (**delicious.com**) is one of the original social bookmarking sites (see Figure 20). Delicious lets you group related links and organize them into "bundles." So if you've collected several links to websites about different places to go to over spring break, you can collect all those links into one bundle about vacations. Or if you want to see what links others may have found about interesting vacations, you could search Delicious with the term *vacations* to see other vacation-related bundles.

Another social bookmarking site is Diigo (**diigo.com**). Diigo differs from Delicious by allowing you to annotate the pages with highlights and sticky notes. Through Diigo, you can archive web pages so they are always available. ■

trends in IT

Doing Business on a Shoestring—Thanks to the Internet

Let's say you think that flip-flops in school colors would be a popular product. Your school's bookstore carries everything else with the school's colors and logo, but not flip-flops. You've asked your friends and several classmates, and most of them say they would buy flip-flops in the school's colors. So what do you do next? How do you move from product concept to selling a physical product?

Before the Internet, it would have been much more difficult and expensive to get your product produced and distributed. First, you would have had to find someone to design your flip-flops. Then, to make the flip-flops, you would have had to find a manufacturer, who may have required a high minimum order (maybe tens of thousands of pairs of flip-flops). You also would have needed a package design, marketing brochures, a company logo, a storage facility, and more. Finally, the largest hurdle would have been to convince a brick-and-mortar retailer, such as your campus bookstore, to carry your product.

Today, however, the Internet brings the power of the global economy right to your door (see Figure 21). For product design and manufacturing, you can visit a site like Alibaba (**alibaba.com**), which helps entrepreneurs locate manufacturers of all sorts of products. Many manufacturers are happy to work with small business owners to custom-design products. So if you find a flip-flop style you like, you probably can get it customized with your school colors.

But what happens if the bookstore doesn't want to sell your flip-flops? If this happens, you can set up a website to sell them yourself. Of course, you may need help doing this, in which case you can locate skilled professionals by using sites such as Guru (**guru.com**) or Elance (**elance.com**). You simply create a description of the job you need done (such as logo design for a flip-flop company), post it on the site, and invite freelancers to bid on your job. You then contact the freelancers who look promising, review samples of their work, and decide on someone who can help you—and at a competitive price. After your website is designed and up and running, you can place your business on social networking sites, such as Facebook, to help potential customers discover your product and spread the word about your great flip-flops. You probably already have lots of friends on Facebook who attend your school and would be good potential customers.

Another hurdle is determining where you'll store your product and who will package and ship it to customers. If your parents' basement isn't large enough, you can outsource warehousing and order fulfillment to **Amazon.com**. Amazon will (for a fee) warehouse your inventory and then package and ship it when customer orders are received. Orders don't have to come through Amazon's site (although that is an option); you can provide ordering information collected on your site to Amazon, and Amazon will take care of the rest.

Although there is always a cost to starting up a business, up-front costs are much lower when you take advantage of the global marketplace and the Internet. So, take that brilliant idea you have and turn it into a business today!

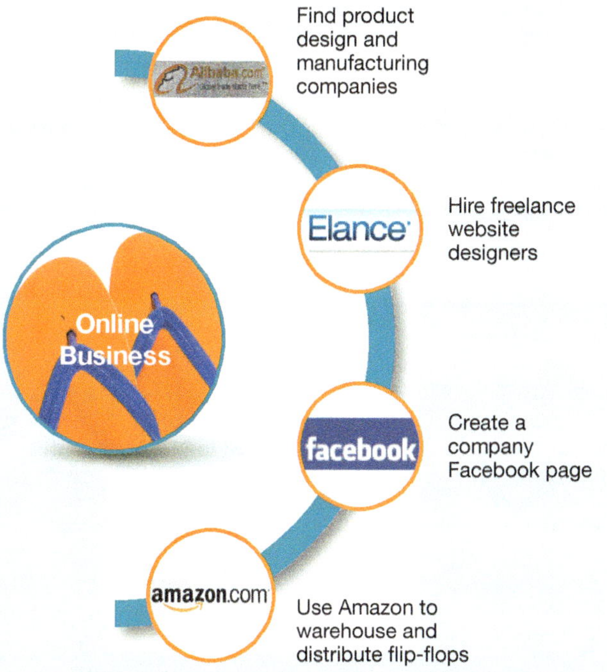

FIGURE 21 By using the services of only a few websites, you can create and distribute products, such as your own line of custom flip-flops. *(M4OS Photos/Alamy; Elance, Inc.; Kevin Britland/Alamy; Anatolii Babii/Alamy; nito/Shutterstock)*

searching the web EFFECTIVELY

You've most likely "Googled" something today, and if you did, your search is one of over five billion searches today. Google is the world's most popular **search engine**—a set of programs that searches the web for keywords (specific words you wish to look for or *query*) and then returns a list of the sites on which those keywords are found. In fact, Google has become so popular that its name is synonymous with looking for information on the web. Other popular search engines include Yahoo!, Bing, and Ask.com. But there are even more options for searching the web.

For some web searches, it might be better to use a **subject directory**, which is a structured outline of websites organized by topics and subtopics. By drilling down through the topics and subtopics, you can narrow down to a list of meaningful websites to look through. For example, if you wanted to know about exhibits of 3-D photography, you might click Arts>Visual Arts>Photography>3-D>Exhibits in a subject directory. In Yahoo's subject directory (**dir.yahoo.com**), the result would be a list of relevant websites about 3-D photography exhibits. The website ipl2 (**ipl2.org**) has a subject directory that combines resources from the Internet Public Library and the Librarians' Internet Index websites (see Figure 22). (ipl2 also has a feature through which you can ask a librarian a question.)

If you can't decide which search engine is best, you may want to try a metasearch engine. **Metasearch engines**, such as Dogpile (**dogpile.com**; see Figure 22), search other search engines rather than individual websites. Figure 23 lists search engines and subject directories that are alternatives to Google, Yahoo!, and Bing.

Using Search Engines Effectively

How do search engines work? Search engines have three components:

1. The first component is a program called a *spider*, which constantly collects data on the web, following links in websites and reading web pages. Spiders get their name because they crawl over the web using multiple "legs" to visit many sites simultaneously.
2. As the spider collects data, the second component of the search engine, an *indexer program*, organizes the data into a large database.
3. When you use a search engine, you interact with the third component: the *search engine software*. This software searches the indexed data, pulling out relevant information according to your search.

The resulting list appears in your web browser as a list of hits—sites that match your search.

Why don't I get the same results from all search engines? Each search engine uses a unique formula, or *algorithm*, to formulate the search and create the resulting index of related sites. In addition, search engines differ in how they rank the search results. Most search engines rank their results based on the frequency of the appearance of your queried keywords in websites as well as the location of those words in the sites. This means that sites that include the keywords in their URL or site name most likely appear at the top of the results list. An important part of a company's marketing strategy

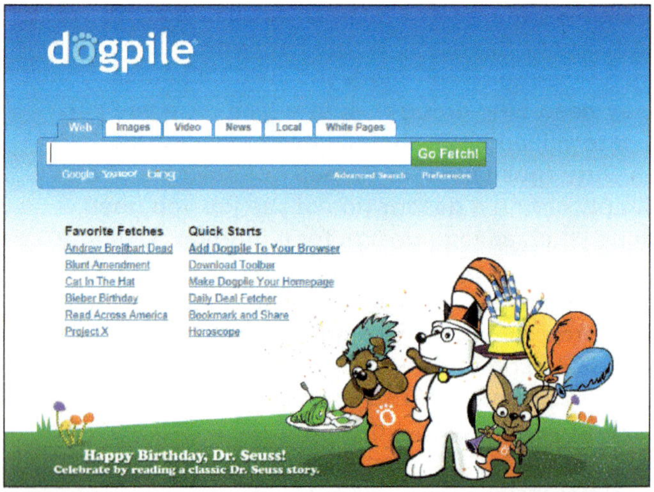

FIGURE 22 ipl2 and Dogpile are alternatives to Google. ipl2 (**ipl2.org**) is a subject directory that lists resources by subject, and Dogpile (**dogpile.com**) is a metasearch engine that searches Google, Yahoo!, and Bing. *(Courtesy of iPL2; Courtesy of InfoSpace, Inc./Blucora)*

FIGURE 23

Beyond Google: Alternative Search Engines and Subject Directories

Bing **bing.com**	Web search engine from Microsoft
ChaCha **chacha.com**	Uses live people who help you search; free of charge. Also available by texting your questions to 242242.
CompletePlanet **aip.completeplanet.com**	"Deep web" directory that searches databases not normally searched by typical search engines.
Dogpile **dogpile.com**	Metasearch engine that searches Google, Yahoo!, and Bing.
Excite **excite.com**	Website that in addition to having keyword search capabilities includes links to information on a wide variety of topics including travel, weather, concert tickets, and top news items.
Info.com **info.com**	Metasearch engine that searches Google, Yahoo!, Bing, and Yandex (a Russian search engine).
InfoMine **infomine.ucr.edu**	Subject directory of academic resources with keyword search engine capabilities.
ipl2 **ipl2.org**	Subject directory that combines resources from the Internet Public Library and the Librarians' Internet Index websites.
Oolone **oolone.com**	Visual search engine that displays images rather than text as a result of a keyword search.
Open Directory Project **dmoz.org**	Human-edited subject directory with keyword search capabilities. Maintained by a global community of volunteer editors.
Yippy **yippy.com**	Metasearch engine that groups similar results into topics called clusters (for example, NBA, College Basketball, Photo Gallery, and Articles would be some resulting clusters if you use the search term *basketball*). Clicking on any of these clusters results in listing those sites specific to that subset of basketball.

Note: For a complete list of search engines, go to **searchengineguide.com**

is search engine optimization, which is designing the corporate website to ensure it ranks near the top of a search.

Search engines also differ as to which sites they search. For instance, Google and Bing search nearly the entire web, whereas specialty search engines search only sites that are relevant to a particular topic or industry. Specialty search engines exist for almost every industry or interest. DailyStocks (**dailystocks.com**) is a search engine used primarily by investors that searches for corporate information. Search Engine Watch (**searchenginewatch.com**) has a list of many specialty search engines, organized by industry.

Can I use a search engine to search just for images and videos? With the increasing popularity of multimedia, search engines such as Google, Bing, and Yahoo! let you search the web for digital images and audio and video files. After putting in your search term, select Video from Google's top menu to display only the search results that are videos. You can further narrow down the video selection by using the filtering tools. Blinkx (**blinkx.com**) is a video search engine that helps you sift through all the video posted on the web (see Figure 24).

How can I refine my searches for better results? You've probably searched for something on Google and gotten back a list of hits that includes thousands—even millions—of web pages that have no relevance to the topic you're interested in. Initially, Boolean operators were needed to help refine a search. **Boolean operators** are words such as *AND, NOT,* and *OR* that describe the relationships between keywords in a search. With the simple addition of a few words or constraints,

ACTIVE HELPDESK

Using Subject Directories and Search Engines

In this Active Helpdesk call, you'll play the role of a helpdesk staffer, fielding calls about how to search the Internet using search engines and subject directories, as well as how to use advanced search options to search the web more effectively.

ACTIVE HELPDESK

Getting Around the Web

In this Active Helpdesk call, you'll play the role of a helpdesk staffer, fielding calls about web browsers, URLs, and how to use hyperlinks and other tools to get around the web.

you can narrow your search results to a more manageable and more meaningful list.

Are there other helpful search strategies? Other strategies can help refine your searches when entering your search phrases:

- **Search for a phrase.** To search for an exact phrase, place quotation marks around your keywords. The search engine will look for only those websites that contain the words in *that exact order*. For example, if you want information on the movie *The Green Hornet* and you type these words without quotation marks, your search results will contain pages that include either of the words *Green* and *Hornet*, although not necessarily in that order. Typing *"The Green Hornet"* in quotation marks guarantees that search results will include this exact phrase.
- **Search within a specific website.** To search just a specific website, you can use the search keyword, then *site:* followed by the website's URL. For example, searching with *processor site:* www.wired.com returns results about processors from the Wired.com website. The same method works for entire classes of sites in a given top-level domain or country code.
- **Use a wild card.** The asterisk ("*") is a wild card, or placeholder, feature that is helpful when you need to search with unknown terms. Another way to think about the wild card search feature is as a "fill in the blank." For example, searching with *Congress voted * on the * bill* might bring up an article about the members of Congress who voted *no* on the *healthcare* bill or a different article about the members of Congress who voted *yes* on the *energy* bill.

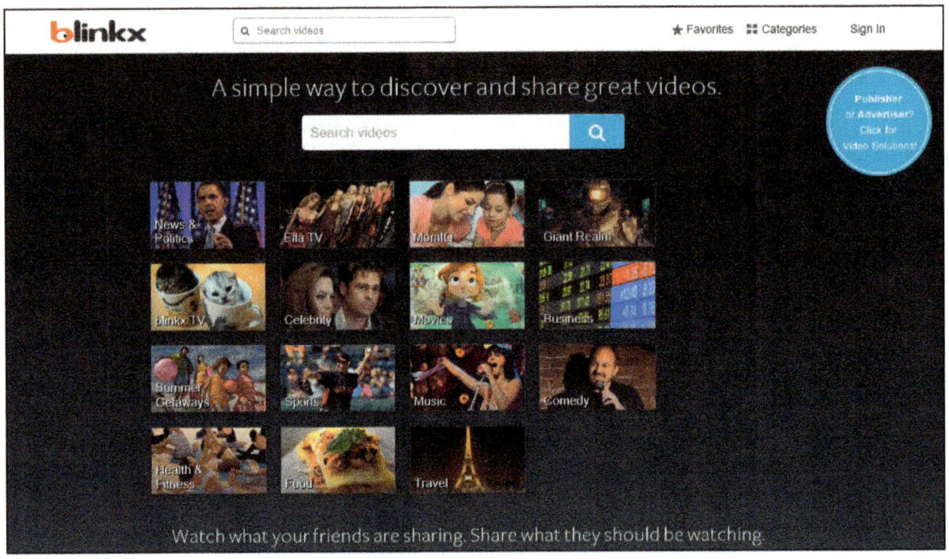

(blinkx)

FIGURE 24 Blinkx is a video search engine that helps you sift through the increasing number of videos on the web. *(Courtesy of Blinkx)*

BITS&BYTES

Searching to Do Good

Wouldn't it be great to benefit others just by searching the web? Now there's an easy way to "do good" with every search. Goodsearch (**goodsearch.com**) is a Yahoo!-powered search engine that donates half of its revenues (approximately a penny per search) to approved U.S. charities and schools that users designate. The money Goodsearch donates comes from the site's advertisers. More than 100,000 charitable organizations are being helped by Goodsearch, but if the organization you're interested in isn't on the list, as long as it's a registered U.S. not-for-profit organization, you can apply to have it added. Goodsearch has expanded its program to online shopping and dining out.

You can also contribute to your favorite charity by shopping online through Goodshop (**goodshop.com**). Instead of going directly to your favorite online store, go to Goodshop first, find and click through to the store of your choice, and start shopping. Participating stores donate up to 30% of the purchased amount. Similarly, through the GoodDining program, dine at a participating restaurant and a percentage of your bill will go to your cause. So, search, shop, and eat—and do some good!

How else can I customize my searches? Many other specialty search strategies and services are available. By clicking on Search tools in Google's menu at the top of a Google search, you can restrict search results by time, location, and even reading level (see Figure 25). You can also click on the Apps button in Google's main page, then click the "More" and "Even more from Google" options for all the specialized search products Google offers (see Figure 26):

- *Scholar* searches scholarly literature such as peer-reviewed papers, theses, and publications from academic organizations. Each search result contains bibliographic information as well.
- *Custom Search* lets you create a customized search engine to search only a selected set of sites tailored to your needs. You can add this specialized search engine to a website or blog or design it for a specific organization.
- *Google Shopping* lets you search by product rather than by company. So if you're interested in buying a digital camera, Google Shopping lists cameras by popularity and provides information on the stores that carry the cameras, along with the average price.

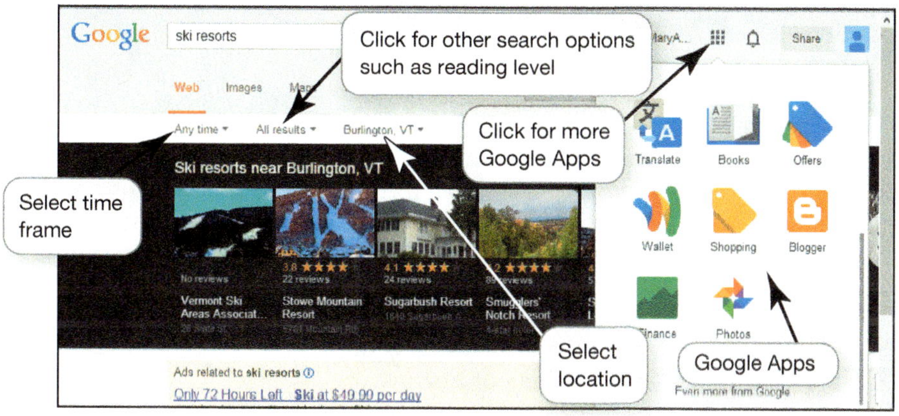

FIGURE 25 Use Google's search tools to restrict the time frame, the location, and even the reading level of your search results. *(Courtesy of Google, Inc.)*

- *Alerts* let you know by e-mail when content that you specify has been updated, so you can monitor a developing news story or be aware of breaking news about your favorite sports team, for example.

Evaluating Websites

How can I make sure a website is appropriate to use for research? When you're using the Internet for research, you shouldn't assume that everything you find is accurate and appropriate to use. The following is a list of questions to consider before you use an Internet resource; the answers to these questions will help you decide whether you should consider a website to be a good source of information:

- **Authority:** Who is the author of the article or the sponsor of the site? If the author is well known or the site is published by a reputable news source (such as the *New York Times*), then you can feel more confident using it as a source than if you are unable to locate such information. *Note:* Some sites include a page with information about the author or the site's sponsor.
- **Bias:** Is the site biased? The purpose of many websites is to sell products or services or to persuade rather than inform. These sites, though useful in some situations, present a biased point of view. Look for sites that offer several sets of facts or consider opinions from several sources.
- **Relevance:** Is the information on the site current? Material can last a long time on the web. Some research projects (such as historical accounts) depend on older records. However, if you're writing about cutting-edge technologies, you need to look for the most recent sources. Therefore, look for a date on information to make sure it is current.
- **Audience:** For what audience is the site intended? Ensure that the content, tone, and style of the site match your needs. You probably wouldn't want to use information from a site geared toward teens if you're writing for adults, nor would you use a site that has a casual style and tone for serious research.
- **Links:** Are the links available and appropriate? Check out the links provided on the site to determine whether they're still working and appropriate for your needs. Don't assume that the links provided are the only additional sources of information. Investigate other sites on your topic, as well. You should also be able to find the same information on at least three different websites to help verify the information is accurate. ■

SOUND BYTE
Finding Information on the Web

In this Sound Byte, you'll learn how and when to use search engines and subject directories. Through guided tours, you'll learn effective search techniques, including how to use Boolean operators and metasearch engines.

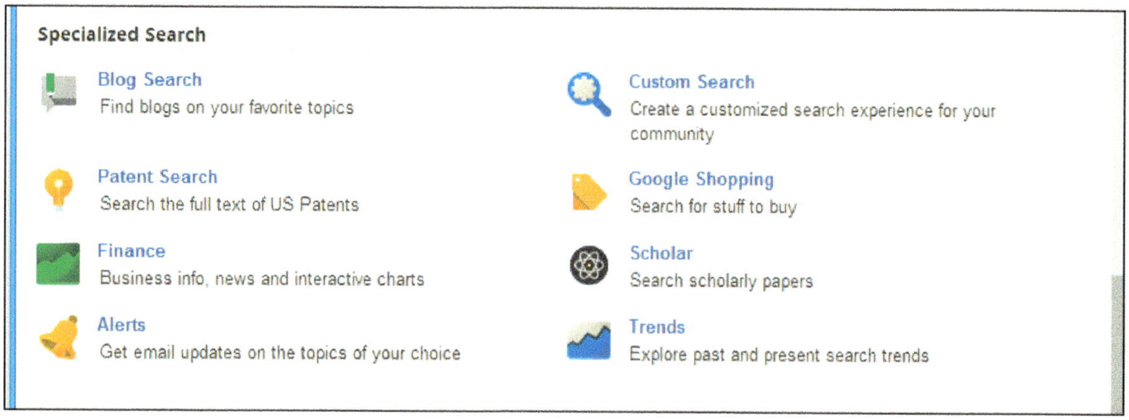

FIGURE 26 Google's Specialized Search Tools. *(Courtesy of Google, Inc.)*

ethics in IT Plagiarism and Copyright Violation: What Can You Borrow from the Internet?

Despite having so much information easily available on the web, using it without receiving proper permissions is not only wrong but can also be illegal. So what can you borrow from the web and what must you seek permission to use? Consider these scenarios:

1. You find a political cartoon that would be terrific in a PowerPoint presentation you're creating for your civics class. You copy it into your presentation.
2. Your hobby is writing children's books, which you later sell online. Most of what you create is your content, but sometimes you borrow story ideas from other children's books and just change a few characters or situations. You do not obtain permission from the originators of the story ideas you borrow.
3. You're pressed for time and need to do research for a paper due tomorrow. You find information on an obscure website and copy it into your paper without documenting the source.
4. You download a song from the Internet and incorporate it into a PowerPoint presentation for a school project. Because you assume everyone knows the song, you don't credit it in your sources.

Which of the preceding scenarios represent copyright violations? Which represent plagiarism? The distinctions between these scenarios are narrow in some cases, but it's important to understand the differences.

Plagiarism occurs when you use someone else's ideas or words and represent them as your own. In today's computer society, it's easy to copy information from the Internet and paste it into a Word document, change a few words, and call it your own. To avoid plagiarism, properly crediting all information you obtain from the Internet by using quotation marks around all words you borrow directly, and credit your sources for any ideas you paraphrase or borrow.

WriteCheck (**writecheck.com**) is a website specifically for students to help check for plagiarism violations (see Figure 27). The site compares your document to a database of publications, books, and web content and identifies possible plagiarism violations. Although some common phrasing may be truly coincidental, real and purposeful plagiarism is reasonably easy to identify. Students can use WriteCheck before submitting an assignment to ensure their papers are free from plagiarism and avoid the serious consequences of this offense.

Copyright violation is more serious because it, unlike plagiarism, is punishable by law. Copyright law assumes that all original work is copyrighted even if the work does not display the copyright symbol (©). Copyright violation occurs when you use another person's material for your own personal economic benefit or when you take away from the economic benefit of the originator. In most cases, citing the source is not sufficient; you need to seek and receive written permission from the copyright holder.

There are exceptions to this rule. There is no copyright on government documents, so you can download and reproduce material from any government website. The British Broadcasting Corporation (BBC) is also beginning to digitize and

FIGURE 27 Students can compare their work to a database of publications in sites such as WriteCheck to check for unintended plagiarism. *(Keith Morris/Alamy)*

make available its archives of material to the public without copyright restrictions. Teachers and students receive special consideration that falls under a provision called *academic fair use*. As long as the material is being used for educational purposes only, limited copying and distribution is allowed.

One standard applied to academic fair use is the effect the use has on the potential market. For example, a student can include a cartoon in a PowerPoint presentation without seeking permission from the artist. However, to avoid plagiarism, you still must credit your sources of information.

So, do you now know which of the four scenarios above are plagiarism or copyright violations? Let's review them.

1. You are not in violation because the use of the cartoon is for educational purposes and falls under the academic fair use provision. You must still credit the source, however.
2. You are in violation of copyright laws because you are presenting others' ideas for children's stories as your own and receiving personal economic benefit from them.
3. You are guilty of plagiarism because you copied content from another source and implied it was your own work.
4. Again, because your copying is for a school project, you are not in violation of copyright laws because of the academic fair use provision. However, it's always important to document your sources.

Before moving on to the Chapter Review:
- **Watch Replay Video 2** .
- Then check your understanding of what you've learned so far.

check your understanding//

For a quick review to see what you've learned so far, answer the following questions. Visit **pearsonhighered.com/techinaction** to check your answers.

multiple choice

1. What is the name for a list of links you've visited within a website?
   - **a.** favorites
   - **b.** breadcrumb trail
   - **c.** bookmarks
   - **d.** social bookmarks
2. Which is NOT a component of a search engine?
   - **a.** spider
   - **b.** indexer program
   - **c.** subject directory
   - **d.** search engine software
3. When using the Internet for research, you
   - **a.** can assume that everything you find is accurate and appropriate.
   - **b.** should evaluate sites for bias and relevance.
   - **c.** can assume the author is an authority on the subject matter.
   - **d.** can assume that the links provided on the site are the only additional sources of information.
4. Which of the following is not an Internet protocol?
   - **a.** ARPANET
   - **b.** HTTP
   - **c.** FTP
   - **d.** BitTorrent
5. Country codes are what part of a URL?
   - **a.** sub-top-level domain
   - **b.** top-level domain
   - **c.** path
   - **d.** protocol

true–false

_______ **1.** A search engine that searches other search engines is called a SuperSearch engine.

_______ **2.** You can share your favorite sites with others through social bookmarking.

critical thinking

1. **File-Swapping Ethics**

   Downloading free music, movies, and other electronic media from the Internet, although illegal, still occurs on sites such as BitTorrent.
   - **a.** Do you think you should have the ability to download free music files of your choice? Do you think the musicians who oppose online music sharing have made valid points?
   - **b.** Discuss the differences you see between sharing music files online and sharing CDs with your friends.
   - **c.** The current price to buy a song online is about $1. Is this a fair price? If not, what price would you consider fair?
2. **The Power of Google**

   Google is the largest and most popular search engine on the Internet today. Because of its size and popularity, some people claim that Google has enormous power to influence a web user's search experience solely by its website-ranking processes. What do you think about this potential power? How could it be used in negative or harmful ways?
   - **a.** Some websites pay search engines to list them near the top of the results pages. These sponsors therefore get priority placement. What do you think of this policy?
   - **b.** What effect (if any) do you think that Google has on website development? For example, do you think website developers intentionally include frequently searched words in their pages so that they will appear in more hits lists?

Continue

Chapter Review

summary//

The Internet and How It Works

1. What is the origin of the Internet?

- The Internet is the largest computer network in the world, connecting millions of computers.
- Government and military officials developed the early Internet as a reliable way to communicate in the event of war. Eventually, scientists and educators used the Internet to exchange research.
- Today, we use the Internet and the web (which is a part of the Internet) to shop, research, communicate, and entertain ourselves.

2. How does data travel on the Internet?

- A computer (or other device) connected to the Internet acts as either a client (a computer that asks for information) or a server (a computer that receives the request and returns the information to the client).
- Data travels between clients and servers along a system of communication lines or pathways. The largest and fastest of these pathways form the Internet backbone.
- To ensure that data is sent to the correct computer along the pathways, IP addresses (unique ID numbers) are assigned to all computers connected to the Internet.

Communicating and Collaborating on the Web

3. How can I communicate and collaborate using Web 2.0 technologies?

- Web 2.0 can be described as the social web, in which the user is also a participant. Before Web 2.0 technologies were in place, we were only able to be passive users of the web.
- Examples of Web 2.0 technologies include social networking, blogs, wikis, podcasts, and webcasts. Social networking enables you to communicate and share information with friends as well as meet and connect with others.
- Blogs are journal entries posted to the web that are generally organized by a topic or area of interest and are publicly available. Generally, one person writes the blog, and others can comment on the journal entries.
- Video logs are personal journals that use video as the primary content in addition to text, images, and audio.
- Wikis are a type of website that allows users to collaborate on content—adding, removing, or editing it.
- Podcasts are audio or video content that is available over the Internet. Users subscribe to receive updates to podcasts.
- Webcasts are broadcasts of audio or video content over the Internet. Most webcasts are distributed in real time, unlike podcasts that are usually prerecorded and made available for download.

4. How can I communicate using e-mail and instant messaging?

- Communication was one of the reasons the Internet was developed and is one of the primary uses of the Internet today.
- E-mail allows users to communicate electronically without the parties involved being available at the same time, whereas instant-messaging services are programs that enable you to communicate in real time with others who are online.

Web Entertainment

5. What multimedia files are found on the web, and what software is needed to access those files?

- Multimedia is anything that involves one or more forms of media in addition to text, such as graphics, audio, and video clips.
- Sometimes you need a special software program called a *plug-in* (or *player*) to view and hear multimedia files. Plug-ins are often installed in new computers or are offered free of charge at developer's websites.

Conducting Business over the Internet: E-Commerce

6. What is e-commerce, and what online safeguards are available?

- E-commerce is the business of conducting business online.
- E-commerce includes transactions between businesses (B2B), between consumers (C2C), and between businesses and consumers (B2C).
- Because more business than ever before is conducted online, numerous safeguards have been put in place to ensure that transactions are protected. Some important safeguards to keep in mind include looking for indicators that the website is secure; shopping at well-known, reputable sites; and avoiding making online transactions on public computers.

Accessing and Moving Around the Web

7. What is a web browser, and what are a URL and its parts?

- Once you're connected to the Internet, in order to locate, navigate to, and view web pages, you need to install special software called a web browser on your system.
- The most common web browsers are Internet Explorer, Firefox, Google Chrome, and Safari.
- You gain access to a website by typing in its address, called a Uniform Resource Locator (URL).
- A URL is comprised of several parts, including the protocol, the domain, the top-level domain, and paths (or subdirectories).

8. How can I use hyperlinks and other tools to get around the web?

- One unique aspect of the web is that you can jump from place to place by clicking on specially formatted pieces of text or images called *hyperlinks*.
- You can also use the Back and Forward buttons, History lists, breadcrumb trails, and Favorites or Bookmarks to navigate the web.
- Favorites, live bookmarks, and social bookmarking help you return to specific web pages without having to type in the URL and help you organize the web content that is most important to you.

Searching the Web Effectively

8. How do I search the Internet effectively, and how can I evaluate websites?

- A search engine is a set of programs that searches the web using specific keywords you wish to query and then returns a list of the websites on which those keywords are found.
- Search engines can be used to search for images, podcasts, and videos in addition to traditional text-based web content.
- A subject directory is a structured outline of websites organized by topic and subtopic. Metasearch engines search other search engines.
- Not all websites are equal, and some are better sources for research than others. To evaluate whether it is appropriate to use a website as a resource, determine whether the author of the site is reputable and whether the site is intended for your particular needs. In addition, make sure that the site content is not biased, the information on the site is current, and all the links on the site are available and appropriate. If multiple sites offer the same content, this is another indication that the information is accurate.

Be sure to check out the companion website for additional materials to help you review and learn, including a Tech Bytes Weekly newsletter—**pearsonhighered.com/techinaction**. And don't forget the Replay Videos.

key terms//

aggregator
blog (weblog)
Bookmarks
Boolean operators
breadcrumb trail
business-to-business (B2B)
business-to-consumer (B2C)
client
client/server network
consumer-to-consumer (C2C)
domain name
e-commerce (electronic commerce)
e-mail (electronic mail)
e-mail client
Favorites
File Transfer Protocol (FTP)
host
hyperlink
Hypertext Transfer Protocol (HTTP)
instant messaging (IM)
Internet
Internet backbone
Internet Protocol (IP) address
keyword
live bookmark
metasearch engine
multimedia

path (subdirectory)
plug-in (player)
podcast
Really Simple Syndication (RSS)
search engine
secure socket layer
semantic web (Web 3.0)
server
social commerce
social networking
streaming media
subject directory
tagging (social bookmarking)
top-level domain
Uniform Resource Locator (URL)
video log (vlog or video blog)
Web 2.0
web-based e-mail
web browser (browser)
webcast
web server
website
wiki
World Wide Web (WWW or the web)

making the transition to . . . next semester//

1. **Plagiarism**

   Policies Does your school have a plagiarism policy?

   a. Search your school's website to find the school's plagiarism policy. What does it say?

   b. How well do you paraphrase? Find some websites that help test or evaluate your paraphrasing skills.

   c. Create an account at WriteCheck. This website checks your written work against content on the web and produces an originality report. Submit at least three different drafts of your work to WriteCheck to check for any intended or unintended cases of plagiarism before submitting your final work for a grade. What were the results?

2. **Searching Beyond Google**

   While Google is probably your first choice among search engines, there are many other very good search engines that are worth knowing about. Conduct searches for inexpensive travel deals for spring break by using the search engines in the following list. Record your results and a summary of the differences among search engines. Would you choose to use any of these search engines again? Why or why not?

   a. Yippy.com

   b. Dogpile.com

   c. Chacha.com

making the transition to . . . the workplace//

1. **Online Résumé Resources**

   Using a search engine, locate several web resources that offer assistance in writing a résumé. For example, the University of Minnesota (**umn.edu/ohr/careerdev/resources/resume**) has a résumé tutor that guides you as you write your résumé.

   a. What other websites can you find that help you write a résumé?

   b. Do these sites all offer the same services and have the same features?

2. **Evaluating Web 2.0 Content**

   You are aware of the guidelines you should use to evaluate the quality of content on a website, but you find yourself using other kinds of web content such as blogs, wikis, social networking sites, and social bookmarks. Visit **library.albany.edu/usered/eval/evalweb** and review the new guidelines for evaluating web content in the Web 2.0 environment. After reviewing the guidelines, describe the guidelines for evaluating web content at the following sites:

   a. Free research sites such as Google Scholar (**scholar.google.com**)

   b. Document repositories such as California Digital Library (**cdlib.org**)

   c. Blogs and wikis such as TechCrunch (**techcrunch.com**)

d. Social networking sites such as Twitter (**twitter.com**)

e. Social bookmarking sites such as Delicious (**delicious.com**)

f. Multimedia sites such as YouTube (**youtube.com**)

3. **Facebook Privacy and Security**

You most likely share lots of information on Facebook with your friends and family. You're aware of the privacy and security settings, and may think you have your settings established just right. But the problem is that those settings are complex and change on a regular basis, so reviewing your settings is important to ensure you're not sharing too much. Conduct an Internet search to locate a guide to Facebook privacy that has been published by a reputable source within the past month. (If you're using Google, click on Search tools, click the Any time arrow, and then select Past month.) Go through the guide, and make any necessary changes to your Facebook privacy and security settings. Write a brief report that summarizes the steps in the guide, and note where you had to make changes. End the report by summarizing your thoughts about Facebook's privacy and security settings.

team time//

Collaborating with Technology

Problem

Collaborating on projects with team members is a regular part of business and academia. Many great tools are available that facilitate online collaboration, and it's important to be familiar with them. In this Team Time, each team will create a group report on a specific topic, using online collaboration tools, and compare and rate the tools and the collaboration process.

Process

Split your group into teams. To appreciate fully the benefits of online collaboration, each team should have at least five or six members. Each group will create a team report on a topic that is approved by your instructor. As part of the report, one group member should record the process the group took to create the report, including a review of the tools used and reflections on the difficulties encountered by the group.

1. Conduct a virtual meeting. Agree on an online meeting and video collaboration tool such as Skype, Google+ Hangouts, ooVoo, or Tinychat and conduct a group chat. In this phase, outline your group project strategy and delegate work responsibilities.
2. Share documents and collaborate online. Your group must create one document that is accessible to every member at all times. Gone are the days of e-mailing parts of documents to a group member who will assemble the parts. Explore document-sharing sites such as Google Docs, Evernote, OneDrive, or Dropbox and collaboratively create your group document. All members are responsible for reviewing the entire document.
3. After the group reports are created, the class should decide which online sharing site (such as Dropbox or OneDrive) will be used so teams can make their reports available to the other teams for comments.

Conclusion

After all the team group reports have been completed and shared, discuss the following with your class: What is the benefit of using online collaboration technology to create group projects? How did collaboration technologies help or hinder the team process?

ethics project//

Plagiarism

In this exercise, you'll research and then role-play a complicated ethical situation. The role you play may or may not match your own personal beliefs, but your research and use of logic will enable you to represent whichever view is assigned. An arbitrator will watch and comment on both sides of the arguments, and together the team will agree on an ethical solution.

Problem

Plagiarism, or portraying another's work as your own, has been around for a long time and extends well beyond the classroom. For example, Nick Simmons, the son of Gene Simmons (from KISS) and a member of A&E's *Family Jewels* reality series, created a comic book series, *Incarnate*. Radical Publishing picked up the series but quickly stopped publication when Internet messages accused the author of copying from other similar series. Similarly, the Australian band Men at Work was cited for copying a melody from "Kookaburra Sits in the Old Gum Tree" for its 1980s hit "Down Under" and owes the owner years of royalties.

Research Areas to Consider

- Plagiarism violations
- Comic book series *Incarnate*
- Australian band Men at Work
- Plagiarism consequences

Process

1. Divide the class into teams.
2. Research the areas cited above and devise a scenario in which someone has violated plagiarism rules.
3. Team members should write a summary that provides background information for their character—for example, author, publisher, or arbitrator—and that details their character's behaviors to set the stage for the role-playing event. Then team members should create an outline to use during the role-playing event.
4. Team members should arrange a mutually convenient time to meet for the exchange, using a virtual meeting tool or by meeting in person.
5. Team members should present their case to the class or submit a PowerPoint presentation for review by the rest of the class, along with the summary and resolution they developed.

Conclusion

As technology becomes ever more prevalent and integrated into our lives, more and more ethical dilemmas will present themselves. Being able to understand and evaluate both sides of an argument, while responding in a personally or socially ethical manner, will be an important skill.

Glossary

aggregator A software program that finds and retrieves the latest update of web material (usually podcasts) according to your specifications.

blog A personal log or journal posted on the web; short for *web log*.

bookmarks Features in some browsers that place markers of websites' Uniform Resource Locators (URLs) in an easily retrievable list.

Boolean operator A word used to refine logical searches. For Internet searches, the words AND, NOT, and OR describe the relationships between keywords in the search.

breadcrumb trail A navigation aid that shows users the path they have taken to get to a web page or where the page is located within the website; it usually appears at the top of a page.

business-to-business (B2B) E-commerce transactions between businesses.

business-to-consumer (B2C) E-commerce transactions between businesses and consumers.

client A computer that requests information from a server in a client/server network (such as your computer when you are connected to the Internet).

client/server network (server-based network) A type of network that uses servers to deliver services to computers that are requesting them (clients).

consumer-to-consumer (C2C) E-commerce transactions between consumers through online sites such as eBay.

domain name A part of a Uniform Resource Locator (URL). Domain names consist of two parts: the site's host and a suffix that indicates the type of organization (example: popsci.com, where *popsci* is the domain name and *com* is the suffix).

e-commerce (electronic commerce) The process of conducting business online for purposes ranging from fund-raising to advertising to selling products.

e-mail (electronic mail) Internet-based communication in which senders and recipients correspond.

e-mail client A software program that runs on a computer and is used to send and receive e-mail through an Internet service provider's server.

Favorites A feature in Microsoft Internet Explorer that places a marker of a website's Uniform Resource Locator (URL) in an easily retrievable list in the browser's toolbar. (Called Bookmarks in some browsers.)

File Transfer Protocol (FTP) A protocol used to upload and download files from one computer to another over the Internet.

host The portion of a domain name that identifies who maintains a given website. For example, berkeley.edu is the domain name for the University of California at Berkeley, which maintains that site.

hyperlink A type of specially coded text that, when clicked, enables a user to jump from one location, or web page, to another within a website or to another website altogether.

Hypertext Transfer Protocol (HTTP) The protocol that allows files to be transferred from a web server so that you can see them on your computer by using a browser.

instant messaging (IM) A program that enables users to communicate online in real time with others who are also online.

Internet A network of networks that's the largest network in the world, connecting billions of computers globally.

Internet Protocol (IP) address The means by which all computers connected to the Internet identify each other. It consists of a unique set of four numbers separated by dots, such as 123.45.178.91.

keyword (1) A specific word a user wishes to query (or look for) in an Internet search. (2) A specific word that has a predefined meaning in a particular programming language.

live bookmark A bookmark that delivers updates as soon as they become available, using Really Simple Syndication (RSS).

metasearch engine A search engine, such as Dogpile, that searches other search engines rather than individual websites.

multimedia Anything that involves one or more forms of media plus text.

path (subdirectory) The information after the slash that indicates a particular file or path (or subdirectory) within the website.

plug-in (player) A small software program that "plugs in" to a web browser to enable a specific function—for example, to view and hear certain multimedia files on the web.

podcast A clip of audio or video content that's broadcast over the Internet using compressed audio or video files in formats such as MP3.

Really Simple Syndication (RSS) An XML-based format that allows frequent updates of content on the World Wide Web.

search engine A set of programs that searches the web for specific words (or keywords) you wish to query (or look for) and that then returns a list of the websites on which those keywords are found.

Secure Sockets Layer (SSL) A network security protocol that provides for the encryption of data transmitted using the Internet. The current versions of all major web browsers support SSL.

semantic web (Web 3.0) An evolving extension of the World Wide Web in which information is defined in such a way as to make it more easily readable by computers.

server A computer that provides resources to other computers on a network.

social commerce A subset of e-commerce that uses social networks to assist in marketing and purchasing products.

social bookmark (tagging) A keyword or term that Internet users assign to a web resource such as a web page, digital image, or video.

social networking A means by which people use the Internet to communicate and share information among their immediate friends and to meet and connect with others through common interests, experiences, and friends.

subject directory A structured outline of websites organized by topics and subtopics.

top-level domain The suffix, often of three letters (such as .com or .edu), in the domain name that indicates the kind of organization the host is.

Uniform Resource Locator (URL) A website's unique address; an example is microsoft.com.

video log (vlog or video blog) A personal online journal that uses video as the primary content in addition to text, images, and audio.

Web 2.0 Tools and web-based services that emphasize online collaboration and sharing among users.

web-based e-mail A type of e-mail system that's managed by a web browser and that allows access to e-mail from the web.

web browser (browser) Software installed on a computer system that allows individuals to locate, view, and navigate the web.

webcast The broadcast of audio or video content over the Internet. Unlike a podcast, a webcast is not updated automatically.

website A location on the web.

wiki A type of website that allows anyone visiting the site to change its content by adding, removing, or editing the content.

World Wide Web (WWW or the web) The part of the Internet used the most. What distinguishes the web from the rest of the Internet are (1) its use of common communication protocols (such as Transmission Control Protocol/Internet Protocol, or TCP/IP) and special languages (such as the HyperText Markup Language, or HTML) that enable different computers to talk to each other and display information in compatible formats and (2) its use of special links (called hyperlinks) that enable users to jump from one place to another in the web.

Securing Your System: Protecting Your Digital Data and Devices

Securing Your System: Protecting Your Digital Data and Devices

Major Threats to Your Digital Assets

Cybercrime and Identity Theft

OBJECTIVE

1. What is cybercrime, and who perpetrates it?

Protecting Yourself from Computer Viruses

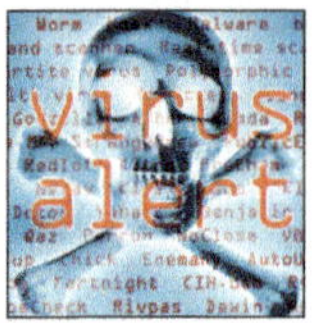

OBJECTIVES

2. What are the types of viruses from which I need to protect my computer?
3. What can I do to protect my computer from viruses?

Active Helpdesk: Avoiding Computer Viruses

Sound Byte: Protecting Your Computer

Protecting Digital Assets from Hackers

OBJECTIVES

4. How can hackers attack my computing devices, and what harm can they cause?
5. What is a firewall, and how does it keep my computer safe from hackers?
6. How do I create secure passwords and manage all of my passwords?
7. How can I surf the Internet anonymously and use biometric authentication devices to protect my data?

Active Helpdesk: Understanding Firewalls

Sound Byte: Installing a Personal Firewall

Protecting Your Digital Property from Yourself

Managing Online Annoyances

OBJECTIVE

8. How do I manage online annoyances such as spyware and spam?

Keeping Your Data Safe

OBJECTIVES

9. What data do I need to back up, and what are the best methods for doing so?
10. What is social engineering, and how do I avoid falling prey to phishing?

Sound Byte: Managing Computer Security with Windows Tools

Protecting Your Physical Computing Assets

OBJECTIVE

11. How do I protect my physical computing assets from environmental hazards, power surges, and theft?

Sound Byte: Surge Protectors

For all media in this chapter go to **pearsonhighered.com/techinaction** or **MyITLab**.

(iKandy/Shutterstock; Dimitri Vervits/ImageState/Alamy; Lauren Nicole/Getty Images; D. Hurst/Alamy; SVLuma/Shutterstock; Shutterstock)

HOW COOL IS THIS?

You have a lot of **information** in your **cell phone**. What happens if you **lose your phone**, damage it beyond repair, or want to **switch phones**? Transferring data can be very time-consuming, or even impossible, if you lose your phone. Apple's iOS devices do a good job of backing up your settings either in iTunes or iCloud. But what about backing up Android devices? Not all settings and apps are backed up on Google's sites. So, apps like **Helium (Premium)** provide a solution by allowing you to **back up settings**, contacts, notes, tasks, bookmarks, calendars, music, videos, and photos from your Android phone to popular **cloud sites** such as Dropbox, Box, or Google Drive. Then, if your phone is ever lost, stolen, or damaged, or if you are just upgrading to the latest model, you can easily **transfer** your information to a new or replacement phone. So install a backup app on your Android phone today and enjoy some peace of mind!

(bannosuke/Fotolia; Courtesy of Google, Inc.)

Scan here for more info

Major Threats to Your Digital Assets

The media is full of stories about malicious computer programs damaging computers, criminals stealing people's identities online, and attacks on corporate websites bringing major corporations to a standstill. These are examples of cybercrime. In this part of the chapter, we'll discuss the three most serious types of cybercrime you need to worry about: identity theft, computer viruses, and hackers.

cybercrime and IDENTITY THEFT

Cybercrime is any criminal action perpetrated primarily through the use of a computer. The existence of cybercrime means that computer users must take precautions to protect themselves. The FBI maintains a website (**fbi.gov/about-us/investigate/cyber/cyber**) specifically to inform the public about types of cybercrimes and methods of protecting yourself.

Who perpetrates computer crimes? Cybercriminals are individuals who use computers, networks, and the Internet to perpetrate crime. Anyone with a computer and the wherewithal to arm him- or herself with the appropriate knowledge can be a cybercriminal.

What kinds of cybercrimes are conducted over the Internet? The Internet Crime Complaint Center (IC3) is a partnership between the FBI and the National White Collar Crime Center (NW3C). In 2012 (the latest year for which data was available at this text's publication), the IC3 received almost 289,000 complaints related to Internet crime. Four common categories of complaints received are shown in Figure 1. FBI–related scams involve people pretending to represent official organizations, such as the FBI or Homeland Security, to defraud. Nonauction scams involve running auctions of merchandise that does not really exist, wherein the perpetrators just collect funds and disappear without delivering the promised goods. Advance fee fraud involves

FIGURE 1

Common Types of Cybercrimes Reported to the IC3 in 2012

(Peter Kim/Fotolia; RabidBadger/Fotolia; © viperagp/Fotolia; Donets/Fotolia)

convincing individuals to send money as a "good faith" gesture to enable them to receive larger payments in return. The scammers then disappear with the advance fees. Although these complaints relate to some type of fraud, other complaints received involve equally serious matters such as computer intrusions (hacking), child pornography, and blackmail.

What is the most financially damaging cybercrime plaguing individuals? Theft of personal data such as bank account numbers and credit/debit card numbers is of most concern to individuals because this information is usually used for fraudulent purposes. **Identity theft** occurs when a thief steals personal information such as your name, address, Social Security number, birth date, bank account number, and credit card information and runs up debts in your name. Many victims of identity theft spend months, or even years, trying to repair their credit and eliminate fraudulent debts.

What types of scams do identity thieves perpetrate? The nefarious acts cover a wide range:

- Counterfeiting your existing credit and debit cards
- Requesting changes of address on your bank and credit card statements, which makes detecting fraudulent charges take longer
- Opening new credit cards and bank accounts in your name and then writing bad checks and not paying off the credit card balances (ruining your credit rating in the process)
- Obtaining medical services under your name (you might lose coverage later if the thief's treatment exceeds the limits of your policy's covered services)
- Buying a home with a mortgage in your name, then reselling the house and absconding with the money (leaving you with the debt)

Many people believe that the only way your identity can be stolen is by a computer. However, the Federal Trade Commission (**ftc.gov**) has identified other methods thieves use to obtain others' personal information:

- Stealing purses and wallets, in which people often keep personal information such as their ATM PIN codes
- Stealing mail or looking through trash for bank statements and credit card bills
- Posing as bank or credit card company representatives and tricking people into revealing sensitive information over the phone
- Installing skimming devices on ATM machines that record information, such as account numbers and passcodes

Although foolproof protection methods don't exist, there are precautions that will help you minimize your risk, which we'll discuss later in this chapter.

With all the news coverage about identity theft and other cybercrimes, aren't people being more cautious? Although most people are aware of spam, a survey by the Messaging Anti-Abuse Working Group (MAAWG) found that half of e-mail users in North America and Europe have opened spam, some of which are designed to trick you into divulging sensitive information. The MAAWG also discovered that 46% of people who opened spam did so intentionally—out of idle curiosity, to follow links to unsubscribe to unwanted e-mails (which only brings more spam), or because they are interested in the product being touted.

Does cybercrime include the theft of computing devices? Although theft of computer equipment is not classified as a cybercrime (it is considered larceny), the theft of tablets, smartphones, notebook computers, and other portable computing devices is on the rise. The resale value for used electronic equipment is high, and the equipment can be easily sold online. ■

computer VIRUSES

A computer **virus** is a computer program that attaches itself to another computer program (known as the *host* program) and attempts to spread to other computers when files are exchanged. Creating and disseminating computer viruses is one of the most widespread types of cybercrimes. Some viruses cause only minor annoyances, whereas others cause destruction or theft of data. Many viruses are designed to gather sensitive information such as credit card numbers.

Why are viruses such a threat to my security? Computer viruses are threatening because they are engineered to evade detection. Viruses normally attempt to hide within the code of a host program to avoid detection. And viruses are not just limited to computers. Smartphones, tablet computers, and other devices can be infected with viruses. Viruses such as SpyEye Mobile Banking are used to trick users into downloading an infected file to their phones, which then steals their online banking information.

I have an Apple computer, so I don't need to worry about viruses, do I? This is a popular misconception! Everyone, even Apple users, needs to worry about viruses. As the OS X and iOS operating systems have gained market share, the amount of virus attacks against Apple operating systems is on the rise.

What do computer viruses do? A computer virus's main purpose is to replicate itself and copy its code into as many other host files as possible. This gives the virus a greater chance of being copied to another computer system so that it can spread its infection. However, computer viruses require human interaction to spread. Although there might be a virus in a file on your computer, a virus normally can't infect your computer until the infected file is opened or executed.

Although virus replication can slow down networks, it's not usually the main threat. The majority of viruses have secondary objectives or side effects, ranging from displaying annoying messages on the computer screen to destroying files or the contents of entire hard drives.

Catching a Virus

How does my computer catch a virus? If your computer is exposed to a file infected with a virus, the virus will try to copy itself and infect a file on your computer.

Downloading infected audio and video files from peer-to-peer file-sharing sites is a major source of virus infections. Shared flash drives are also a common source of virus infection, as is e-mail. Just opening an e-mail message usually won't infect your computer with a virus, although some new viruses are launched when viewed in the preview pane of your e-mail software. Downloading and running (executing) a file that's attached to the e-mail are common ways that your computer becomes infected. Thus, be extremely wary of e-mail attachments, especially if you don't know the sender. Figure 2 illustrates the steps by which computer viruses are often passed from one computer to the next:

1. An individual writes a virus program, attaches it to a music file, and posts the file to a file-sharing site.
2. Unsuspecting Bill downloads the "music file" and infects his computer when he listens to the song.
3. Bill sends his cousin Fred an e-mail with the infected "music file" and contaminates Fred's tablet.
4. Fred syncs his phone with his tablet and infects his phone when he plays the music file.
5. Fred e-mails the file from his phone to Susan, one of his colleagues at work. Everyone who copies files from Susan's infected work computer, or whose computer is networked to Susan's computer, risks spreading the virus.

What types of viruses exist? Although thousands of computer viruses and variants exist, they can be grouped into six broad categories based on their behavior and method of transmission.

Boot-Sector Viruses

What are boot-sector viruses? A **boot-sector virus** replicates itself onto a hard drive's master boot record. The **master boot record** is a program that executes whenever a computer boots up, ensuring that the virus will be loaded into memory immediately, even before some virus protection programs can load. Boot-sector viruses are often transmitted by a flash drive left in a USB port. When the computer boots up with the flash drive connected, the computer tries to launch a master boot record from the flash drive, which is usually the trigger for the virus to infect the hard drive.

Logic Bombs and Time Bombs

What are logic bombs and time bombs? A **logic bomb** is a virus that is triggered when certain logical conditions are met, such as opening a file or starting a program a certain number of times. A **time bomb** is a virus that is triggered by the passage of time or on a certain date. For example, the Michelangelo virus was a famous time bomb that was set to trigger every year on March 6, Michelangelo's birthday. The effects of logic bombs and time bombs range from the display of annoying messages on the screen to the reformatting of the hard drive, which causes complete data loss.

Worms

What is a worm? Although often called a virus, a **worm** is subtly different. Viruses require human interaction to spread, whereas worms take advantage of file transport methods, such

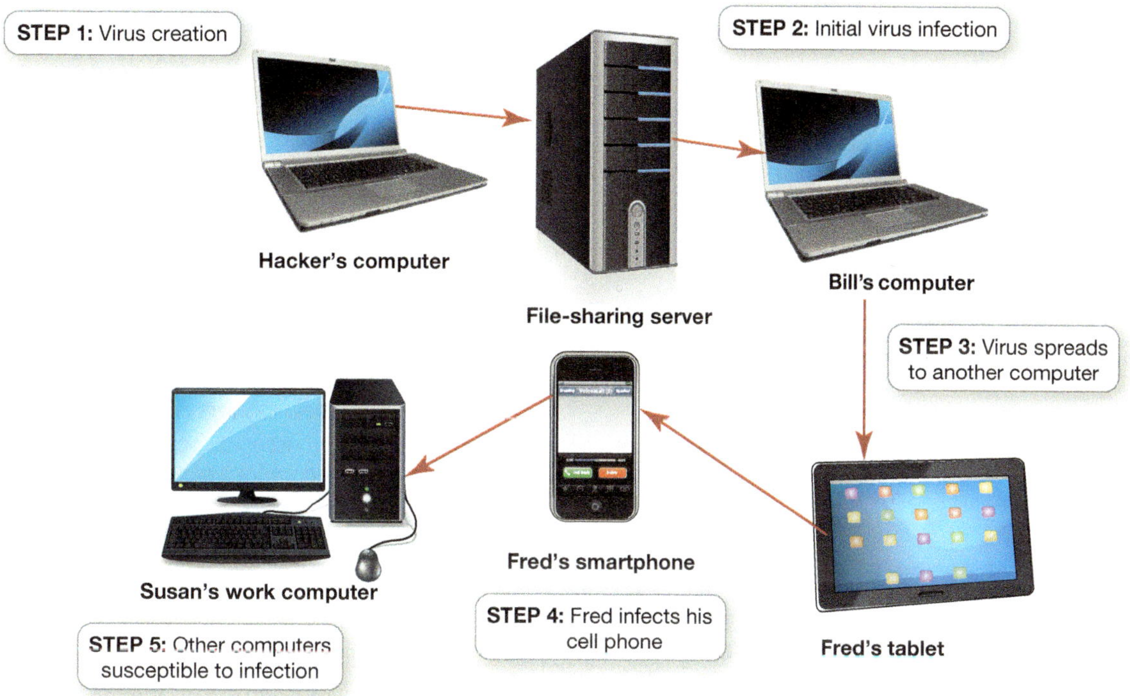

FIGURE 2 Computer viruses are passed from one unsuspecting user to the next.

as e-mail or network connections, to spread on their own. A virus infects a host file and waits until that file is executed to replicate and infect a computer system. A worm, however, works independently of host file execution and is much more active in spreading itself. When the Palevo worm broke out in 2013, it was reported to be infecting 500 computers per hour. It spread through Yahoo! Messenger and used contacts in Yahoo! Messenger accounts to spread itself to other victims.

Script and Macro Viruses

What are script and macro viruses? Some viruses are hidden on websites in the form of scripts. A **script** is a series of commands—actually, a miniprogram—that is executed without your knowledge. Scripts are often used to perform useful, legitimate functions on websites, such as collecting name and address information from customers. However, some scripts are malicious. For example, you might click a link to display a video on a website, which causes a script to run that infects your computer with a virus.

A **macro virus** is a virus that attaches itself to a document that uses macros. A *macro* is a short series of commands that usually automates repetitive tasks. However, macro languages are now so sophisticated that viruses can be written with them. In 1999, the Melissa virus became the first major macro virus to cause problems worldwide.

E-Mail Viruses

What is an e-mail virus? In addition to being a macro virus, the Melissa virus was the first practical example of an e-mail virus. **E-mail viruses** use the address book in the victim's e-mail system to distribute the virus. In the case of the Melissa virus, anyone opening an infected document triggered the virus, which infected other documents on the victim's computer. Once triggered, the Melissa virus sent itself to the first 50 people in the e-mail address book on the infected computer.

Encryption Viruses

What are encryption viruses? When **encryption viruses** infect your computer, they run a program that searches for common types of data files, such as Microsoft Word and Excel files, and compresses them using a complex encryption key that renders your files unusable. You then receive a message that asks you to send money to an account if you want to receive the program to decrypt your files. The flaw with this type of virus, which keeps it from being widespread, is that law enforcement officials can trace the payments to an account and may possibly be able to catch the perpetrators. Figure 3 summarizes the major categories of viruses.

Additional Virus Classifications

How else are viruses classified? Viruses can also be classified by the methods they take to avoid detection by antivirus software:

- A **polymorphic virus** changes its own code or periodically rewrites itself to avoid detection. Most polymorphic viruses infect a particular type of file such as .EXE files, for example.
- A **multipartite virus** is designed to infect multiple file types in an effort to fool the antivirus software that is looking for it.

FIGURE 3

Major Categories of Viruses

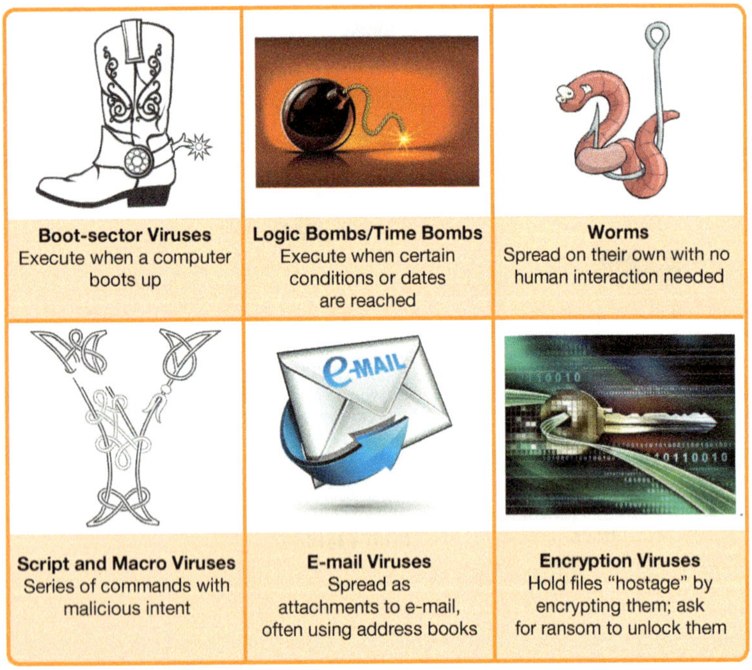

(tribalium81/Fotolia; LoopAll/Fotolia; dedMazay/Fotolia; Theo Malings/Fotolia; Beboy/Fotolia; Andrea Danti/Fotolia)

- **Stealth viruses** temporarily erase their code from the files where they reside and then hide in the active memory of the computer. This helps them avoid detection if only the hard drive is being searched for viruses. Fortunately, current antivirus software scans memory as well as the hard drive.

Virus Symptoms

How can I tell if my computer is infected with a virus? Sometimes it can be difficult to definitively tell whether your computer is infected with a virus. However, if your computer displays any of the following symptoms, it may be infected with a virus:

1. Existing program icons or files suddenly disappear. Viruses often delete specific file types or programs.
2. You start your browser and it takes you to an unusual home page (i.e., one you didn't set) or it has new toolbars.
3. Odd messages, pop-ups, or images are displayed on the screen, or strange music or sounds play.
4. Data files become corrupt. (However, note that files can become corrupt for reasons other than a virus infection.)
5. Programs stop working properly, which could be caused by either a corrupted file or a virus.
6. Your system slows down or takes a long time to boot up. ■

ACTIVE HELPDESK

Avoiding Computer Viruses

In this Active Helpdesk call, you'll play the role of a helpdesk staffer, fielding calls about different types of viruses and what users should do to protect their computer from them.

BITS&BYTES

CAPTCHA: Keeping Websites Safe from Bots

Automated programs called *bots* (or web robots) are used to make tasks easier on the Internet. For example, search engines use bots to search and index web pages. Unfortunately, bots can also be used for malicious or illegal purposes because they can perform some computing tasks faster than humans. For example, bots can be used on ticket-ordering sites to buy large blocks of high-demand concert tickets. They are also often used to post spam in the comment sections of blogs. Fortunately, website owners can deploy CAPTCHA software (see Figure 4) to prevent such bot activities.

CAPTCHA (Completely Automated Public Turing Test to Tell Computers and Humans Apart) programs generate distorted text and require that it be typed into a box. Because bots can't yet be programmed to read distorted text, which most people can, the CAPTCHA program can verify that a human is performing the task being tested. If you want to try integrating a CAPTCHA program into your website (to protect your e-mail address), go to **google.com/recaptcha**, which offers free CAPTCHA tools to help you protect your data.

FIGURE 4 CAPTCHA programs like this one verify that a human, not a bot, is performing the requested task. *(Courtesy of the Carnegie Mellon University Press)*

preventing virus INFECTIONS

Antivirus software is specifically designed to detect viruses and protect your computer and files from harm. Symantec, Kaspersky, AVG, and McAfee are among the companies that offer highly rated antivirus software packages. Antivirus protection is also included in comprehensive Internet security packages such as Norton Internet Security, Kaspersky Internet Security, and McAfee Total Protection. These software packages also help protect you from threats other than computer viruses. For example, Windows 8 includes Windows Defender, which defends against malware as well as viruses.

Antivirus Software

How often do I need to run antivirus software? Although antivirus software is designed to detect suspicious activity on your computer at all times, you should run an active virus scan on your entire system at least once a week. By doing so, all files on your computer will be checked for undetected viruses.

Current antivirus programs run scans in the background when your CPU is not being heavily utilized. But you can also configure the software to run scans at times when you aren't using your system—for example, when you're asleep (see Figure 5). (However, it's important to note that your computer has to be on and not in sleep mode for these virus scans to take place.) Alternatively, if you suspect a problem, you can launch a scan and have it run immediately.

How does antivirus software work? The main functions of antivirus software are as follows:

- *Detection:* Antivirus software looks for virus signatures in files. A **virus signature** is a portion of the virus code that's unique to a particular computer virus. Antivirus software scans files for these signatures when they're opened or executed and identifies infected files and the type of virus infecting them.
- *Stopping virus execution:* If the antivirus software detects a virus signature or suspicious activity, such as the

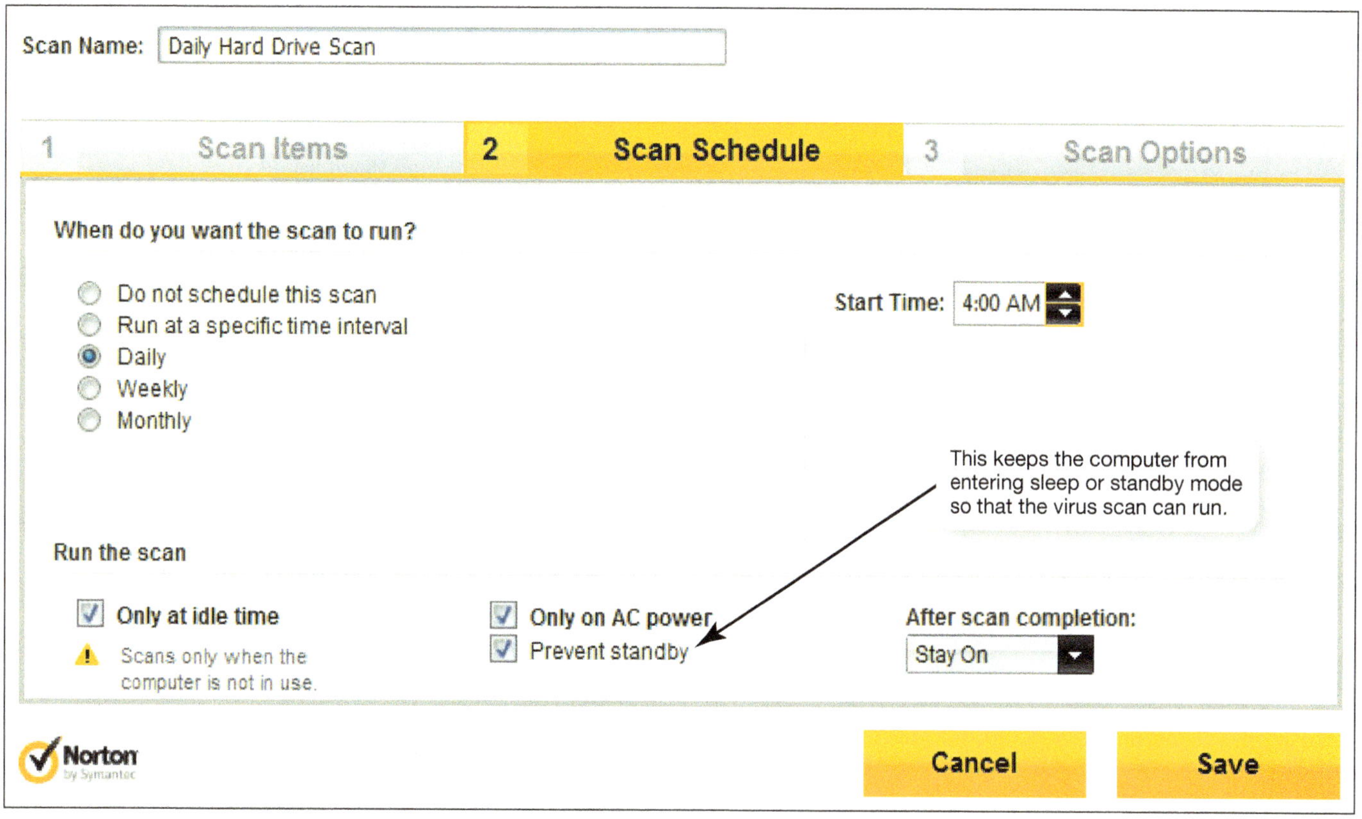

FIGURE 5 In Norton Internet Security, you can set up virus scans to run automatically. This computer will be scanned every day at 4 a.m. *(Reprinted with permission of Symantec Corporation)*

launch of an unknown macro, it stops the execution of the file and virus and notifies you that it has detected a virus. It also places the virus in a secure area on your hard drive so that it won't spread to other files; this procedure is known as **quarantining**. Usually, the antivirus software then gives you the choice of deleting or repairing the infected file. Unfortunately, antivirus programs can't always fix infected files to make them usable again. You should keep backup copies of critical files so that you can restore them in case a virus damages them irreparably.

- *Prevention of future infection:* Most antivirus software will also attempt to prevent infection by inoculating key files on your computer. In **inoculation**, the antivirus software records key attributes about your computer files, such as file size and date created, and keeps these statistics in a safe place on your hard drive. When scanning for viruses, the antivirus software compares the attributes of the files with the attributes it previously recorded to help detect attempts by virus programs to modify your files.

Does antivirus software always stop viruses? Antivirus software catches *known* viruses effectively. However, new viruses are written all the time. To combat unknown viruses, modern antivirus programs search for suspicious virus-like activities as well as virus signatures. To minimize your risk, you should keep your antivirus software up to date.

My new computer came with antivirus software installed, so shouldn't I already be protected? Most new computers do come with antivirus software preinstalled. However, these are usually trial versions of the software that only provide updates to the software for a limited period of time, usually 90 or 180 days. After that, you have to buy a full version of the software to ensure you remain protected from new viruses.

How do I make sure my antivirus software is up to date? Most antivirus programs have an automatic update feature that downloads updates for virus signature files every time you go online (see Figure 6). Also, the antivirus software usually shows the status of your update subscription so that you can see how much time you have remaining until you need to buy another version of your software.

What should I do if I think my computer is infected with a virus? Boot up your computer using the antivirus installation disc. This should prevent most virus programs from loading and will allow you to run the antivirus software directly from your disk drive. (*Note:* If you download your antivirus software from the Internet, copy it to a DVD in case you have problems in the future.) If the software does detect viruses, you may want to research them further to determine whether your antivirus software will eradicate them completely or whether you'll need to take additional manual steps to eliminate the viruses. Most antivirus company websites, such as the Symantec site (**symantec.com**), contain archives of information on viruses and provide step-by-step solutions for removing them.

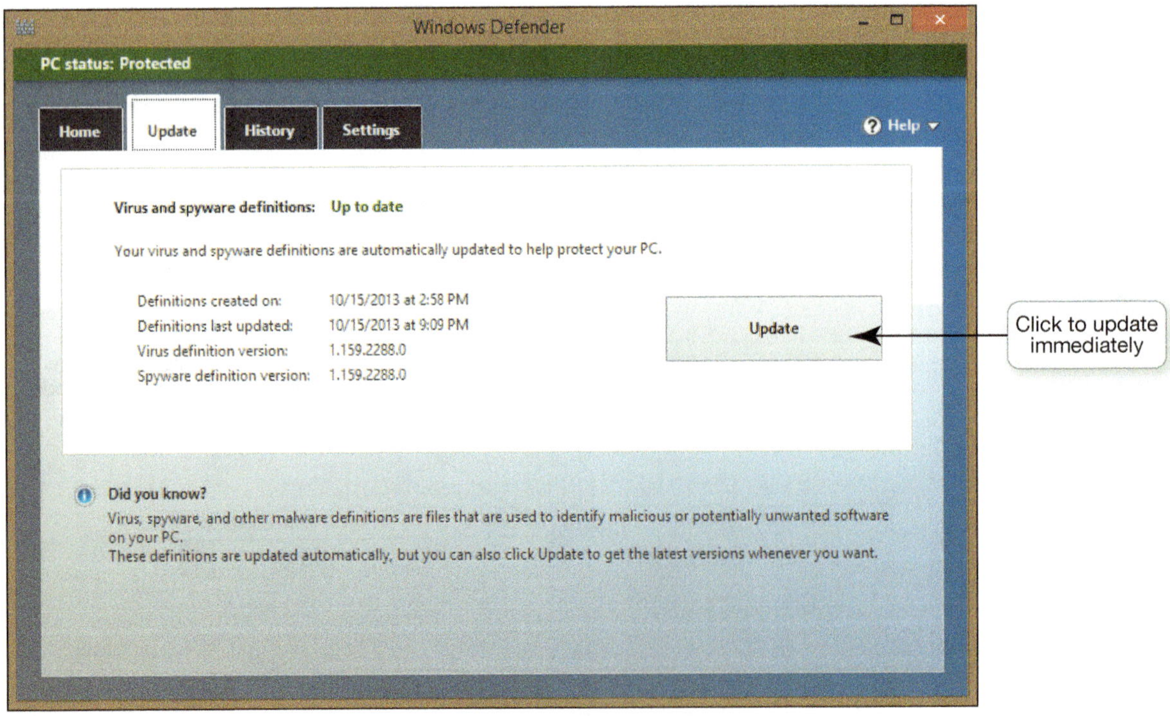

FIGURE 6 Antivirus software, such as Windows Defender, provides for automatic updates but also allows manual updates.

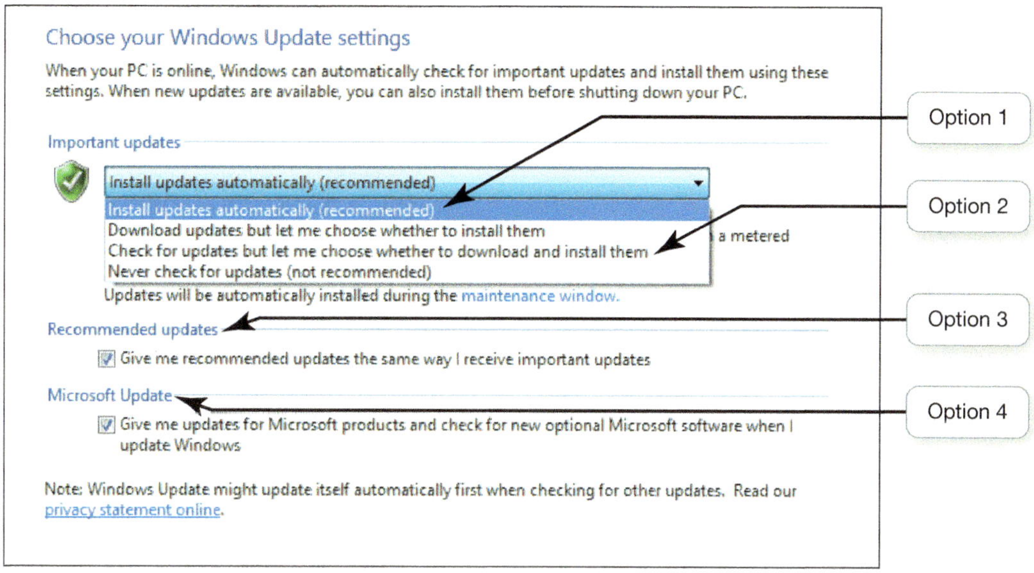

FIGURE 7 The Windows Update screen makes it easy for users to configure Windows to update itself.

>To enable automatic updates, access the Control Panel, select **System and Security**, *click the* **Windows Update** *link, and then click the* **Change Settings** *link.*

How do I protect my phone from viruses? Because smartphones and other mobile devices run operating systems and contain files, they are susceptible to infection by viruses. Cybercriminals are now hiding viruses in legitimate-looking apps for download to mobile devices. Most antivirus software companies now offer antivirus software specifically designed for mobile devices, such as Lookout Mobile Security, which Samsung is now installing on its Android phones.

Software Updates

Why does updating my operating system (OS) software help protect me from viruses? Many viruses exploit weaknesses in operating systems. Malicious websites can be set up to attack your computer by downloading harmful software onto your computer. According to research conducted by Google, this type of attack, known as a **drive-by download**, affects almost 1 in 1,000 web pages. To combat these threats, make sure your OS is up to date and contains the latest security patches. You can update your Windows OS with an automatic update utility called Windows Update. When you enable automatic updates, your computer searches for updates on the Microsoft website every time it connects to the Internet. Mac OS X has a similar utility for gathering updates.

> SOUND BYTE
> **Protecting Your Computer**
> In this Sound Byte, you'll learn how to use a variety of tools to protect your computer, including antivirus software and Windows utilities.

Do OS updates only happen automatically? The default option in Windows is to receive updates automatically. There are several other options you can choose from in Windows, as shown in Figure 7. The following options are noteworthy:

- *Option 1: Install updates automatically.* Selecting this option will automatically download and install updates at a time you have specified. *We strongly recommend that you select this option.*
- *Option 2: Check for updates but let me choose whether to download and install them.* This is an appropriate choice only if you have low bandwidth Internet access. Because downloads over dial-up can take a long time, you need to control when they will occur. But you need to be extra vigilant with this option because you may forget to install important updates.
- *Option 3: Give me recommended updates*. This option ensures you receive recommended (optional) updates as well as critical (necessary) updates.
- *Option 4: Microsoft Update.* This option ensures you receive updates for other Microsoft products besides Windows, such as Microsoft Office.

If you keep both your antivirus and OS software up to date, you'll help prevent viruses from infecting your computer. ■

understanding HACKERS

Although there's a great deal of disagreement as to what a hacker actually is, especially among hackers themselves, a **hacker** is most commonly defined as anyone who unlawfully breaks into a computer system—either an individual computer or a network (see Figure 8).

Are there different kinds of hackers? Some hackers are offended by being labeled as criminals and therefore attempt to classify different types of hackers as follows:

- **White-hat hackers** (or **ethical hackers**) break in to systems for nonmalicious reasons, such as to test system security vulnerabilities or to expose undisclosed weaknesses. They believe in making security vulnerabilities known either to the company that owns the system or software or to the general public, often to embarrass a company into fixing a problem.
- **Black-hat hackers** break into systems to destroy information or for illegal gain. The terms *white hat* and *black hat* are references to old Western movies in which the heroes wore white hats and the outlaws wore black hats.
- **Grey-hat hackers** are a bit of a cross between black and white—they often illegally break into systems merely to flaunt their expertise to the administrator of the system they penetrated or to attempt to sell their services in repairing security breaches.

Regardless of the hackers' opinions, the laws in the United States and in many other countries consider *any* unauthorized access to computer systems a crime.

"Oh, we used to use a crystal ball, but hacking into your credit files is much more informative!"

FIGURE 8 Hackers can find lots of personal information about you on the Internet. *(Wildt, Chris/Cartoonstock)*

Problems Hackers Can Cause

Could a hacker steal my debit card or bank account number? Hackers often try to break in to computers or websites that contain credit card information. If you perform financial transactions online, such as banking or buying goods and services, you probably do so using a credit or debit card. Credit card and bank account information can thus reside on your hard drive or an online business's hard drive and may be detectable by a hacker.

Aside from your home computer, you have personal data stored on various websites. For example, many sites require that you provide a login ID and password to gain access. Even if this data isn't stored on your computer, a hacker may be able to capture it when you're online by using a *packet analyzer (sniffer)* or a *keylogger* (a program that captures all keystrokes made on a computer).

What's a packet analyzer? Data travels through the Internet in small pieces called *packets*. The packets are identified with an IP address, in part to help identify the computer to which they are being sent. Once the packets reach their destination, they're reassembled into cohesive messages. A **packet analyzer (sniffer)** is a program deployed by hackers that looks at (or sniffs) each packet as it travels on the Internet—not just those addressed to a particular computer, but all packets coming across a particular network. For example, a hacker might sit in a coffee shop and run a packet sniffer to capture sensitive data (such as debit/credit card numbers) from patrons using the coffee shop's free wireless network. Wireless networks such as these can be particularly vulnerable to this type of exploitation if encryption of data isn't enabled when the networks are set up.

What do hackers do with the information they "sniff"? Once a hacker has your debit/credit card information, he or she can use it to purchase items illegally or can sell the number to someone who will. If a hacker steals the login ID and password to an account where you have your bank card information stored (such as eBay or Amazon), he or she can also use your account to buy items and have them shipped to him- or herself instead of to you. If hackers can gather enough information in conjunction with your credit card information, they may be able to commit identity theft.

Although this sounds scary, you can easily protect yourself from packet sniffing by installing a firewall (which we discuss later in this chapter) and using data encryption on a wireless network.

Trojan Horses and Rootkits

Besides stealing information, what other problems can hackers cause if they break into my computer? Hackers often use individuals' computers as a staging area for mischief. To commit widespread computer attacks, for example, hackers need to control many computers at the same time. To this end, hackers often use Trojan horses to install other programs on computers. A **Trojan horse** is a program that appears to be something useful or desirable, like a game or a screen saver, but while it runs, it does something malicious in the background, without your knowledge (see Figure 9).

What damage can Trojan horses do? Often, the malicious activity perpetrated by a Trojan horse program is the installation of a backdoor program or a rootkit. **Backdoor programs** and **rootkits** are programs (or sets of programs) that allow hackers to gain access to your computer and take almost complete control of it without your knowledge. Using a backdoor program, hackers can access and delete all the files on your computer, send e-mail, run programs, and do just about anything else you can do with your computer. A computer that a hacker controls in this manner is referred to as a **zombie**. Zombies are often used to launch *denial-of-service attacks* on other computers.

Denial-of-Service Attacks

What are denial-of-service attacks? In a **denial-of-service (DoS) attack**, legitimate users are denied access to a computer system because a hacker is repeatedly making requests of that computer system through a computer he or she has taken over as a zombie. A computer system can handle only a certain number of requests for information at one time. When it is flooded with requests in a DoS attack, it shuts down and refuses to answer any requests for information, even if the requests are from a legitimate user. Thus, the computer is so busy responding to the bogus requests for information that authorized users can't gain access.

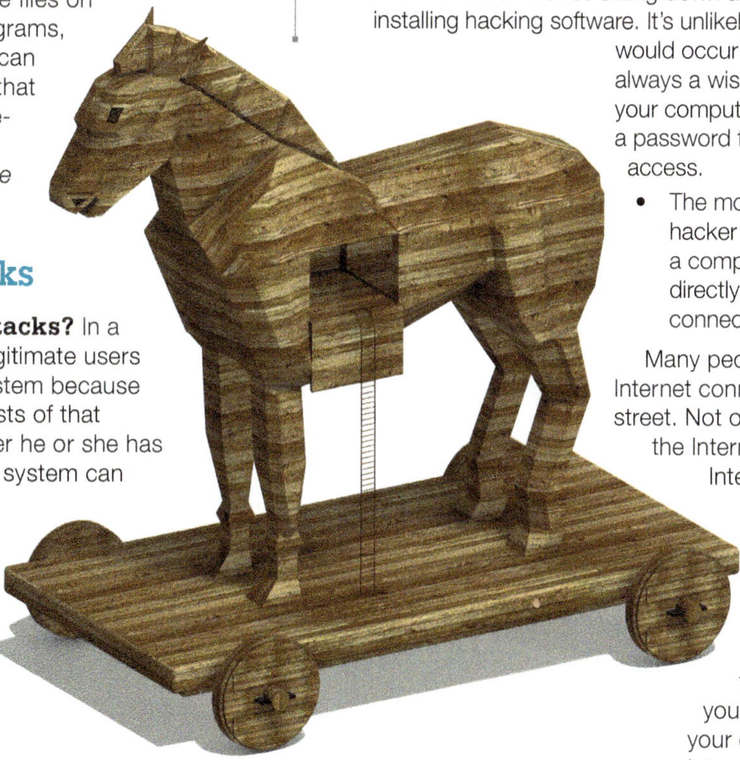

FIGURE 9 The term *Trojan horse* derives from Greek mythology and refers to the wooden horse that the Greeks used to sneak into the city of Troy and conquer it. Therefore, computer programs that contain a hidden, and usually dreadful, "surprise" are referred to as Trojan horses. *(Ralf Kraft/Fotolia)*

Couldn't a DoS attack be traced back to the computer that launched it? Launching a DoS attack on a computer system from a single computer is easy to trace. Therefore, most savvy hackers use a **distributed denial-of-service (DDoS) attack**, which launches DoS attacks from more than one zombie (sometimes thousands of zombies) at the same time.

Figure 10 illustrates how a DDoS attack works. A hacker creates many zombies and coordinates them so that they begin sending bogus requests to the same computer at the same time. Administrators of the victim computer often have a great deal of difficulty stopping the attack because it comes from so many computers. Often, the attacks are coordinated automatically by botnets. A **botnet** is a large group of software programs (called *robots* or *bots*) that runs autonomously on zombie computers. Some botnets have been known to span 1.5 million computers.

Because many commercial websites receive revenue from users, either directly (such as via subscriptions to online games) or indirectly (such as when web surfers click on advertisements), DDoS attacks can be financially distressing for the owners of the affected websites.

How Hackers Gain Computer Access

How exactly does a hacker gain access to a computer? Hackers can gain access to computers directly or indirectly:

- Direct access involves sitting down at a computer and installing hacking software. It's unlikely that such an attack would occur in your home, but it's always a wise precaution to set up your computer so that it requires a password for a user to gain access.
- The most likely method a hacker will use to access a computer is to enter indirectly through its Internet connection.

Many people forget that their Internet connection is a two-way street. Not only can you access the Internet, but people on the Internet can access your computer. Think of your computer as a house. Common sense tells you to lock your home's doors and windows to deter theft when you aren't there. Hooking your computer up to the Internet without protection is like leaving the front door to your house wide open. Your computer obviously doesn't have doors and windows like a house, but it does have logical ports.

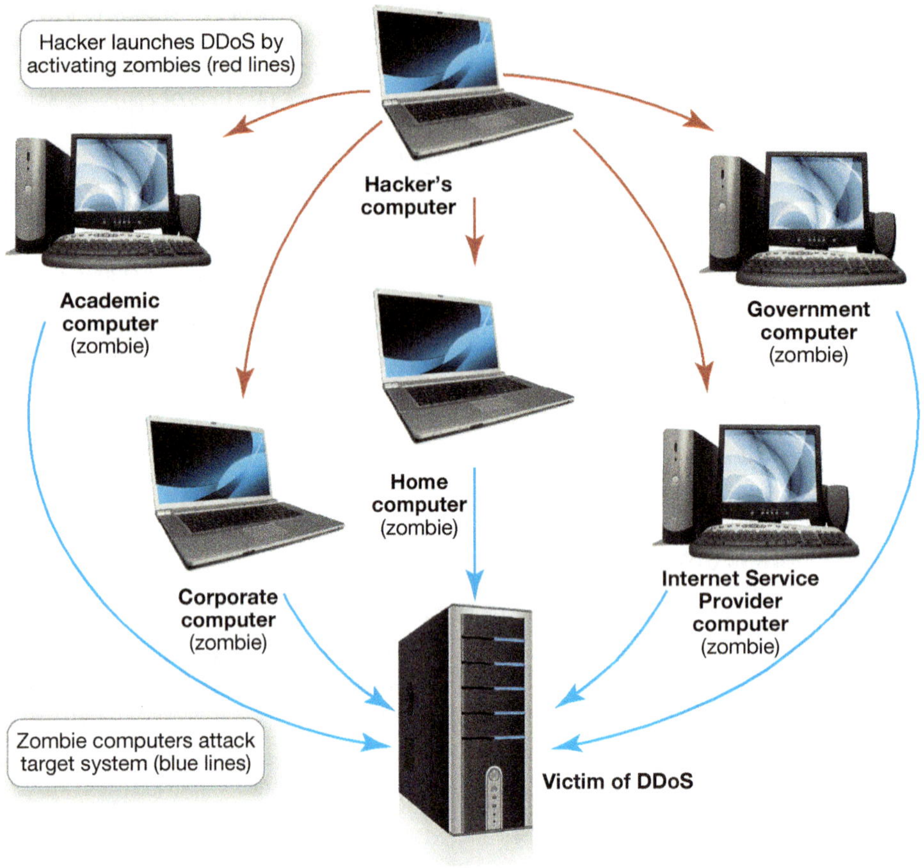

FIGURE 10 Zombie computers are used to facilitate a DDoS attack.

BITS&BYTES

Are Your Photos Helping Criminals Target You?

All cell phones today contain GPS chips. The cameras in phones often use information gathered from the GPS chips to encode information onto photos in the form of geotags. A **geotag** is a piece of data attached to a photo that indicates your latitude and longitude when you took the photo. Geotagging is useful for applications that can take advantage of this information, but problems arise when you share geotagged photos on the web.

If you post a lot of photos, cybercriminals and cyberstalkers can use the information from the geotags on your photos to figure out the patterns of your movements. They may be able to ascertain when you're at work or that you're currently on vacation, which leads them to determine prime times for burglarizing your home. Some sites such as Facebook and Twitter have measures in place to limit the amount of geotagged information that can be seen in photos in order to prevent their users from unwittingly revealing personal information. However, many photo-sharing sites don't have such protections in place.

The safest thing to do is not tag your photos with geotags in the first place. It's usually easy to disable location tracking on your smartphone. For instance, on the iPhone, on the Settings screen, select General, then Location Services, and choose Off. So stop geotagging your photos, and make it tougher for the cybercriminals to figure out your movements. For photos that already have geotags, you can remove them using software such as BatchPurifier or Geotag Remover.

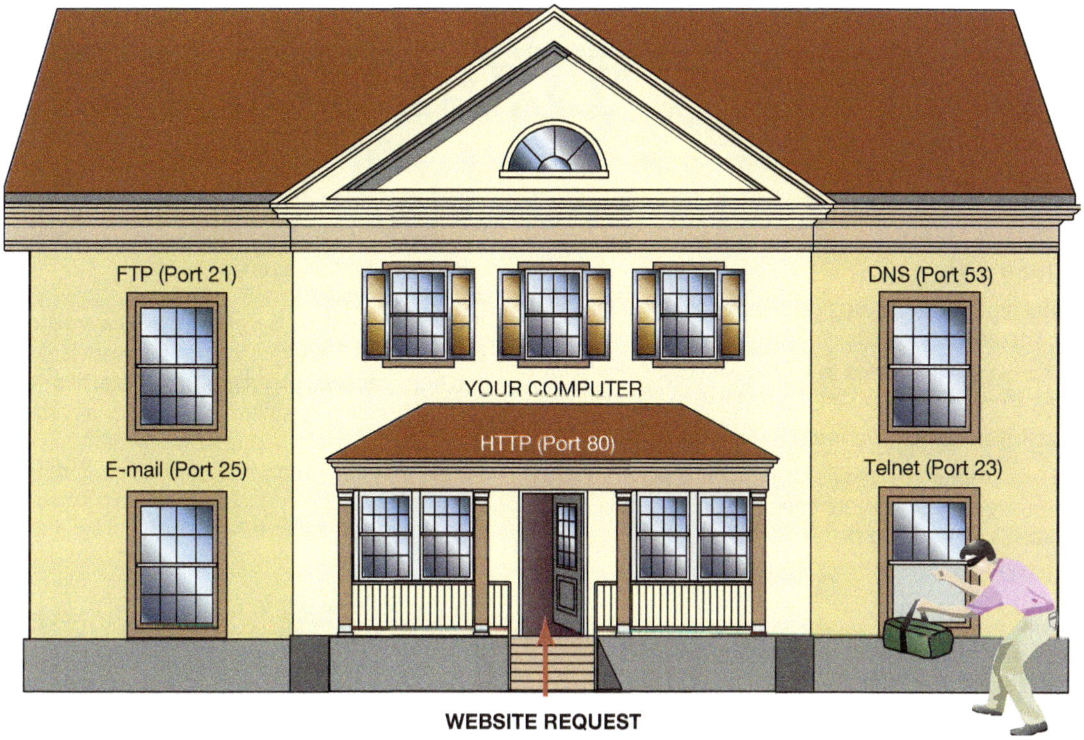

FIGURE 11 Open logical ports are an invitation to hackers.

What are logical ports? Logical ports are virtual—that is, not physical—communications gateways or paths that allow a computer to organize requests for information, such as web page downloads or e-mail routing, from other networks or computers. Unlike physical ports, such as USB ports, you can't see or touch a logical port; it's part of a computer's internal organization.

Logical ports are numbered and assigned to specific services. For instance, logical port 80 is designated for hypertext transfer protocol (HTTP), the main communications protocol for the web. Thus, all requests for information from your browser to the web flow through logical port 80. Open logical ports, like open windows in a home, invite intruders, as illustrated in Figure 11. Unless you take precautions to restrict access to your logical ports, other people on the Internet may be able to access your computer through them.

Fortunately, you can thwart most hacking problems by installing a firewall, which we discuss next.

restricting access to your DIGITAL ASSETS

Keeping hackers at bay is often just a matter of keeping them out. You can achieve this by:

- Preventing hackers from accessing your computer (usually through your Internet connection)
- Protecting your digital information in such a way that it can't be accessed (by using passwords, for example)
- Hiding your activities from prying eyes

In this section, we explore strategies for protecting access to your digital assets and keeping your Internet-surfing activities from being seen by the wrong people.

Firewalls

What is a firewall? A **firewall** is a software program or hardware device designed to protect computers from hackers. It's named after a housing construction feature that slows the spread of fires from house to house. A firewall specifically designed for home networks is called a **personal firewall**. By using a personal firewall, you can close open logical ports to invaders and potentially make your computer invisible to other computers on the Internet.

Which is better, a software firewall or a hardware firewall? Both hardware and software firewalls will protect you from hackers. One type isn't better than the other. Although installing either a software or a hardware firewall on your home network is probably sufficient, you should consider installing both for maximum protection. This will provide you with additional safety, just as wearing multiple layers of clothing helps keep you warmer in the winter than a single layer.

Types of Firewalls

What software firewalls are there? Both Windows and OS X include reliable firewalls. The Windows Action Center is a good source of information about the security settings on your computer (see Figure 12), including the status of your firewall. Security suites such as Norton Internet Security, McAfee Internet Security, and ZoneAlarm Internet Security Suite also

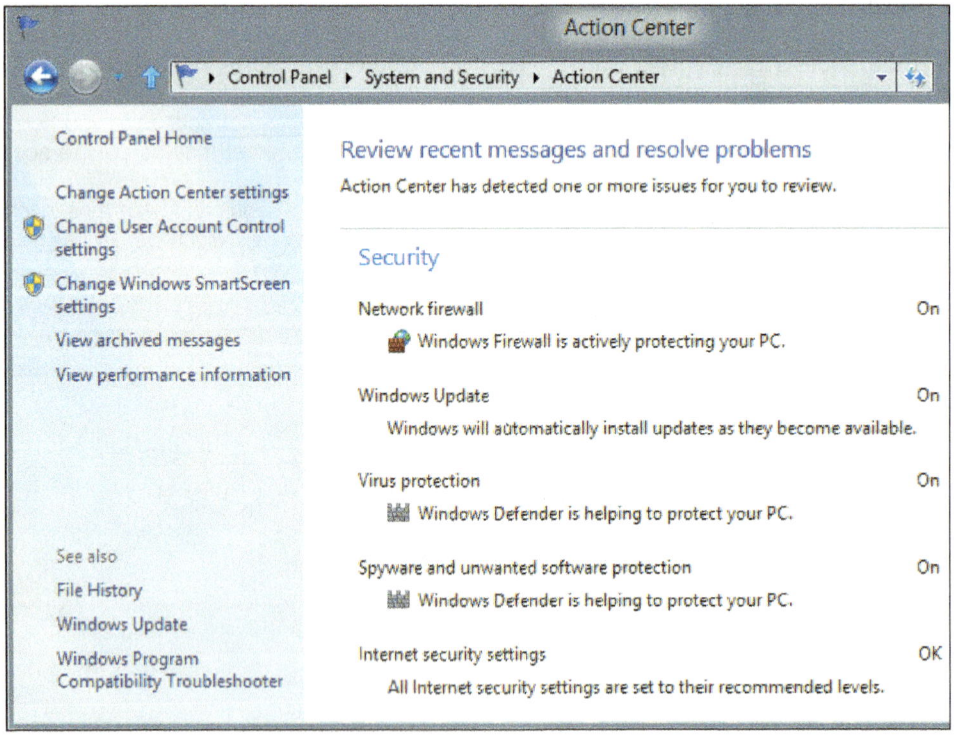

FIGURE 12 The security section of the Windows Action Center provides the status of programs protecting your computer.

>*To view the Action Center, access the Control Panel, select* **System and Security**, *and then click the* **Action Center** *link.*

include firewall software. Although the firewalls that come with Windows and OS X will protect your computer, firewalls included in security suites often come with additional features such as monitoring systems that alert you if your computer is under attack.

If you're using a security suite that includes a firewall, the suite should disable the firewall that came with your OS. Two firewalls running at the same time can conflict with each other and cause your computer to slow down or freeze up.

What are hardware firewalls? You can also buy and configure hardware firewall devices. Many routers sold for home networks include firewall protection. Just like software firewalls, the setup for hardware firewalls is designed for novices, and the default configuration on most routers keeps unused logical ports closed. Documentation accompanying routers can assist more-experienced users in adjusting the settings to allow access to specific ports if needed.

How Firewalls Work

How do firewalls protect you from hackers? Firewalls are designed to restrict access to a network and its computers. Firewalls protect you in two major ways:

1. By blocking access to logical ports and
2. By keeping your computer's network address secure

How do firewalls block access to your logical ports? Certain logical ports are very popular in hacker attacks. To block access to logical ports, firewalls examine data packets that your computer sends and receives. Data packets contain information such as the address of the sending and receiving computers and the logical port that the packet will use. Firewalls can be configured so that they filter out packets sent to specific logical ports in a process known as **packet filtering**. Firewalls are also often configured to ignore requests that originate from the Internet asking for access to certain ports. This process is referred to as **logical port blocking**. By using filtering and blocking, firewalls keep hackers from accessing your computer (Figure 13).

How do firewalls keep your network address secure? Every computer connected to the Internet has a unique address called an *Internet Protocol address (IP address)*. Data is routed to the correct computer on the Internet based on the IP address. This is similar to how a letter finds its way to your mailbox. You have a unique postal address for your home. If a hacker finds out the IP address of your computer, he or she can locate it on the Internet and try to break into it. This is similar to how a conventional thief might target your home after finding out you collect antique cars by using your street address to locate your house.

Your IP address for your home network is assigned to your router by your Internet service provider (ISP), but each device on your home network also has an IP address. Firewalls use a process called **network address translation (NAT)** to assign internal IP addresses on a network. The internal IP addresses are used only on the internal network and therefore can't be detected by hackers. For hackers to access your computer, they must know your computer's internal IP address. With a NAT–capable router/firewall installed on your network, hackers are unable to access the internal IP address assigned to your computer, so your computer is safe. You can use NAT in your home by purchasing a hardware firewall with NAT capabilities. Many routers sold for home use are also configured as firewalls, and many feature NAT.

ACTIVE HELPDESK
Understanding Firewalls

In this Active Helpdesk call, you'll play the role of a helpdesk staffer, fielding calls about how hackers can attack networks and what harm they can cause as well as what a firewall does to keep a computer safe from hackers.

Knowing Your Computer Is Secure

How can I tell if my computer is at risk? For peace of mind, you can visit websites that offer free services that test your computer's vulnerability. One popular site is Gibson Research Corporation (**grc.com**). The company's ShieldsUP and LeakTest programs are free and easy to run and can pinpoint security vulnerabilities in a system connected to the Internet. If you get a clean report from these programs, your

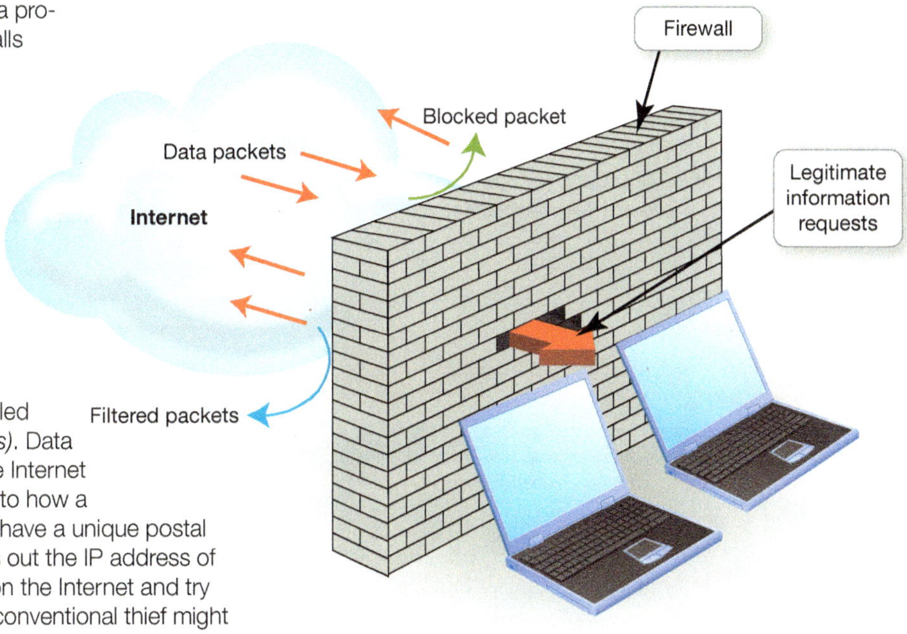

FIGURE 13 Firewalls use filtering and blocking to keep out unwanted data and keep your network safe. *(Intelligent Computer Solutions)*

> **SOUND BYTE**
> **Installing a Personal Firewall**
> Firewalls provide excellent protection against hackers on a home network. In this Sound Byte, you'll learn how to install and configure software firewalls to protect your computer.

system is probably not vulnerable to attack. See the Try This section in this chapter for instructions on how to test your system.

What if I don't get a clean report from the testing program? If the testing program detects potential vulnerabilities and you don't have a firewall, you should install one as soon as possible. If the firewall is already configured and common ports (such as those shown in Figure 14) are identified as being vulnerable, consult your firewall documentation for instructions on how to close or restrict access to those ports.

Password Protection and Password Management

How can I best use passwords to protect my computer? You no doubt have many passwords you need to remember to access your digital life. However, creating strong passwords—ones that are difficult for hackers to guess—is an essential piece of security that people sometimes overlook. Password-cracking programs have become more sophisticated. In fact, some commonly available programs can test more than one million password combinations per second! Creating a secure password is therefore more important than ever.

Many people use extremely weak passwords. The Imperva Application Defense Center, a computer-security research organization, conducted a review of 32 million passwords that were used at the website **rockyou.com**. More than 345,000 people were using "12345," "123456," or "123456789" as their password. And almost 62,000 people were using "password"! Passwords such as these are easy for hackers to crack.

FIGURE 14

Common Logical Ports

PORT NUMBER	PROTOCOL USING THE PORT
21	FTP (File Transfer Protocol) control
23	Telnet (unencrypted text communications)
25	SMTP (Simple Mail Transfer Protocol)
53	DNS (domain name system)
80	HTTP (Hypertext Transfer Protocol)
443	HTTPS (HTTP with Transport Layer Security [TLS] encryption)

Websites that need to be very secure, such as those for financial institutions, usually have strong defenses to prevent hackers from cracking passwords. But sites that need less security, such as casual gaming or social networking sites, might have less protection. Hackers attack poorly defended sites for passwords because many people use the same password for every site they use. So if a hacker can get your password from a poorly secured gaming site, they might be able to access your bank account with the same password.

Creating Passwords

What constitutes a strong password? Strong passwords are difficult for someone to guess. Follow these guidelines to create strong passwords (see Figure 15):

- Don't use easily deduced components related to your life, such as parts of your name, your pet's name, your street address, or the name of the website or institution for which you are creating the password (i.e., don't use "Citibank" for your online banking password).
- Use a password that is at least 14 characters long. Longer passwords are more difficult to deduce. Consider using a passphrase that is even longer.
- Don't use words found in the dictionary.
- Use a mix of upper- and lowercase letters and symbols (such as # or %).
- Never tell anyone your password or write it down in a place where others might see it, like in your wallet or purse.
- Change your passwords on a regular basis, such as monthly or quarterly. Your school or your employer probably requires you to change your password regularly. This is also a good idea for your personal passwords.
- Don't use the same password for every account you have.

If you have trouble thinking of secure passwords, there are many password generators available for free, such as the Strong Password Generator (**strongpasswordgenerator.com**).

How can I check the strength of my passwords? You can use online password strength testers, such as the Password Meter (**passwordmeter.com**), to evaluate your passwords. The Password Meter provides guidelines for good passwords and shows you how integrating various elements, such as symbols, affects the strength score of your password.

How do I restrict access to my computer? Windows, OS X, and most other operating systems have built-in password (or passcode) protection for files as well as the entire desktop. After a certain period of idle time, your computer is automatically password locked, and your password must be entered to gain access to the computer. This provides excellent protection from casual snooping if you need to walk away from your computer for a period of time. If someone attempts to log on to your computer without your password, that person won't be able to gain access. It's an especially good idea to use passwords on laptop computers, smartphones, and

FIGURE 15

Strong and Weak Password Candidates

PASSWORD	RATING	GOOD POINTS	BAD POINTS
Joysmithl022	Poor	• Contains upper- and lowercase letters • Contains letters and numbers	• Less than 14 characters • Contains name and birth date
test44drive6car	Mediocre	• 15 characters in length	• Contains three words found in the dictionary • Numbers repeated consecutively
8$RanT%5ydTTtt&	Better	• Good length • Contains upper- and lowercase letters • Contains symbols	• Upper- and lowercase letters repeated consecutively • Still contains one dictionary word (rant)
7R3m3mB3R$5%y38	Best	• All good points from above • Dictionary word (remember) has 3s instead of Es	• None

tablets because this provides additional protection of your data if your device is lost or stolen.

Windows 8 allows you to use picture passwords. You select a picture and then draw three gestures on it—either straight lines, circles, or taps. This picture then works as an additional method for accessing your computer. You just unlock your computer by repeating the gestures (see Figure 16). But if you forget your gestures, you can always access your computer via the conventional password.

Managing Your Passwords

How can I remember all of my complex passwords? Good security practices suggest that you have different passwords for all the different websites that you access and that you change your passwords frequently. The problem with well-constructed passwords is that they can be hard to remember. Fortunately, password-management tools are now available. They take the worry out of forgetting passwords because the password-management software does the remembering for you.

Where can I obtain password-management software? Most current Internet security suites and web browsers make it easy to keep track of passwords by providing password-management tools. For example, Internet Explorer (IE) will remember passwords for you. When you go to a website that requires a login, IE will display a dialog box prompting you to have IE remember the password for the site (see Figure 17). Then, when you return to the site and type in your user name, IE will fill in the password information for you using a process known as auto complete. However, there are some passwords that you shouldn't have your browser remember, such as your online banking password. So be selective when using this feature.

FIGURE 16 Drawing three gestures on your picture (and repeating them once) sets your picture password options in Windows 8.

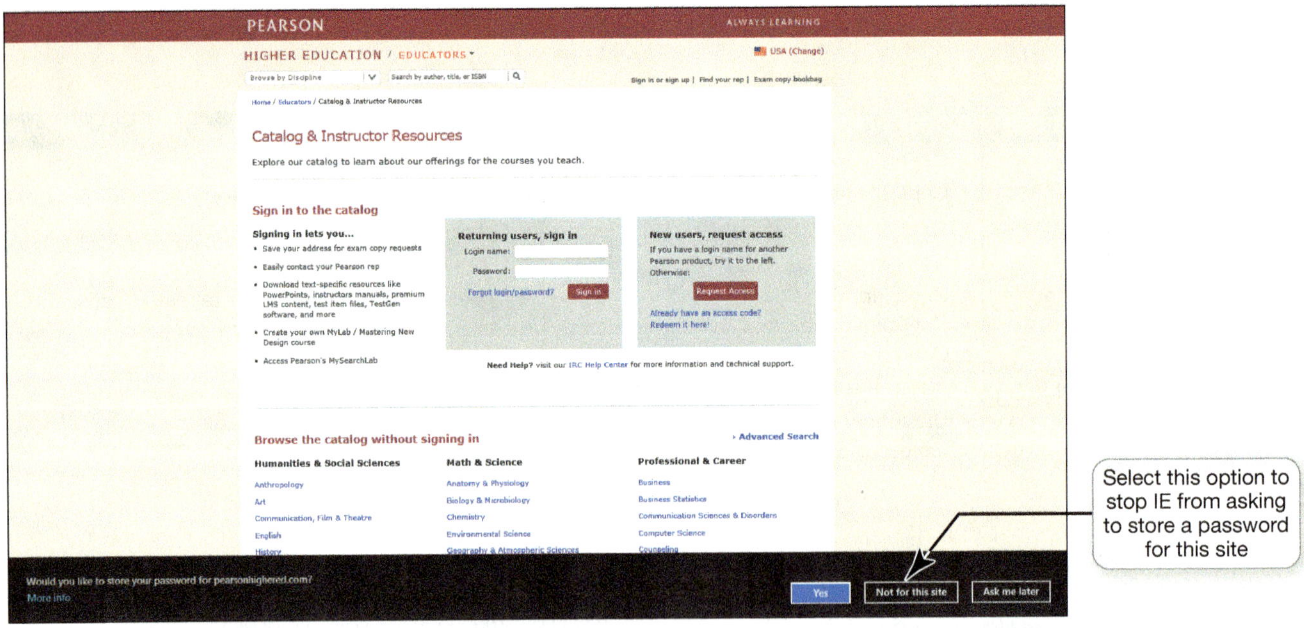

FIGURE 17 The password bar in IE 11 displays whenever you type in a password for a website for which IE hasn't yet stored the password.

Anonymous Web Surfing: Hiding from Prying Eyes

Should I be concerned about surfing the Internet on shared, public, or work computers? If you use shared computers in public places such as libraries, coffee shops, or student unions, you never know what nefarious tools have been installed by hackers on a public computer. When you browse the Internet, traces of your activity are left behind on that computer, often as temporary files. A wily hacker can glean sensitive information long after you've finished your surfing session. In addition, many employers routinely review the Internet browsing history of employees to ensure workers are spending their time on the Internet productively.

What tools can I use to keep my browsing activities private when surfing the Internet? The current versions of Google Chrome, Firefox, and Internet Explorer include privacy tools (called Incognito,

BITS&BYTES

Can't Remember Passwords? Try a Passphrase Instead!

Sure, Tr4h&nj9$WsD2# is a hard-to-guess password. It's also difficult for most people to remember. It's often easier for people to remember a phrase than random strings of characters and numbers. Therefore, *passphrases* can be a useful alternative to passwords.

A passphrase is a string of words that makes some sense to the individual using it so it will be easier to remember. Passphrases usually span 25 or more characters, making them much longer than passwords, which are typically 10 to 14 characters long. Longer passphrases are harder to crack, so the longer the better.

Passphrases should have meaning only to you. You should not use famous quotes, song lyrics, old proverbs or really any phrase that is in common usage or has been published. A phrase related to a memorable event in your past usually works best, such as:

- myfirstcatwasnamedblackieandwandereduptoourdoorwhenIwasfive
- IfirstwentwaterskiinginMainewithmyfriendScottin1997

Unless you have published a memoir with this information in it, personal events should be unknown to other people. Most people find a phrase easier to remember than a complex password. But as with passwords, you should change your passphrase periodically, and don't use the same phrase for every website/system that you access.

Private Browsing, and InPrivate, respectively) that help you surf the web anonymously (see Figure 18). When you choose to surf anonymously, all three browsers open special versions of their browser windows that are enhanced for privacy. When surfing in these windows, records of websites you visit and files you download don't appear in the web browser's history files. Furthermore, any temporary files generated in that browsing session are deleted when you exit the special window.

Are there any other tools I could use to protect my privacy? Portable privacy devices, such as the Ironkey Personal Flash Drive (**ironkey.com**), provide an even higher level of surfing privacy. Simply plug the device into an available USB port on the machine on which you'll be working. All sensitive Internet files, such as cookies, passwords, Internet history, and browser caches, will be stored on the privacy device, not on the computer you're using. Privacy devices such as these often come preloaded with software designed to shield your IP address from prying eyes, making it difficult (if not impossible) for hackers to tell where you're surfing on the Internet. These privacy devices also have password-management tools that store all of your login information and encrypt it so it will be safe if your privacy device falls into someone else's hands.

Is there anything else I can do to keep my data safe on shared computers? Another free practical solution is to take the Linux OS with you on a flash drive and avoid using the public or work computer's OS. The interfaces of many Linux distros look almost exactly like Windows and are easy to use. There are several advantages to using a Linux-based OS on a public or work computer:

- Your risk of picking up viruses and other malicious programs is significantly reduced because booting a computer from a flash drive completely eliminates any interaction with the computer's OS. This, in turn, significantly reduces the chance that your flash drive will become infected by any malware running on the computer.
- Virus and hacking attacks against Linux are far less likely than attacks against Windows. Because Windows has about 90% of the OS market, people who write malware tend to target Windows systems.
- When you run software from your own storage medium, such as a flash drive, you avoid reading and writing to the hard disk of the computer. This significantly enhances your privacy because you don't leave traces of your activity behind.

Pendrivelinux (**pendrivelinux.com**) is an excellent resource that offers many different versions of Linux for download and includes step-by-step instructions on how to install them

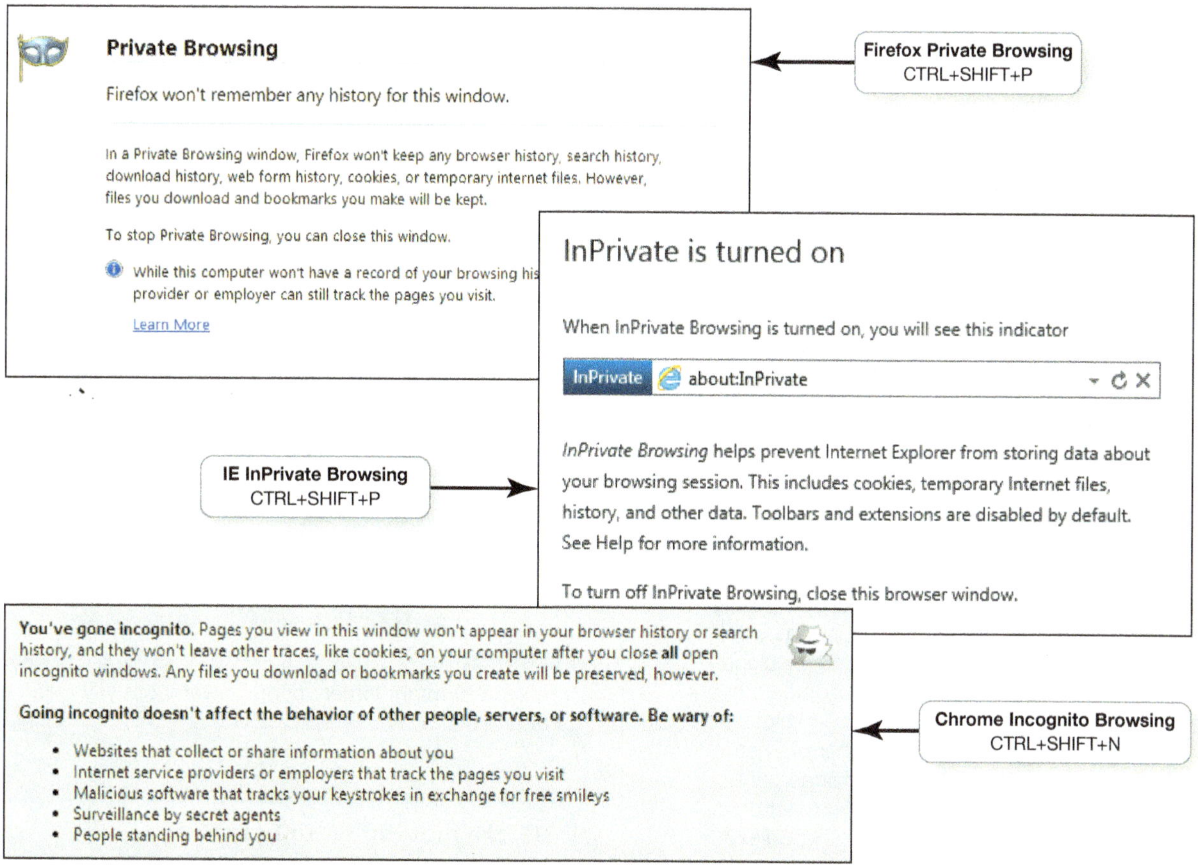

FIGURE 18 The recent versions of the Firefox, Internet Explorer, and Google Chrome browsers all feature privacy tools for web surfing. *((a) Courtesy of the Mozilla Foundation; (c) Courtesy of the Mozilla Foundation)*

on your flash drive (see Figure 19). If you're a Mac user, the gOS version of Linux provides a close approximation of OS X, so you can feel right at home.

Do I need to take special precautions with my tablet devices? Tablets like the iPad run their own proprietary operating systems that differ from the operating systems deployed on laptop and desktop computers. Although tablet operating systems do contain security features, they may not be robust enough to satisfy business users who have a great deal of confidential information on their tablets, especially when the devices are connected to wireless networks. Third-party software developers are now offering many apps to enhance tablet security. Comprehensive suites like IPVanish (**ipvanish.com**) offer features such as government-grade encryption of data, enhanced e-mail security, and anonymous web surfing. So look for security apps that are specifically designed for your tablet device if you often deal with sensitive data on your tablet, such as online banking.

FIGURE 19 **Pendrivelinux.com** can help you load a version of Linux onto a flash drive.
(Courtesy of USB Pen Drive Linux)

Biometric Authentication Devices

Besides passwords, how else can I restrict the use of my computer? A **biometric authentication device** is a device that reads a unique personal characteristic such as a fingerprint or the iris pattern in your eye and converts its pattern to a digital code (see Figure 20). When you use the device, your pattern is read and compared to the one stored on the computer. Only users having an exact fingerprint or iris pattern match are allowed to access the computer.

Because no two people have the same biometric characteristics (fingerprints and iris patterns are unique), these devices provide a high level of security. They also eliminate the human error that can occur in password protection. You might forget your password, but you won't forget to bring your fingerprints when you're working on your computer! Some smartphones, such as the iPhone 5s, now include fingerprint readers. But since Touch ID (the Apple software for fingerprint identification) has already been hacked, you might be safer using a regular password. Other biometric devices, including voice authentication and fingerprint–recognition systems, are now widely offered in notebooks, tablets, and smartphones (such as the Samsung Galaxy phones).

Make sure to use some (or all) of these methods to keep your activities from prying eyes and to restrict access to your digital information. ■

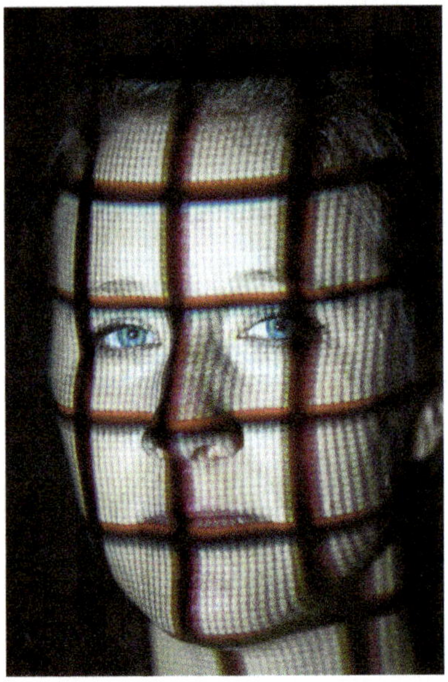

FIGURE 20 Face recognition software is now available on laptops. You might forget your password, but you won't forget to bring your face! *(© Jochen Tack/Alamy)*.

Before moving on to Part 2:
- **Watch Replay Video 1**.
- Then check your understanding of what you've learned so far.

check your understanding//

For a quick review to see what you've learned so far, answer the following questions. Visit **pearsonhighered.com /techinaction** to check your answers.

multiple choice

1. When a hacker steals personal information with the intent of impersonating another individual to commit fraud, it is known as
   - **a.** impersonation theft.
   - **b.** scareware theft.
   - **c.** identity theft.
   - **d.** malware theft.
2. Viruses that activate on certain dates or with the passage of time are known as
   - **a.** boot-sector viruses.
   - **b.** script viruses.
   - **c.** time bombs.
   - **d.** encryption viruses.
3. Firewalls work by closing __________ in your computer.
   - **a.** logical ports
   - **b.** software gaps
   - **c.** logical doors
   - **d.** backdoors
4. An attack that renders a computer unable to respond to legitimate users because it is being bombarded with data requests is known as a __________ attack.
   - **a.** stealth
   - **b.** backdoor
   - **c.** scareware
   - **d.** denial-of-service
5. A large group of software programs used to launch coordinated DoS attacks is known as a __________.
   - **a.** rootkit
   - **b.** botnet
   - **c.** Trojan horse
   - **d.** zombienet

true–false

_____ **1.** Cybercrime is any crime that is carried out with the aid of a computer.

_____ **2.** Hackers that break into systems for nonmalicious reasons, such as to test security systems, are known as black-hat hackers.

critical thinking

1. Protecting Your Data from Viruses and Malware

Consider the following:

- **a.** What security software are you using on your personal computers? (Make sure to list all devices.) Is the security software up to date? If you don't have security software on a certain device (such as your phone), research available software to determine what might be appropriate to protect your device.
- **b.** Have you or a family member ever been the victim of a virus or malware attack? If so, how did you eradicate the problem? Were data or files lost because of the infection?

2. Password Protection

You know from reading this chapter that secure passwords are essential to protecting your digital information. Consider the following:

- **a.** How many online accounts do you have that have passwords? List them. Are the passwords for these accounts secure, based on the suggestions proposed in this chapter? Do you change your passwords on a regular basis?
- **b.** How do you keep track of all of your passwords? Do you use password-management features in your browser? If so, which browser are you using? If you don't use password-management in your browser, what methodology do you use for remembering and tracking your passwords? Have you replaced your passwords with passphrases for added security?

Continue »

TRY THIS Testing Your Network Security

A properly installed firewall should keep you relatively safe from wily hackers. But how do you know if your computer system is safe? Many websites help test your security. In this exercise, we'll use tools provided by Gibson Research Corporation (**grc.com**) to test the strength of your protection.

Step 1 Open a web browser and navigate to **grc.com**. From the pull-down Services menu at the top of the screen, select **ShieldsUP!** *(Courtesy of the Gibson Research Corporation)*

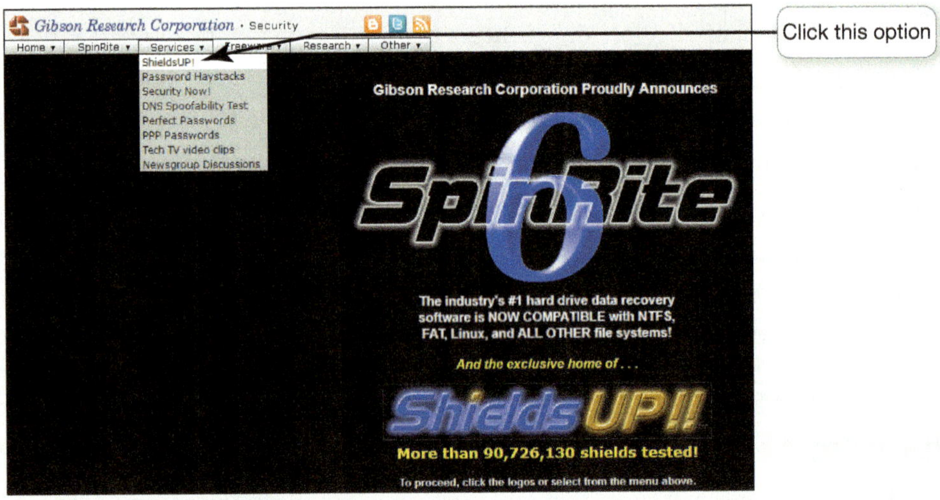

Step 2 On the ShieldsUP! welcome screen, click the **Proceed** button. *(Courtesy of the Gibson Research Corporation)*

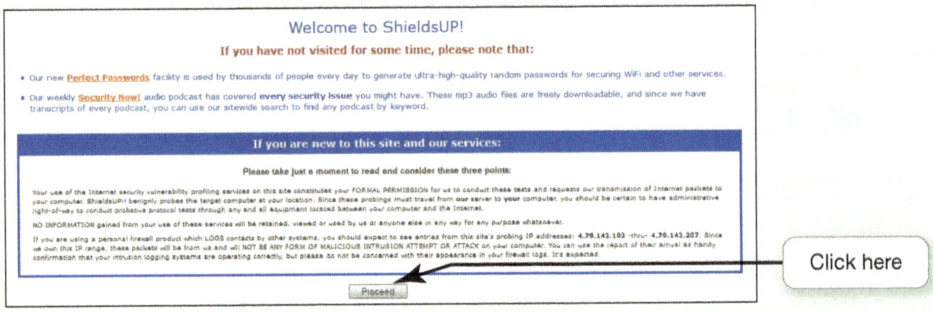

Step 3 Click the **Common Ports** link to begin the security test. It will take a few moments for the results to appear, depending on the speed of your Internet connection. *(Courtesy of the Gibson Research Corporation)*

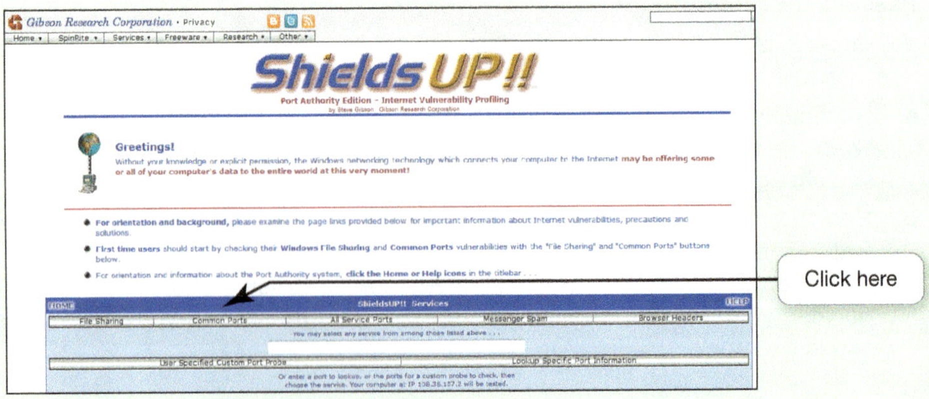

Step 4 Hopefully, you'll see a report indicating that your computer has passed the TruStealth analysis test. This means that your computer is very safe from attack. However, don't panic if your results say **failed for true stealth analysis**. Consider these common issues:

- Ports that only report as being closed will result in a TruStealth analysis failure. As long as all common ports are reporting as stealth or closed, you are well protected. However, if any ports report as being open, this means your computer could be exposed to hackers. Consult your firewall documentation to resolve the problem.
- Another common failure on the TruStealth test is ping reply. This means GRC attempted to contact your computer using a method called ping and it replied to the GRC computer. This is not a serious problem. It just means it's a little easier for a hacker to tell your computer network is there, but that doesn't mean that a hacker can break in. Often your ISP has your home modem configured to reply to ping requests to facilitate remote diagnostics if there is ever a problem with your modem. As long as your ports are closed (or stealthed), your system should still be secure. *(Courtesy of the Gibson Research Corporation)*

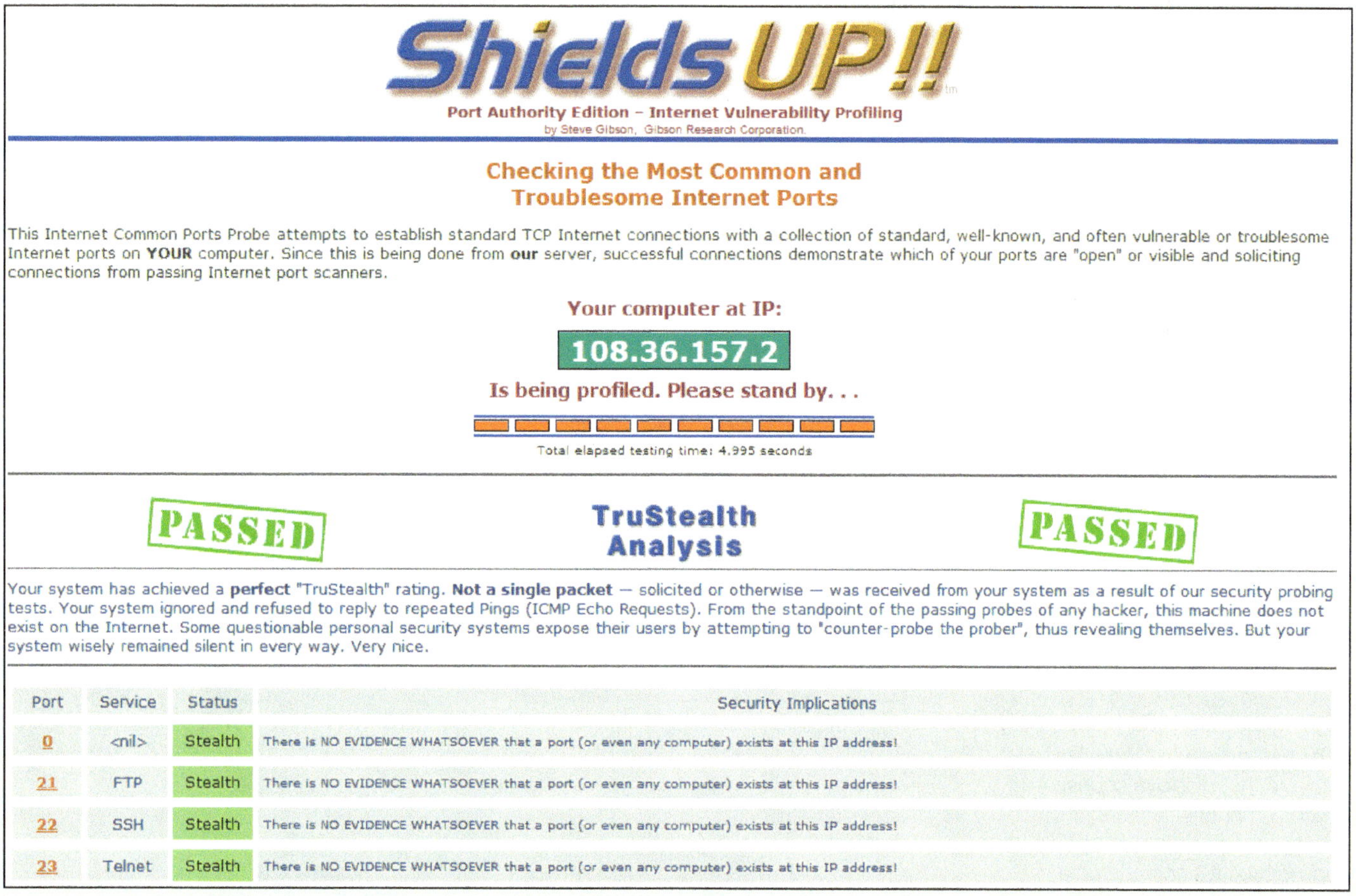

Protecting Your Digital Property from Yourself

Often, we can be our own worst enemies when using computing devices. If you're not careful, you might be taken in by thieves or scam artists who want to steal your digital and physical assets. Being aware of the tricks and traps that criminals use allows you to take steps to avoid being scammed.

managing online ANNOYANCES

Surfing the web, using social networks, and sending and receiving e-mail have become common parts of most of our lives. Unfortunately, the web has become fertile ground for people who want to advertise their products, track our browsing behaviors, or even con people into revealing personal information. In this section, we'll look at ways in which you can manage, if not avoid, these and other online headaches.

Malware: Adware and Spyware

What is malware? Malware is software that has a malicious intent (hence the prefix *mal*). There are three primary forms of malware: adware, spyware, and viruses. Adware and spyware are not physically destructive like viruses and worms, which can destroy data. Known collectively as *grayware*, most malware is intrusive, annoying, or objectionable online programs that are downloaded to your computer when you install or use other online content such as a free program, game, or utility.

What is adware? Adware is software that displays sponsored advertisements in a section of your browser window or as a pop-up box. It's considered a legitimate, though sometimes annoying, means of generating revenue for those developers who do not charge for their software or information. Fortunately, because web browsers such as Firefox, Safari, and Internet Explorer have built-in pop-up blockers, the occurrence of annoying pop-ups has been greatly reduced.

Some pop-ups, however, are legitimate and increase the functionality of the originating site. For example, your account balance may pop up on your bank's website. To control which sites to allow pop-ups on, you can access the pop-up blocker settings in your browser (see Figure 21) and add websites for which you allow pop-ups. Whenever a

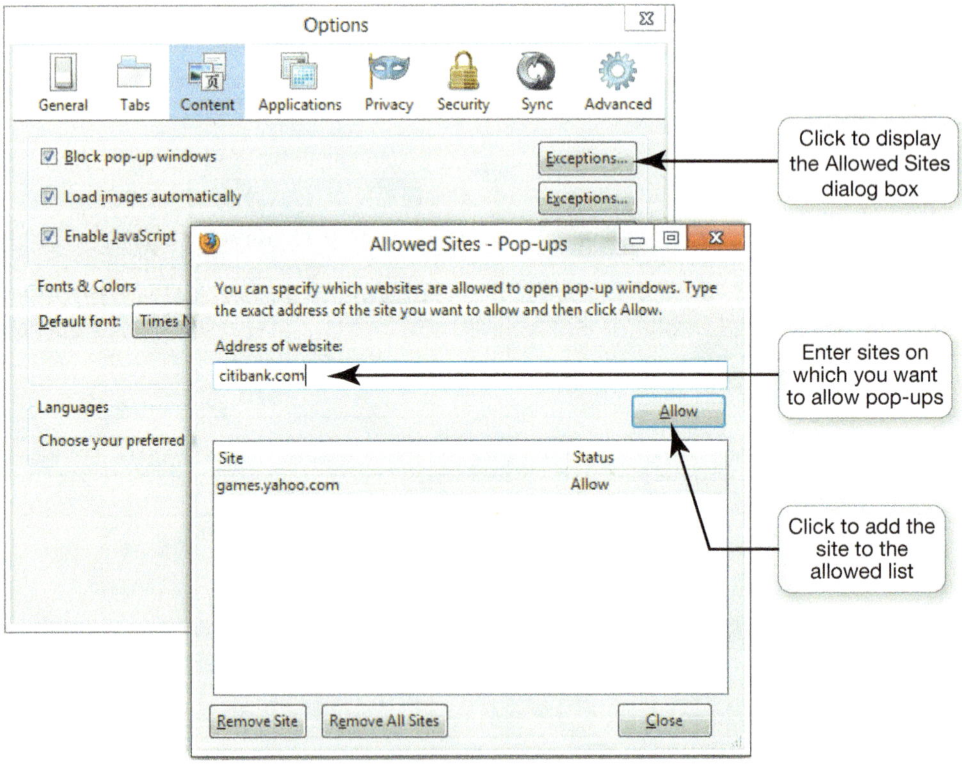

FIGURE 21 Firefox's Allowed Sites - Pop-ups dialog box lets you control which sites you'll allow to display pop-ups. *(Courtesy of the Mozilla Foundation)*

>*To display the pop-up blocker in Firefox, from the Tools menu, select* **Options**, *and then click the* **Content** *tab.*

pop-up is blocked, the browser displays an information bar or plays a sound to alert you. If you feel the pop-up is legitimate, you can choose to accept it.

What is spyware? Spyware is an unwanted piggyback program that usually downloads with other software you install from the Internet and that runs in the background of your system. Without your knowledge, spyware transmits information about you, such as your Internet-surfing habits, to the owner of the program so that the information can be used for marketing purposes. Many spyware programs use tracking cookies (small text files stored on your computer) to collect information. One type of spyware program known as a **keystroke logger (key logger)** monitors keystrokes with the intent of stealing passwords, login IDs, or credit card information.

Can I prevent spyware from spying on me? Anti-spyware software detects unwanted programs and allows you to delete the offending software easily. Most Internet security suites now include anti-spyware software. You can also obtain stand-alone anti-spyware software and run it on your computer to delete unwanted spyware. Because so many variants of spyware exist, your Internet security software may not detect all types that attempt to install themselves on your computer. Therefore, it's a good idea to install one or two additional stand-alone anti-spyware programs on your computer.

Because new spyware is created all the time, you should update and run your anti-spyware software regularly. Windows comes with a program called Windows Defender, which scans your system for spyware and other potentially unwanted software. Malwarebytes Anti-Malware, Ad-Aware, and Spybot–Search & Destroy (all available from **download.com**) are other anti-spyware programs that are easy to install and update. Figure 22 shows an example of Malwarebytes in action.

Spam

How can I best avoid spam? Companies that send out **spam**—unwanted or junk e-mail—find your e-mail address either from a list they purchase or with software that looks for e-mail addresses on the Internet. Unsolicited instant messages are also a form of spam, called *spim*. If you've used your e-mail address to purchase anything online, open an online account, or participate in a social network such as Facebook, your e-mail address eventually will appear on one of the lists that spammers get.

One way to avoid spam in your primary account is to create a free e-mail address that you use only when you fill out forms or buy items on the web. For example, both Windows Mail and Yahoo! let you set up free e-mail accounts. If your free e-mail account is saturated with spam, you can abandon that account with little inconvenience. It's much less convenient to abandon your primary e-mail address.

Another way to avoid spam is to filter it. A **spam filter** is an option you can select in your e-mail account that places known or suspected spam messages into a special folder (called "Spam" or "Junk Mail"). Most web-based e-mail

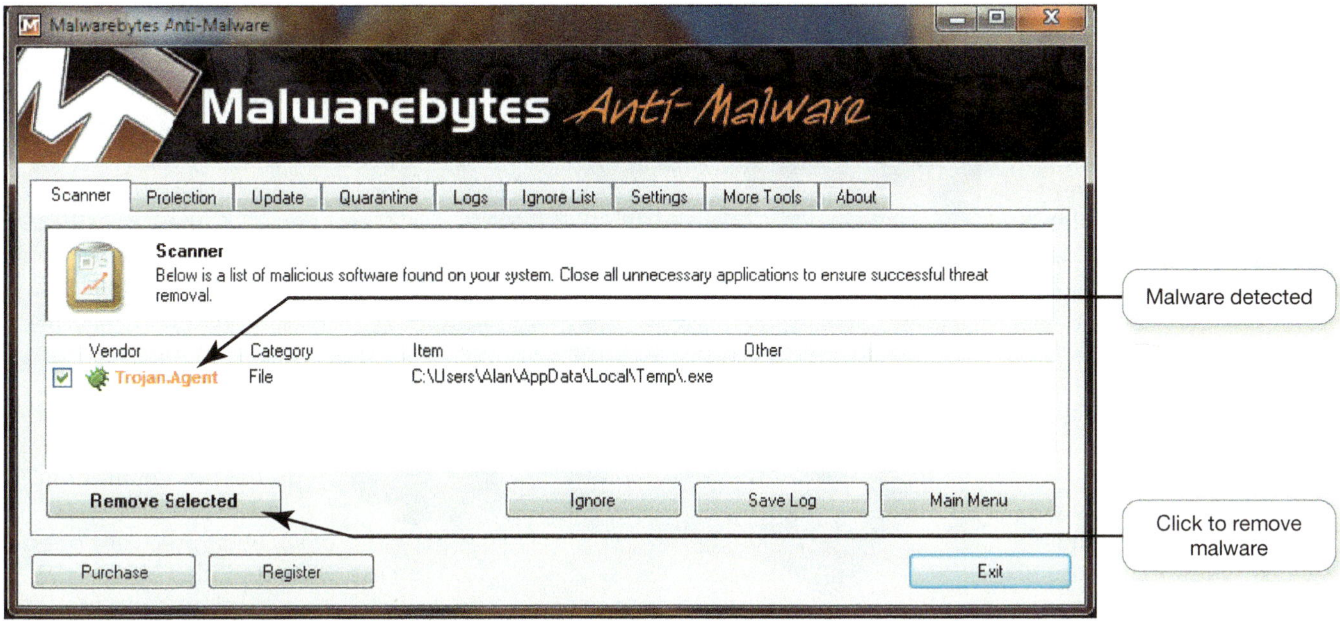

FIGURE 22 After performing a routine scan of a computer, Malwarebytes returns a log of problems found on the system. *(Courtesy of Malwarebytes)*

DIG DEEPER

Computer Forensics: How It Works

On law enforcement TV shows, you often see computer technicians working on suspects' computers to assist detectives in solving crimes. It may look simple, but the science of computer forensics is a complex step-by-step process that ensures evidence is collected within the confines of the law.

Forensic means that something is suitable for use in a court of law. There are many branches of forensic science. For example, forensic pathologists provide evidence about the nature and manner of death in court cases involving deceased individuals. **Computer forensics** involves identifying, extracting, preserving, and documenting computer evidence. Computer forensics is performed by individuals known as *computer forensic scientists*, who rely primarily on specialized software to collect their evidence.

Phase 1: Obtaining and Securing Computer Devices

The first step in a computer forensics investigation is to seize the computer equipment that law enforcement officials believe contains pertinent evidence. Police are required to obtain a warrant to search an individual's home or place of business. Warrants must be very specific by spelling out exactly where detectives can search for evidence and exactly what type of evidence they're seeking. If a warrant indicates that the police may search an individual's home for his laptop computer, they can't then confiscate a tablet computer they notice in his car. It is important to specify in the warrant all types of storage devices where potential evidence might be stored, such as external hard drives, flash drives, and servers.

Once permission to collect the computers and devices containing possible evidence has been obtained, law enforcement officials must exercise great care when collecting the equipment. They need to ensure that no unauthorized persons are able to access or alter the computers or storage devices. The police must make sure the data and equipment are safe; if the equipment is connected to the Internet, the connection must be severed without data loss or damage. It's also important for law enforcement officials to understand that they may not want to power off equipment because potential evidence contained in RAM may be lost. After the devices are collected and secured, the computer forensic scientists take over the next phase of the investigation.

Phase 2: Cataloging and Analyzing the Data

It's critical to preserve the data exactly as it was found, or attorneys may argue that the computer evidence was subject to tampering or altering. Because just opening a file can alter it, the first task is to make a copy of all computer systems and storage devices collected (see Figure 23). The investigators then work from the copies to ensure that the original data always remains preserved exactly as it was when it was collected.

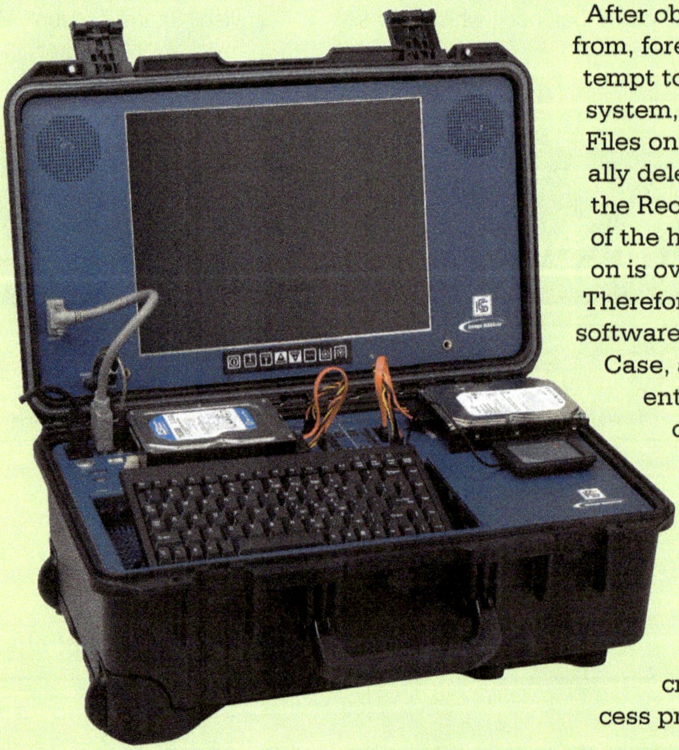

FIGURE 23 Portable devices like the RoadMASSter 3 Data Acquisition and Analysis tool make it easy to copy storage devices at crime scenes. *(Intelligent Computer Solutions)*

After obtaining a copy to work from, forensics professionals attempt to find every file on the system, including deleted files. Files on a computer aren't actually deleted, even if you empty the Recycle Bin, until the section of the hard disk they're stored on is overwritten with new data. Therefore, using special forensic software tools such as SIFT, EnCase, and FTK, the forensic scientists catalog all files found on the system or storage medium and recover as much information from deleted files as they can. Forensic software like FTK can readily detect hidden files and perform procedures to crack encrypted files or access protected files and reveal their contents.

The most important part of the process is

documenting every step. Forensic scientists must clearly log every procedure performed because they may be required to provide proof in court that their investigations did not alter or damage information contained on the systems they examined. Detailed reports should list all files found, how the files were laid out on the system, which files were protected or encrypted, and the contents of each file. Finally, computer forensic professionals are often called on to present testimony in court during a trial.

Criminals are getting more sophisticated and are now employing anti-forensics techniques to foil computer forensic investigators. Although techniques for hiding or encrypting data are popular, the most insidious anti-forensics techniques are programs designed to erase data if unauthorized persons (i.e., not the criminal) access a computer system or if the system detects forensics software in use. When computer forensic investigators detect these countermeasures, they must often use creative methods and custom-designed software programs to retrieve and preserve the data.

Computer forensics is an invaluable tool to law enforcement in many criminal investigations, but only if the correct procedures are followed and the appropriate documentation is prepared.

services, such as Hotmail and Yahoo!, offer spam filters (see Figure 25). Microsoft Outlook also features a spam filter.

You can also buy third-party programs that provide some control over spam, including SPAMfighter, which you can download at **download.com**.

How do spam filters work? Spam filters and filtering software can catch as much as 95% of spam by checking incoming e-mail subject headers and senders' addresses against databases of known spam. Spam filters also check your e-mail for frequently used spam patterns and keywords, such as "for free" and "over 21." Spam filters aren't perfect, and you should check the spam folder before deleting its contents because legitimate e-mail might end up there by mistake. Most programs let you reclassify e-mails that have been misidentified as spam (see Figure 24).

How else can I prevent spam? Here are a few other ways you can prevent spam:

1. Before registering on a website, read its privacy policy to see how it uses your e-mail address. Don't give the site permission to pass on your e-mail address to third parties.
2. Don't reply to spam to remove yourself from the spam list. By replying, you're confirming that your e-mail address is active. Instead of stopping spam, you may receive more.
3. Subscribe to an e-mail forwarding service such as VersaForward (**versaforward.com**) or Sneakemail (**sneakemail.com**). These services screen your e-mail messages, forwarding only those messages you designate as being okay to accept.

Cookies

What are cookies? Cookies are small text files that some websites automatically store on your hard drive when you visit them. When you log on to a website that uses cookies, a cookie file assigns an ID number to your computer. The unique ID is intended to make your return visit to a website more

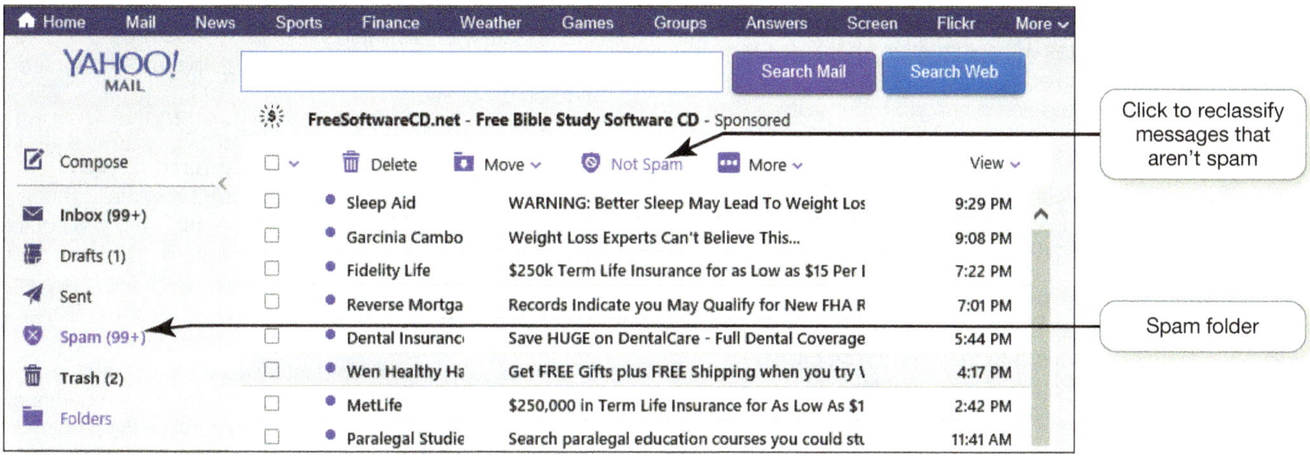

FIGURE 24 In Yahoo! Mail, messages identified as spam are directed into a folder called "Spam" for review and deletion. *(Courtesy of Yahoo, Inc.)*

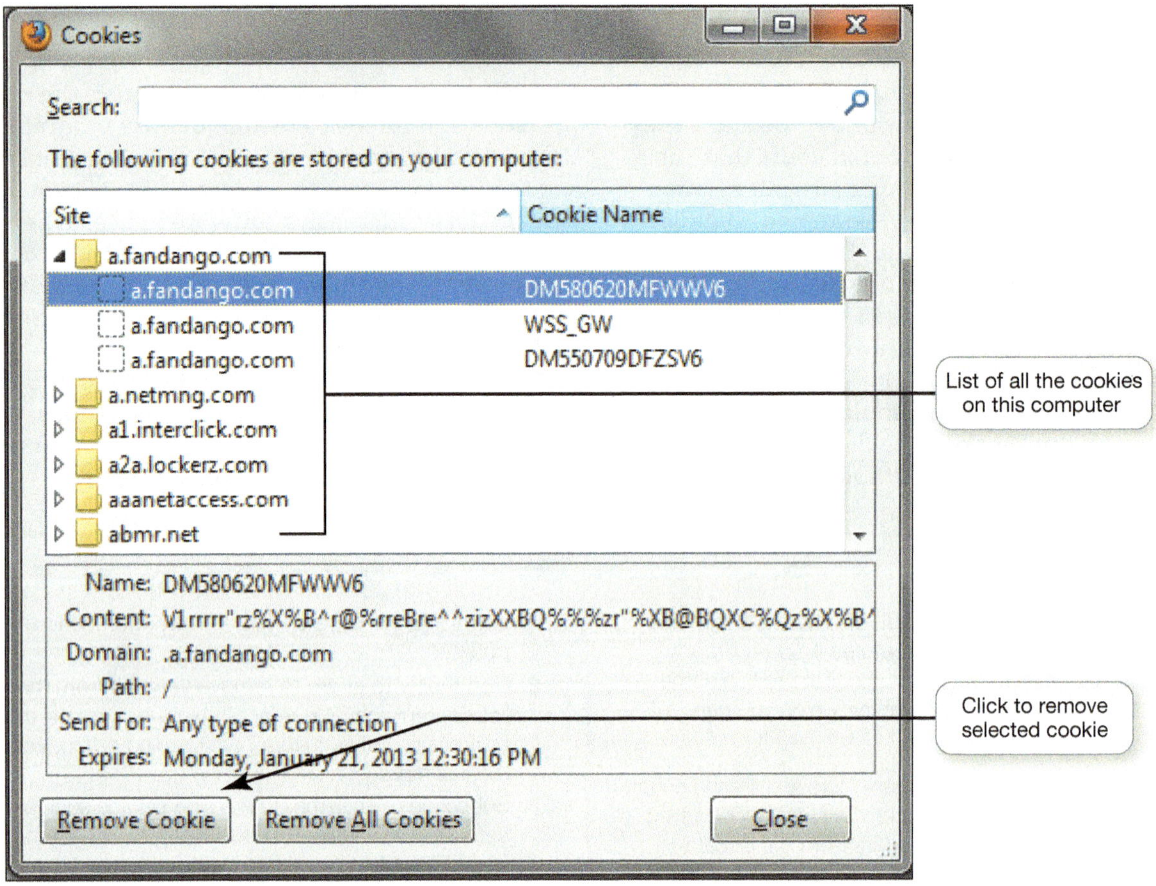

FIGURE 25 Tools are available, either through your browser (Firefox is shown here) or as separate programs, to distinguish between cookies you want to keep and cookies you don't want on your system. *(Courtesy of the Mozilla Foundation)*

>On the Firefox menu toolbar, click **Tools***, click Options, choose the* **Privacy tab***, and then click the* **remove individual cookies** *link to display the Cookies dialog box.*

efficient and better geared to your interests. The next time you log on to that site, the site marks your visit and keeps track of it in its database.

What do websites do with cookie information? Cookies can provide websites with information about your browsing habits, such as the ads you've opened, the products you've looked at, and the time and duration of your visits. Companies use this information to determine the traffic flowing through their website and the effectiveness of their marketing strategy and placement on websites. By tracking such information, cookies enable companies to identify different users' preferences.

Can companies get my personal information when I visit their sites? Cookies do not go through your hard drive in search of personal information such as passwords or financial data. The only personal information a cookie obtains is the information you supply when you fill out forms online.

Do privacy risks exist with cookies? Some sites sell the personal information their cookies collect to web advertisers who are building huge databases of consumer preferences and habits, collecting personal and business information such as phone numbers, credit reports, and the like. The main concern is that advertisers will use this information indiscriminately, thus invading your privacy. And you may feel your privacy is being violated by cookies that monitor where you go on a website.

Should I delete cookies from my hard drive? Cookies pose no *security* threat because it is virtually impossible to hide a virus or malicious software program in a cookie. Because they take up little room on your hard drive, and offer you small conveniences on return visits to websites, there is no great reason to delete them. Deleting your cookie files could actually cause you the inconvenience of reentering data you have already entered into website forms. However, if you're uncomfortable with the accessibility of your personal information, you can periodically delete cookies (as shown in Figure 25) or configure your browser to block certain types of cookies. Software such as Cookie Pal (**kburra.com**) also can help you monitor cookies. ■

ethics in IT You're Being Watched ... But Are You Aware You're Being Watched?

Think you aren't being closely watched by your employer? Think again! A recent survey of employers by the American Management Association and the ePolicy Institute revealed that, of the employers surveyed:

- 73% monitored e-mail messages
- 66% monitored web surfing
- 48% monitored activities using video surveillance
- 45% monitored keystrokes and keyboard time
- 43% monitored computer files in some other fashion

As you can see, there is a high probability that you're being monitored while you work and when you access the Internet via your employer's Internet connection.

The two most frequently cited reasons for employee monitoring are to prevent theft and to measure productivity. Monitoring for theft isn't new—monitoring cameras have been around for years, and productivity monitoring has been used for assembly line workers for decades. However, the Internet has led to a new type of productivity drain of concern to employers. **Cyberloafing**, or cyberslacking, means using your computer for nonwork activities while you're being paid to do your job. Examples of cyberloafing activities include playing games and using social networks. Some employees even do multiple nonwork tasks at the same time, which is known as *multishirking*. Estimates of business productivity losses due to cyberloafing top $50 billion annually.

Do you have a right to privacy in the workplace? Laws such as the 1986 Electronic Communications Privacy Act (ECPA), which prohibits unauthorized monitoring of electronic communications, have been interpreted by the courts in favor of employers. The bottom line is that employers who pay for equipment and software have the *legal* right to monitor their usage (see Figure 26).

So, is it *ethical* for employers to monitor their employees? Certainly, it seems fair that employers ensure they're not the victims of theft and that they're getting a fair day's work from their employees, just as employees have an obligation to provide a fair effort for a fair wage. The ethical issue is whether employees are adequately informed of monitoring policies. Employers have an ethical responsibility (and a legal one as well, depending on the jurisdiction) not to place monitoring devices in sensitive locations such as bathrooms and dressing areas. However, in many states, the employer does not legally need to inform employees in advance that they're being monitored. Conscientious employers include monitoring disclosures in published employee policies to avoid confusion and conflict.

The bottom line? Because employers may have a legal right to monitor you in the workplace, operate under the assumption that everything you do on your work computer is subject to scrutiny and behave accordingly. Do your online shopping at home!

FIGURE 26 George Orwell was right—at least when you're at work! It's legal for employers to monitor your computer usage. *(SVLuma/Shutterstock)*

keeping your DATA SAFE

People are often too trusting or just plain careless when it comes to protecting private information about themselves or their digital data. In this section, we discuss ways to keep your data safe from damage, either accidental or intentional, and to keep unscrupulous individuals from tricking you into revealing sensitive information.

Protecting Your Personal Information

If a complete stranger walked up to you on the street and asked you for your address and phone number, would you give it to him or her? Of course you wouldn't! But many people are much less careful when it comes to sharing sensitive information online. And often people inadvertently share information that they really only intended to share with their friends. With cybercrimes like identify theft rampant, you need to take steps to protect your personal information.

What information should I never share on websites? A good rule of thumb is to reveal as little information as possible, especially if the information would be available to everyone. Figure 27 gives you some good guidelines.

Your Social Security number, phone number, date of birth, and street address are four key pieces of information that identity thieves need to steal an identity. This information should never be shared in a public area on any website.

How can I tell who can see my information on a social network? Social networking sites like Facebook make privacy settings available in your profile settings. If you've never changed your default privacy settings in Facebook, you're probably sharing information more widely than you should.

How can I protect my information on Facebook? To begin, you need to change your privacy settings in your profile from some of the default options. In general, it's a bad idea to make personal information available to the public, although this is a default setting for some items in Facebook (see Figure 28). It's a good idea to set most of the options in your profile's Basic Information section to Friends or to Only Me because, presumably, these are personal details you should wish to share only with friends.

In the Contact Information section, restricting this information only to friends or to yourself is imperative. You don't want scammers contacting you via e-mail or snail mail and trying to trick you into revealing sensitive information.

Backing Up Your Data

How might I damage the data on my computer? The data on your computer faces three major threats:

1. Unauthorized access
2. Tampering
3. Destruction

As noted earlier, a hacker can gain access to your computer and steal or alter your data. However, a more likely scenario is that you'll lose your data unintentionally. You may accidentally delete files. You may drop your laptop on the ground, causing the hard drive to break and resulting in complete data loss. A virus from an e-mail attachment you opened

FIGURE 27

Internet Information-Sharing Precautions

Information Identity Thieves Crave

- Social Security Number
- Full Date of Birth
- Phone Number
- Street Address

Never make this information visible on websites!

Other Sensitive Information

- Full Legal Name
- E-mail Address
- Zip Code
- Gender
- School or Workplace

Only reveal this information to people you know—don't make it visible to everyone!

(Mograph/Fotolia; Kevin Largent/Fotolia)

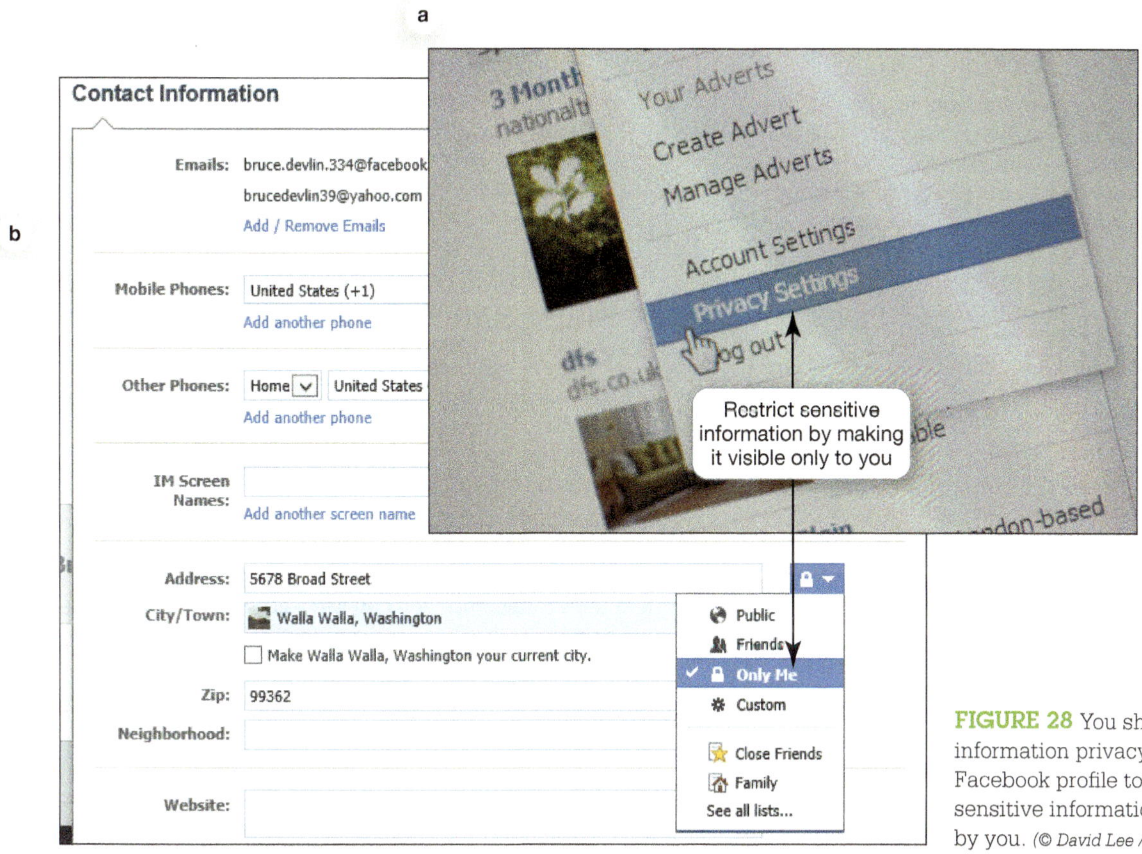

FIGURE 28 You should review the information privacy settings in your Facebook profile to ensure your sensitive information can only be seen by you. *(© David Lee / Alamy)*

may destroy your original file. Your house may catch fire and destroy your computer. Because many of these possibilities are beyond your control, you should have a strategy for backing up your files (see Figure 29). **Backups** are copies of files that you can use to replace the originals if they're lost or damaged.

What types of files do I need to back up? Two types of files need backups:

1. **Program files** include files used to install software, usually found on DVDs or downloaded from the Internet. As long as you have the DVDs in a safe place, you shouldn't need to back up these program files. If you've downloaded a program file from the Internet, however, you should make a copy of the program installation files on a removable storage device as a backup.
2. **Data files** include files you've created or purchased, such as research papers, spreadsheets, music and photo files, contact lists, address books, e-mail archives, and your Favorites list from your browser.

What types of backups can I perform? There are two main options for backing up files:

1. An **incremental backup** (or **partial backup**) involves backing up only files that have changed or have been created since the last backup was performed. Using backup

FIGURE 29

An Effective Backup Strategy

Files to Back Up

- **Program files:** Installation files for productivity software (i.e., Microsoft Office)
- **Data files:** Files you create (term papers, spreadsheets, etc.)

Types of Backups

- **Incremental (partial):** Only backs up files that have changed
- **Image (system):** Snapshot of your entire computer, including system software

Where to Store Backup Files

- Online (in the cloud)
- External hard drives
- Network-attached storage devices or home servers

software that has an option for incremental backups will save time because backing up files that haven't changed is redundant.

2. An **image backup** (or **system backup**) means that all system, application, and data files are backed up, not just the files that changed. Although incremental backups are more efficient, an image backup ensures you capture changes to application files, such as automatic software updates, that an incremental backup might not capture. The idea of imaging is to make an exact copy of the setup of your computer so that in the event of a total hard drive failure you could copy the image to a new hard drive and have your computer configured exactly the way it was before the crash.

Where should I store my backups? To be truly secure, backups must be stored away from where your computer is located and should be stored in at least two different places. You wouldn't want a fire or a flood destroying the backups along with the original data. You have three main choices for where to back up your files (see Figure 30):

1. *Online (in the cloud):* The beauty of online storage is that you don't need to be at your home computer or lug around your external hard drive to access your data. More important, because the information is stored online, it's in a secure, remote location, so data is much less vulnerable to the disasters that could harm data stored in your computer or external hard drive. Free storage options include Microsoft OneDrive (**onedrive.com**) and ADrive (**adrive.com**). However, image backups probably won't fit within the storage limits offered by free providers. For a fee, companies such as Carbonite (**carbonite.com**) and IBackup (**ibackup.com**) provide larger storage capacity.
2. *External hard drives:* External hard drives, or even large-capacity flash drives, are popular backup options that are usually connected to a single computer. Although convenient and inexpensive, using external hard drives for backups still presents the dilemma of keeping the hard drive in a safe location. Also, external hard drives can fail, possibly leading to loss of your backed-up data. Therefore, using an external hard drive for backups is best done in conjunction with an online backup strategy for added safety.
3. *Network-attached storage (NAS) devices and home servers:* NAS devices are essentially large hard drives connected to a network of computers instead of one computer, and they can be used to back up multiple computers simultaneously. Home servers also act as high-capacity NAS devices for automatically backing up data and sharing files.

FIGURE 30

A Comparison of Typical Data Backup Locations

BACKUP LOCATION	PROS	CONS
Online (in the Cloud) 	• Files stored at a secure, remote location • Files/backups accessible anywhere through a browser	• Most free storage sites don't provide enough space for image backups
External Hard Drive 	• Inexpensive, one-time cost • Fast backups with USB 3.0 devices connected directly to your computer	• Could be destroyed in one event (fire/flood) with your computer • Can be stolen • Slightly more difficult to back up multiple computers with one device
Network-Attached Storage (NAS) Device and Home Server 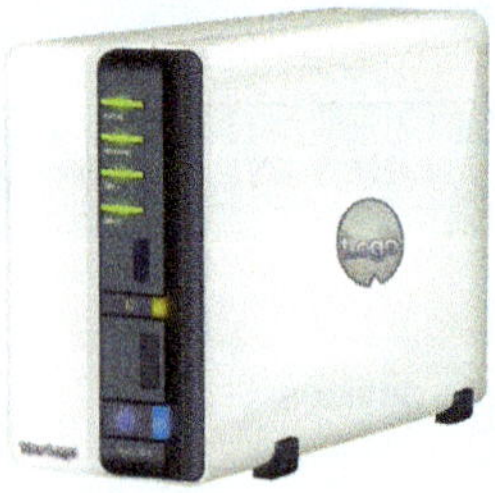	• Makes backups much easier for multiple computing devices	• More expensive than a stand-alone external hard drive • Could be destroyed in one event (fire/flood) with your computer • Can be stolen

(mipan/Fotolia; © Prapass Wannapinij/Fotolia; © darkdesigns/Fotolia)

How often should I back up my data files? You should back up your data files every time you make changes to them, which can be difficult to remember to do. Fortunately, most backup software can be configured to do backups automatically so you don't forget to perform them. For example, with the Windows 8 File History utility, you can have Windows automatically save your data files from your libraries, desktop, contacts, and favorites to an external hard drive or NAS device. The default setting for File History saves files you changed every hour to the backup location you specify. File History even keeps previous versions of the file on the backup drive so you can revert to a previous version of the file if you need to do so.

To set up File History, you first need to connect an external hard drive to your computer or a NAS device to your network. You can then access File History through the Control Panel (in the System and Security group) and set it up (see Figure 31). Once configured, your data files will be backed up as often as you indicate. You can also restore files that you've backed up from the File History utility.

How often should I create an image backup? Because your program and OS files don't change as often as your data files, you can perform image backups on a less frequent basis. You might consider scheduling an image backup of your entire system on a weekly basis, but you should definitely perform one after installing new software.

How do I perform an image backup? Windows 8 includes the System Image Backup utility, which provides a quick and easy way to perform image backups. You can access this utility from the System Image Backup link on the File History screen (see Figure 31). Before starting this utility, make sure your external hard drive or NAS device is connected to your computer or network and is powered on. To set it up, follow these steps:

1. The first screen displayed (see Figure 32a) shows a list of available backup devices. Select a device (usually an external hard drive), and click Next to proceed.

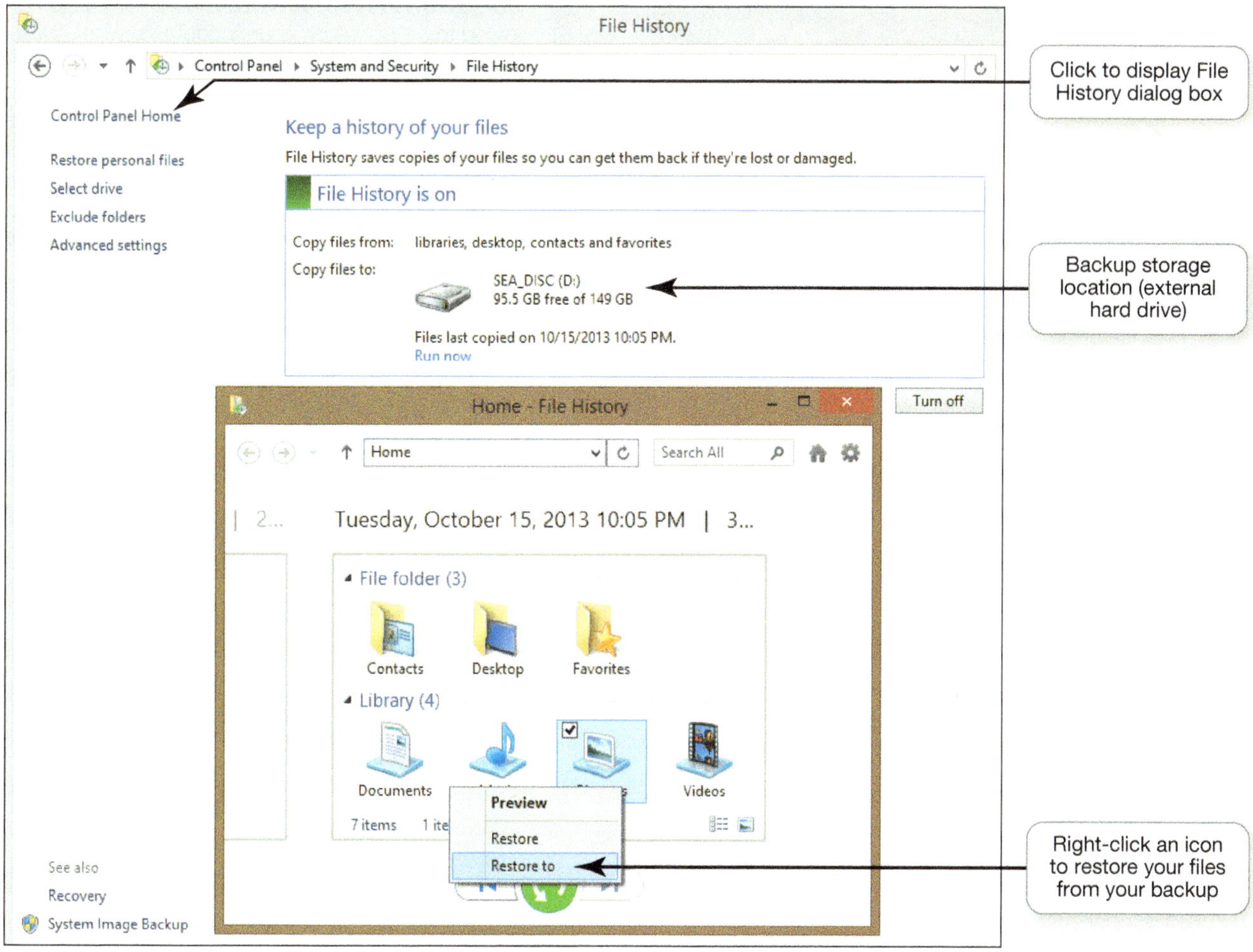

FIGURE 31 You can use the Windows 8 File History utility to back up files and restore files from a previous backup.
>*Access the Control Panel, select the* **System and Security** *group, and then click the* **File History** *link.*

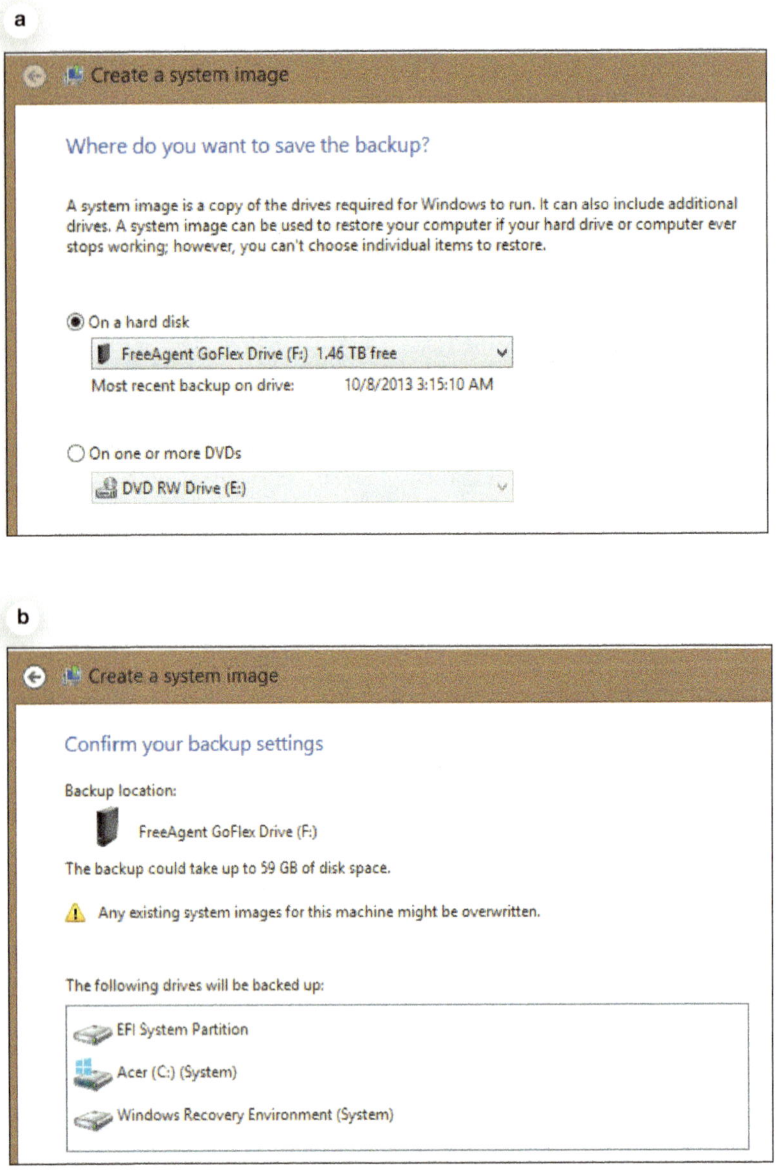

FIGURE 32 The System Image Backup utility allows you to perform an image backup. (a) Select your backup destination. (b) Review options and start the backup.

2. On the following screen (see Figure 32b), you can review your settings Windows decides what to include in your system image backup: all data files and system files on all partitions on your hard drive. When you click the Start Backup button, your system image backup is created on the drive you selected.

From the File History screen, you can access advanced recovery tools (such as creating a system repair backup and System Restore) by clicking the Recovery link. A system repair backup is a copy of files that you can use to boot your computer in case of a serious Windows error.

What about backing up Apple computers? For OS X users, backups are very easy to configure. The Time Machine feature in OS X detects when an external hard drive is connected to the computer or a NAS device is connected to your network. You're then asked if you want this to be your backup drive. If you answer yes, all of your files (including OS files) are automatically backed up to the external drive or NAS device.

Should I back up my files that are stored on my school's network? Most likely, if you're allowed to store files on your school's network, these files are backed up regularly. You should check with your school's network administrators to determine how often they're backed up and how you would request that files be restored from the backup if they're damaged or deleted. But don't rely on these network backups to bail you out if your data files are lost or damaged. It may take days for the network administrators to restore your files. It's better to keep backups of your data files yourself, especially homework and project files, so that you can immediately restore them. ■

SOUND BYTE

Managing Computer Security with Windows Tools

In this Sound Byte, you'll learn how to monitor and control your computer security using features built into the Windows OS.

social ENGINEERING

Social engineering is any technique that uses social skills to generate human interaction that entices individuals to reveal sensitive information. Social engineering often doesn't involve the use of a computer or face-to-face interaction. For example, telephone scams are a common form of social engineering because it is often easier to manipulate someone when you don't have to look at them.

How does social engineering work? Most social engineering schemes use a pretext to lure their victims. **Pretexting** involves creating a scenario that sounds legitimate enough that someone will trust you. For example, you might receive a phone call during which the caller says he is from your bank and that someone tried to use your account without authorization. The caller then tells you he needs to confirm a few personal details such as your birth date, Social Security number, bank account number, and whatever other information he can get out of you. The information he obtains can then be used to empty your bank account or commit some other form of fraud. The most common form of pretexting in cyberspace is *phishing*.

Phishing and Pharming

How are phishing schemes conducted? Phishing (pronounced "fishing") lures Internet users to reveal personal information such as credit card numbers, Social Security numbers, or other sensitive information that could lead to identity theft. The scammers send e-mail messages that look like they're from a legitimate business such as an online bank. The e-mail usually states that the recipient needs to update or confirm his or her account information. When the recipient clicks on the provided link, he or she goes to a website. The site looks like a legitimate site but is really a fraudulent copy that the scammer has created. Once the e-mail recipient enters his or her personal information, the scammers capture it and can begin using it.

Is pharming a type of phishing scam? Pharming is much more insidious than phishing. Phishing requires a positive action by the person being scammed, such as going to a website mentioned in an e-mail and typing in personal information. **Pharming** occurs when malicious code is planted on your computer, either by viruses or by your visiting malicious websites, which then alters your browser's ability to find web addresses. Users are directed to bogus websites even when they enter the correct address of the real website. You end up at a fake website that looks legitimate but is expressly set up for the purpose of gathering information.

How can I avoid being caught by phishing and pharming scams? Follow these guidelines to avoid falling prey to such schemes:

- Never reply directly to any e-mail asking you for personal information.
- Don't click on a link in an e-mail to go to a website. Instead, type the website address in the browser.
- Check with the company asking for the information and only give the information if you're certain it's needed.
- Never give personal information over the Internet unless you know the site is secure. Look for the closed padlock, *https*, or a certification seal such as Norton Secured to help reassure you that the site is secure.
- Use phishing filters. The latest versions of Firefox, Chrome, and Internet Explorer have phishing filters built in, so each time you access a website, the phishing filter checks for the site's legitimacy and warns you of possible web forgeries.
- Use Internet security software on your computer that's constantly being updated.

BITS&BYTES

I Received a Data Breach Letter … Now What?

Data breaches are becoming more common, and companies that are the subject of data breaches now routinely notify customers of data breaches…usually by physical letter, but sometimes via e-mail. Here's what you should do if you receive such a letter:

1. Take it seriously. 22.5% of recipients of these letters become the victim of identity theft per a study by Javelin Strategy and Research.
2. Contact one of the three big credit bureaus (Equifax, Experian, and TransUnion) and have a fraud alert put on your credit report. This alerts people accessing your credit report that your identity information has been stolen and that the person who is applying for credit in your name might be an imposter.
3. For even better security, contact all three credit bureaus and have a credit freeze put on your credit reports. This prevents anyone (even you) from getting credit in your name. You can always unfreeze your accounts later if you need to apply for credit yourself.
4. Review your credit reports regularly. You are entitled to one free credit report per year from each of the three big agencies. Go to **annualcreditreport.com** and request a report from one of the agencies. Repeat the process every 4 months from a different agency. Review the reports for any suspicious activity.

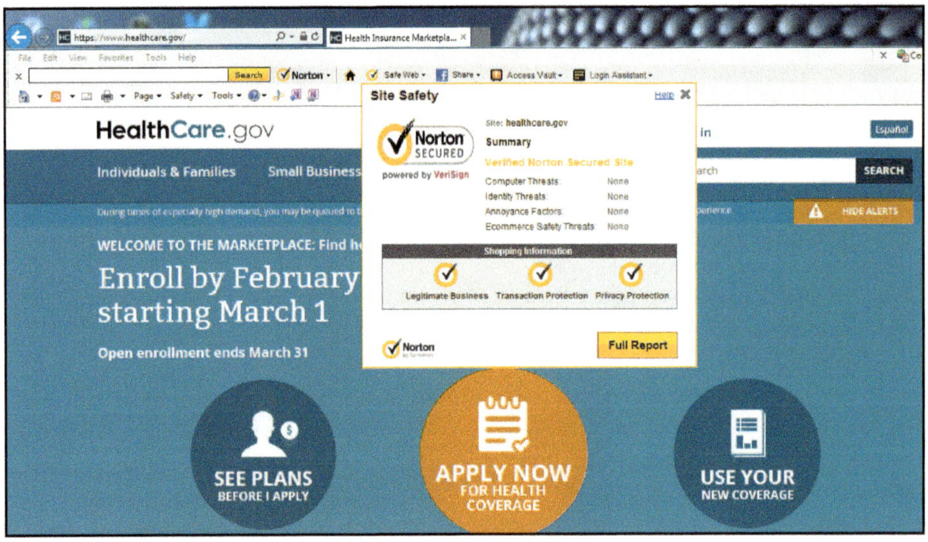

FIGURE 33 Not sure whether you're on the Healthcare.gov website or a cleverly disguised phishing site? Norton Site Safety reassures you that all is well. *(Courtesy of HealthCare.gov; Courtesy of the Symantec Corporation)*

Most Internet security packages can detect and prevent pharming attacks. The major Internet security packages—for example, McAfee and Norton (see Figure 33)—also offer phishing-protection tools. When you have the Norton Toolbar displayed in your browser, you're constantly informed about the legitimacy of the site you are visiting.

Scareware

What is scareware? Scareware is a type of malware that downloads onto your computer and tries to convince you that your computer is infected with a virus (see Figure 34) or other type of malware. Pop-ups, banners, or other annoying types of messages will flash on your screen saying frightening things like, "Your computer is infected with a virus . . . immediate removal is required." You're then directed to a website where you can buy fake removal or antivirus tools that provide little or no value. Panda Security estimates that scareware scams generate in excess of $34 million a month for cybercriminals. Some scareware even goes so far as to encrypt your files and then demand that you pay to have them unencrypted, which is essentially extortion.

Scareware is a social engineering technique because it uses people's fear of computer viruses to convince them to part with their money. Scareware is often designed to be extremely difficult to remove from your computer and to interfere with the operation of legitimate security software. Scareware is usually downloaded onto your computer from infected websites or Trojan horse files.

How do I protect myself against scareware? Most Internet security suites, antivirus, and anti-malware software packages now detect and prevent the installation of scareware. But make sure you never click on website banners or pop-up boxes that say "Your computer might be infected, click here to scan your files" because these are often the starting points for installing malicious scareware files on your computer. ■

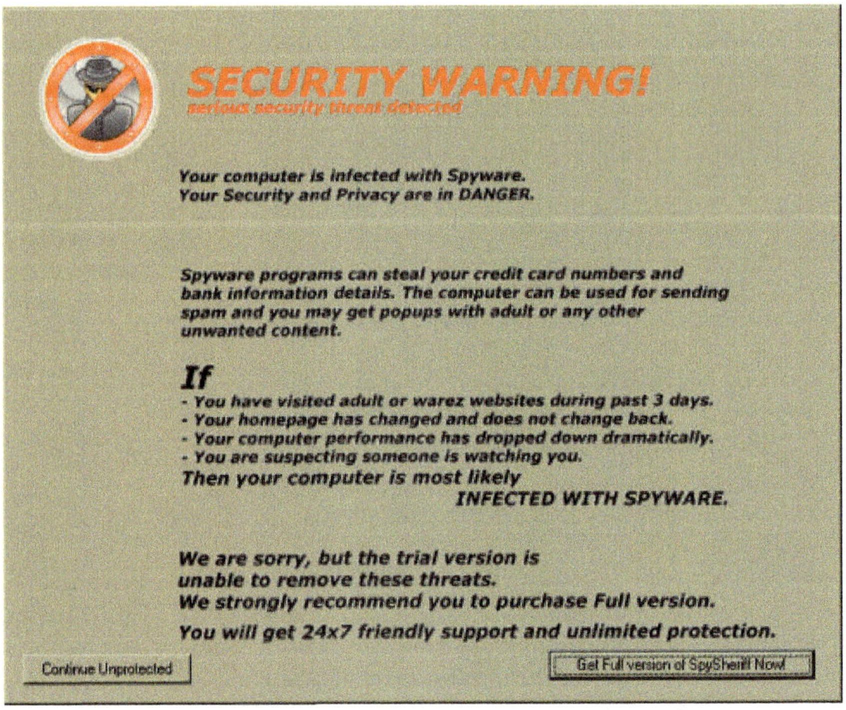

FIGURE 34 Preying on people's fears, scareware attempts to convince you that your computer is infected with a virus and you need to purchase a "solution." *(Courtesy of McAfee, Inc.)*

trends in IT

Computers in Society: Spear Phishing: The Bane of Data Breaches

Most people have vast amounts of personal data residing in the databases of the various companies with which they conduct business. Amazon.com has your credit card and address information. Your bank has your Social Security number, birth date, and financial records. Your local supermarket probably has your e-mail address from when you joined its loyalty club to receive grocery discounts. All this data in various places puts you at risk when companies responsible for keeping your data confidential suffer a data breach.

A **data breach** occurs when sensitive or confidential information is copied, transmitted, or viewed by an individual who isn't authorized to handle the data. Data breaches can be intentional or unintentional. Intentional data breaches occur when hackers break into digital systems to steal sensitive data. Unintentional data breaches occur when companies controlling data inadvertently allow it to be seen by unauthorized parties, usually due to some breakdown in security procedures or precautions.

Unfortunately, data breaches appear to be quite common, as there always seems to be another one in the news. In April 2013, Living Social, a daily deal website, notified 50 million customers that its systems had been breached and that names, e-mail addresses, and dates of birth had been exposed. Fortunately, the system that held customer credit card information had not been hacked. Data breaches such as this one pose serious risks to the individuals whose data has been compromised, even if financial data is not involved. The data thieves now have the basis with which to launch targeted social engineering attacks even if they just have contact information, such as e-mail addresses.

With regular phishing techniques, cybercriminals just send out e-mails to a wide list of e-mail addresses, whether they have a relationship with the company or not. For example, a criminal might send out a general phishing e-mail claiming that a person's Citibank checking account had been breached. People who receive this e-mail that don't have any accounts at Citibank should immediately realize this is a phishing attack and ignore the instructions to divulge sensitive data.

But when cybercriminals obtain data on individuals that includes information about which companies those individuals have a relationship with, they can engage in much more targeted attacks known as **spear phishing**. Spear phishing e-mails are sent to people known to be customers of a company and have a much greater chance of successfully getting individuals to reveal sensitive data. If cybercriminals obtain a list of e-mail addresses of customers from Barclays Bank, for example, they can ensure that the spear phishing e-mails purport to come from Barclays and will include the customer's full name. This type of attack is much more likely to succeed in fooling people than just random e-mails sent out to thousands of people who might not have a relationship with the company mentioned in the phishing letter.

So how can you protect yourself after a data breach? You need to be extra suspicious of any e-mail correspondence from companies involved in the data breach. Companies usually never contact you by e-mail or phone asking you to reveal sensitive information or reactivate your online account by entering confidential information. Usually, these requests come via regular snail mail.

So, if you receive any e-mails or phone calls from companies you deal with purporting to have problems with your accounts, your best course of action is to delete the e-mail or hang up the phone. Then contact the company that supposedly has the problem by a phone number that you look up yourself either in legitimate correspondence from the company (say, the toll-free number on your credit card statement) or in the phone book. The representatives from your company can quickly tell if a real problem exists or if you were about to be the victim of a scam.

protecting your physical COMPUTING ASSETS

Your computer, tablet, and phone aren't useful to you if they're damaged. Therefore, it's essential to select and ensure a safe environment for these devices. This includes protecting them from environmental factors, power surges, power outages, and theft.

Environmental Factors

Why is the environment critical to the operation of my computer equipment? Computers are delicate devices and can be damaged by the adverse effects of abuse or a poor environment. Sudden movements, such as a fall, can damage your computing device's internal components. You should make sure that your computer sits on a flat, level surface, and if it's a laptop or a tablet, you should carry it in a protective case.

Electronic components don't like excessive heat or excessive cold. Don't leave computing devices and phones in a car during especially hot or cold weather because components can be damaged by extreme temperatures. Unfortunately, computers generate a lot of heat, which is why they have fans to cool their internal components. Chill mats that contain cooling fans and sit underneath laptop computers are useful accessories for dissipating heat. Make sure that you place your desktop computer where the fan's intake vents, usually found on the rear of the system unit, are unblocked so air can flow inside.

Naturally, a fan drawing air into a computer also draws in dust and other particles, which can wreak havoc on your system. Therefore, keep the room in which your computer is located as clean as possible. Finally, because food crumbs and liquid can damage keyboards and other computer components, consume food and beverages away from your computer.

FIGURE 35 Surge protectors such as this one are critical for protecting your electronic devices. *(aberenyi/Fotolia)*

Power Surges

What is a power surge? Power surges occur when electrical current is supplied in excess of normal voltage. Old or faulty wiring, downed power lines, malfunctions at electric company substations, and lightning strikes can all cause power surges. A **surge protector** is a device that protects your computer against power surges (see Figure 35).

Note that you should replace your surge protectors every two to three years. Also, after a major surge, the surge protector will no longer function and must be replaced. And it's wise to buy a surge protector that includes indicator lights, which illuminate when the surge protector is no longer functioning properly. Don't be fooled by old surge protectors—although they can still function as multiple-outlet power strips, they deliver power to your equipment without protecting it.

Besides my computer, what other devices need to be connected to a surge protector? All electronic devices in the home that have solid-state components, such as TVs, stereos, printers, and smartphones (when charging), should be connected to a surge protector. However, it can be inconvenient to use individual surge protectors on everything. A more practical method is to install a **whole-house surge protector** (see Figure 36). Whole-house surge protectors function like other surge protectors, but they protect *all* electrical devices in the house. Typically, you'll need an electrician to install a whole-house surge protector, which will cost $300 to $400 (installed).

Is my equipment 100% safe when plugged into a surge protector? Lightning strikes can generate such high voltages that they can overwhelm a surge

> SOUND BYTE
> **Surge Protectors**
>
> In this Sound Byte, you'll learn about the major features of surge protectors and how they work. You'll also learn about the key factors you need to consider before buying a surge protector, and you'll see how easy it is to install one.

FIGURE 36 A whole-house surge protector is usually installed at the breaker panel or near the electric meter.

protector. As tedious as it sounds, unplugging electronic devices during an electrical storm is the only way to achieve absolute protection.

Deterring Theft

What do I need to worry about if my computing device is stolen? Because they're portable, laptops, tablets, and phones are easy targets for thieves. You have four main security concerns with mobile devices:

1. Keeping them from being stolen
2. Keeping data secure in case they are stolen
3. Finding a device if it is stolen
4. Remotely recovering and wiping data off a stolen device

Keep Them Safe: Alarms

What type of alarm can I install on my mobile device? Motion alarm software is a good, inexpensive theft deterrent. Free software such as LAlarm (**lalarm.com**) is effective for laptops. Apps such as Motion Alarm and Alarmomatic help secure your iPad or iPhone. Alarm software either detects motion, like your device being picked up, or sounds near your device and then sets off an ear-piercing alarm until you enter the disable code. Thieves normally don't like it when attention is drawn to their activities, so alarms can be a very effective theft deterrent.

Keeping Mobile Device Data Secure

How can I secure the data on my mobile devices? Encrypting the data on your mobile device can make it extremely difficult, if not impossible, for thieves to obtain sensitive data from your stolen equipment. *Encryption* involves transforming your data using an algorithm that can only be unlocked by a secure code (or key). Encrypted data is impossible to read unless it's decrypted, which requires a secure password, hopefully known only to you.

Safe is an app that provides 256-bit encryption, which is very hard to crack, for data and images on your iPhone and iPad. If your password is not entered, no one can access the data and images on your iPhone or iPad. Mobile StrongBox is a similar app for Android devices. SensiGuard and SafeHouse are available for laptop computers to provide encryption for files or even entire hard drives.

Software Alerts and Data Wipes

How can my computer help me recover it when it is stolen? You've probably heard of LoJack, the theft-tracking device used in cars. Similar systems now exist for computers. Tracking software such as LoJack for Laptops (**absolute.com**), PC PhoneHome, and Mac PhoneHome (**brigadoonsoftware.com**) enables your computer to alert authorities to the computer's location if it is stolen. A similar tracking app for Android and iOS devices is iHound.

To enable your mobile device to help with its own recovery, you install the tracking software on your device. The software contacts a server at the software manufacturer's website each time the device connects to the Internet. If your device is stolen, you notify the software manufacturer. The software manufacturer instructs your device to transmit tracking information, such as an IP address, WiFi hotspot, or cell tower location, that will assist authorities in locating and retrieving the mobile device.

What if the thieves find the tracking software and delete it? The files and directories holding the software aren't visible to thieves looking for such software, so they probably won't know the software is there. Furthermore, the tracking software is written in such a way that even if the thieves tried to reformat the hard drive, it would detect the reformat and hide the software code in a safe place in memory or on the hard drive. This works because some sectors of a hard drive are not rewritten during most reformatting. That way, the tracking software can reinstall itself after the reformatting is complete.

What if my device can't be recovered by the authorities? In the event that your laptop can't be recovered, software packages are available that provide for remote recovery and deletion of files. LoJack for Laptops has these features and allows you to lock your device to keep the thieves from accessing it or to remotely wipe its contents by deleting all your data from your laptop.

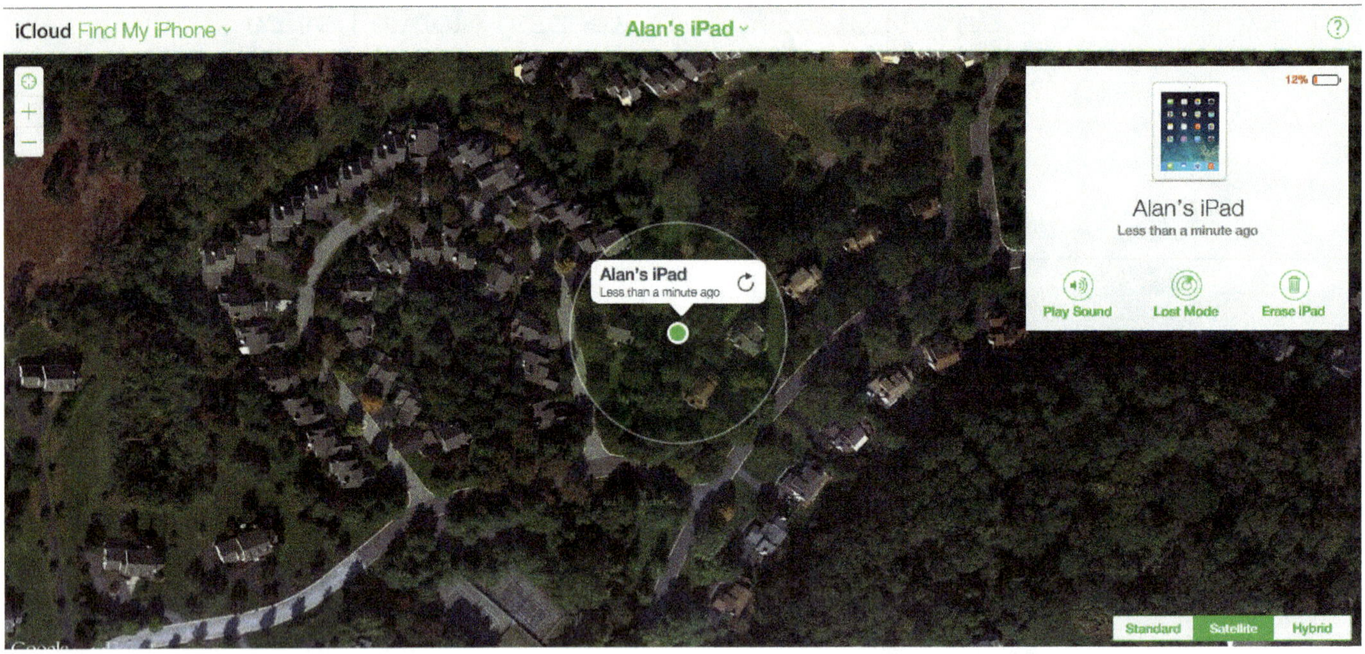

FIGURE 37 The Find My iPhone app can really help if your iOS device goes astray. You can play a sound to help you find it (if it's misplaced where you are), display a message on the device (Lost Mode), or erase all data on the device. *(Courtesy of Apple, Inc.)*

FIGURE 38

Computer Security Checklist

Virus and Spyware Protection

- Is antivirus and anti-spyware software installed on all your devices?
- Is the antivirus and anti-spyware software configured to update itself automatically and regularly?
- Is the software set to scan your device on a regular basis (at least weekly) for viruses and spyware?

Firewall

- Do all your computers and tablets have firewall software installed and activated before connecting to the Internet?
- Is your router also able to function as a hardware firewall?
- Have you tested your firewall security by using the free software available at grc.com?

Software Updates

- Have you configured your operating systems (Windows, OS X, iOS) to install new software patches and updates automatically?
- Is other software installed on your device, such as Microsoft Office or productivity apps, configured for automatic updates?
- Is the web browser you're using the latest version?

Protecting Your Devices

- Are all computing devices protected from electrical surges?
- Do your mobile devices have alarms or tracking software installed on them?

For all iOS devices, Apple offers the Find My iPhone service, which is now part of iCloud. Enabling this service on your device provides you with numerous tools that can assist you in recovering and protecting your mobile devices. Did you forget where you left your iPad? Just sign in with your Apple ID at the iCloud website to see a map showing the location of your iPad (see Figure 37). You can also remotely send a message to be displayed on your lost device, such as your phone number and a reward offer, so that someone who finds it will know what to do. If you can't recover the device, you can remotely password lock it so no one can use it or, if necessary, wipe all the data off the device to completely protect your privacy. With iOS 7, additional security is in place to keep thieves from using your phone. Your Apple ID and password are required to turn off Find My iPhone or to use the phone again after it has been erased.

How can I ensure that I've covered all aspects of protecting my digital devices? Figure 38 provides a guide to ensure you haven't missed critical aspects of security. If you've addressed all of these issues, you can feel reasonably confident that your data and devices are secure. ■

Before moving on to the Chapter Review:
- **Watch Replay Video 2** .
- Then check your understanding of what you've learned so far.

check your understanding//

For a quick review to see what you've learned so far, answer the following questions. Visit **pearsonhighered.com /techinaction** to check your answers.

multiple choice

1. A technique that uses illegally obtained information about individuals to perform targeted attacks in the hopes of getting them to reveal sensitive information is known as
   - **a.** spear phishing.
   - **b.** pretexting.
   - **c.** keystroke logging.
   - **d.** logic bombing.
2. A backup of all files on your computer, which is essentially a snapshot of exactly how your computer looks at a particular point in time, is known as a(n)
   - **a.** total backup.
   - **b.** incremental backup.
   - **c.** image backup.
   - **d.** global backup.
3. Software that transmits information about you, such as your Internet surfing habits, back to a third party is known as
   - **a.** scareware.
   - **b.** spyware.
   - **c.** adware.
   - **d.** trackingware.
4. Small text files that some websites automatically store on your computer's hard drive are known as
   - **a.** greyware.
   - **b.** spam.
   - **c.** adware.
   - **d.** cookies.
5. A social engineering technique in which you send people an e-mail for the purpose of inducing them into revealing sensitive information is known as
   - **a.** pretexting.
   - **b.** phishing.
   - **c.** pharming.
   - **d.** key logging.

true–false

_____ **1.** Sending e-mails to lure people into revealing personal information is a technique known as pharming.

_____ **2.** Using a surge protector will even protect your computer from massive surges such as lightning strikes.

critical thinking

1. **Restricting Information to Keep You Safe**

   Many countries, such as China, have laws that control the content of the Internet and restrict their citizens' access to information. The United States, with the exception of specific areas such as cyberbullying and child pornography, doesn't currently take steps to restrict its citizens' access to the Internet. Unfortunately, this freedom of information does carry some cost because some information on the web can potentially be dangerous to the general public.

   - **a.** Do you think the U.S. government should censor information on the web, such as instructions for making weapons, to protect the general public? Why or why not? If you think there should be some censorship, do you think such a law would violate the First Amendment right to free speech? Explain your answer.
   - **b.** Would you be willing to live with a lower level of information access to increase your sense of well-being? What topics do you feel would make you feel more secure if they were censored?

Continue

Chapter Review

summary//

Cybercrime and Identity Theft

1. What is cybercrime, and who perpetrates it?

- Cybercrime, is any type of crime perpetrated via a computer or a website.
- Major types of cybercrime are identity theft, credit card fraud, computer viruses, illegal access of computer systems, and auction fraud.
- Cybercriminals use computers, the Internet, and computer networks to commit their crimes.

Protecting Yourself from Computer Viruses

2. What are the types of viruses from which I need to protect my computer?

- A computer virus is a program that attaches itself to another program and attempts to spread to other computers when files are exchanged.
- Computer viruses can be grouped into six categories: (1) boot-sector viruses, (2) logic bombs and time bombs, (3) worms, (4) scripts and macro viruses, (5) e-mail viruses, and (6) encryption viruses. Once run, viruses perform their malicious duties in the background and are often invisible to the user.

3. What can I do to protect my computer from viruses?

- The best defense against viruses is to install antivirus software. You should update the software on a regular basis and configure it to examine all e-mail attachments for viruses. You should periodically run a complete virus scan on your computer to ensure that no viruses have made it onto your hard drive.

Protecting Digital Assets from Hackers

4. How can hackers attack my computing devices, and what harm can they cause?

- A hacker is defined as anyone who breaks into a computer system unlawfully. Hackers can use software to break into almost any computer connected to the Internet, unless proper precautions are taken.
- Once hackers gain access to a computer, they can potentially (1) steal personal or other important information, (2) damage and destroy data, or (3) use the computer to attack other computers.

5. What is a firewall, and how does it keep my computer safe from hackers?

- Firewalls are software programs or hardware devices designed to keep computers safe from hackers. By using a personal firewall, you can close to invaders open logical ports and potentially make your computer invisible to other computers on the Internet.

6. How do I create secure passwords and manage all of my passwords?

- Secure passwords contain a mixture of upper- and lowercase letters, numbers, and symbols and are at least 14 characters long. Passwords should not contain words that are in the dictionary or easy-to-guess personal information, like your pet's name.
- Online password checkers can be used to evaluate the strength of your passwords.
- Utilities built into web browsers and Internet security software can be used to manage your passwords and alleviate the need to remember numerous complex passwords.

7. How can I surf the Internet anonymously and use biometric authentication devices to protect my data?

- The current versions of popular browsers include tools, such as Google Chrome's Incognito feature, that hide your surfing activities by not recording websites that you visit or files that you download in your browser's history files.
- Biometric authentication devices use a physical attribute that is not easily duplicated to control access to data files or computing devices. Some laptops and smartphones today feature fingerprint readers and facial-recognition software to control access.

Managing Online Annoyances

8. How do I manage online annoyances such as spyware and spam?

- The web is filled with annoyances such as spam, pop-ups, cookies, spyware, and scams such as phishing that make surfing the web frustrating and sometimes dangerous.
- Installing anti-malware software tools helps to prevent, detect, and/or reduce spam, adware, and spyware.

Keeping Your Data Safe

9. What data do I need to back up, and what are the best methods for doing so?

- Data files created by you, such as Word and Excel files, or purchased by you, such as music files, need to be backed up in case they're inadvertently deleted or damaged. Application software, such as Microsoft Office, may need to be reinstalled if files are damaged, so backups, such as the DVDs the application came on, must be maintained.
- An incremental backup means only files that have changed or been created since the last backup was performed will be backed up. Image backups copy all system, application, and data files regardless of whether they changed since the last backup.
- Websites such as ADrive and OneDrive are great for backing up individual files. External hard drives are popular choices for holding image backups of your entire system, as are online (cloud) storage sites. Windows and OS X contain solid backup tools that help automate backup tasks.

10. What is social engineering, and how do I avoid falling prey to phishing?

- Social engineering schemes use human interaction, deception, and trickery to fool people into revealing sensitive information such as credit card numbers and passwords.
- Phishing schemes usually involve e-mails that direct the unwary to a website that appears to be legitimate, such as a bank site, but that is specifically designed to capture personal information for committing fraud. To avoid phishing scams, you should never reply directly to any e-mail asking you for personal information and never click on a link in an e-mail to go to a website.
- Don't fall for scareware scams that attempt to frighten you by pretending there is something wrong with your computer.

Protecting Your Physical Computing Assets

11. How do I protect my physical computing assets from environmental hazards, power surges, and theft?

- Computing devices should be kept in clean environments free from dust and other particulates and should not be exposed to extreme temperatures (either hot or cold).
- You should protect all electronic devices from power surges by hooking them up through surge protectors, which will protect them from most electrical surges that could damage the devices.
- Mobile devices can be protected from theft by installing software that will (1) set off an alarm if the computer is moved; (2) help recover the computer, if stolen, by reporting the computer's whereabouts when it is connected to the Internet; and/or (3) allow you to lock or wipe the contents of the digital device remotely.

Be sure to check out the companion website for additional materials to help you review and learn, including a Tech Bytes Weekly newsletter—**pearsonhighered.com/techinaction**. And don't forget the Replay Videos.

key terms//

adware
antivirus software
backdoor program
backup
biometric authentication device
black-hat hacker
boot-sector virus
botnet
computer forensics
cookie
cybercrime
cybercriminal
cyberloafing
data breach
data file
denial-of-service (DoS) attack
distributed denial-of-service (DDoS) attack
drive-by download
e-mail virus
encryption virus
firewall
geotag
grey-hat hacker
hacker
identity theft
image backup (system backup)
incremental backup (partial backup)
inoculation
keystroke logger (keylogger)
logical port
logical port blocking
logic bomb
macro virus
malware
master boot record
multipartite virus
network address translation (NAT)
packet analyzer (sniffer)
packet filtering
personal firewall
pharming
phishing
polymorphic virus
pretexting
program file
quarantining
rootkit
scareware
script
social engineering
spam
spam filter
spear phishing
spyware
stealth virus
surge protector
time bomb
Trojan horse
virus
virus signature
white-hat hacker (ethical hacker)
whole-house surge protector
worm
zombie

making the transition to . . . next semester//

1. **Backup Procedures**

   You know you should have a good backup strategy in place for your key data. Consider the following:

   a. How often do you back up critical data files, such as homework files? What type of device do you use for backing up files? Where do you store the backups to ensure they won't be destroyed if a major disaster (such as a fire) destroys your computer? Do you use online sites for file backups?

   b. List the applications (such as Microsoft Office) that are currently installed on your computer. Where is the media (DVDs) for your application software stored? For any software you purchased in an Internet download, have you burned a copy of the installation files to DVD/Blu-ray disc in case you need to reinstall the software?

   c. Have you ever made an image backup of your entire system? If so, what software do you use for image backups? If not, research image backup software on the Internet and find an appropriate package to use. Suppose you need to purchase an additional backup device to hold your image backup. Find one that is appropriate. What is the total cost of the software and hardware you will need to implement your image backup strategy?

2. **Shouldn't Protection Be Included?**

   The Uniform Commercial Code, which governs business in every state except Louisiana, covers the implied warranty of merchantability. The warranty's basic premise is that a company selling goods guarantees that its products will do what they are designed to do (i.e., a car will transport you from place to place) and that there are no significant defects in the product. But computers are routinely sold with only trial versions of anti-malware software.

   a. Computer hardware manufacturers don't make OS software, but they sell computers that would be unusable without an OS. What responsibility do they have in regard to providing anti-malware protection to their customers?

   b. Does the failure of OS manufacturers to include anti-malware tools constitute a breach of the implied warranty of merchantability? Why or why not?

3. **Botnet Awareness**

   Botnets are serious computer infestations that affect large numbers of computers at one time. Still, many students are unaware of this threat even as botnets strike college campuses. Research botnets and prepare a short flyer for your classmates that explains the threats posed by botnets and the software that can be used to detect them.

making the transition to . . . the workplace//

1. **Tracking Employees**

   Many corporations provide mobile devices to their employees who work outside the office. With apps such as Footprints (from Sollico Software) and GPS tracking (from LOCiMOBILE), it's easy for employers to track the whereabouts of their employees by tracking the location of their mobile devices. Consider the following:

   a. How would you feel about your boss tracking your movements during the day? Should employers have to disclose to employees that they're being tracked? Should employers have the right to track employees to ensure they're not slacking off during work hours?

   b. Should the tracking software have an option to allow employees to disable the tracking feature temporarily? Under what circumstances should it be permissible for an employee to turn off employer tracking?

2. **Computer Security Careers**

   Computer security professionals are among the highest-paid employees. Using employment sites such as **Monster.com**, **computerjobs.com**, and **dice.com**, research computer security jobs available in the state where your school is located (try searching "computer security"). Select three entry-level computer security jobs from different employers and prepare a document comparing the following: What are the educational requirements? What job skills are required? How much prior work experience are firms looking for? Are programming skills required?

team time//

Protecting a Network

Problem

Computer networks with high-speed connections to the Internet are common in most businesses and government agencies today. However, along with easy access to computing devices and the web comes the danger of theft of digital assets.

Task

An alumnus of your school has just been placed in charge of the computer department of his county government offices. The network contains a mixture of computers running Windows 7, Windows Vista, and OS X. Lacking recent experience in computing threats, he approached your instructor for help in ensuring that his computers and network are adequately protected from viruses, malware, and hackers. Because the county is currently experiencing a spending freeze, he is hoping that there may be free software available that can adequately shield his employees' computers from harm.

Process

1. Break the class into three teams. Each team will be responsible for investigating one of the following issues:
   a. **Antivirus software:** Research alternatives that can be used to protect the computers in the office from virus infection. Find at least three alternatives and support your recommendations with reviews (from publications such as *PC Magazine* or *PC World*) that evaluate free packages and compare them to commercial solutions.
   b. **Anti-malware software:** Research free packages that will offer protection from malware. Locate at least three alternatives and determine whether the recommended software can be updated automatically. (Many free versions require manual updates.) Most companies that provide free malware protection also offer commercial packages (for a fee) that provide automatic updates. You may want to recommend that the county purchase software to ensure that a minimum of employee intervention is needed to keep the software up to date.
   c. **Firewalls:** Determine if the firewall software provided with Windows 7, Windows Vista, and OS X is reliable. If your research shows that it is reliable, prepare documentation (for all three operating systems) for the county employees to check and see if their firewalls are properly configured. If you determine that additional firewall software is needed, research free firewall software and locate at least three software options that can be deployed by the county.
2. Present your findings to the class and discuss the pros and cons of free and commercial software. Provide your instructor with a report suitable for eventual presentation to the manager of the county office network.

Conclusion

With the proliferation of viruses and malware, it is essential to protect computers and networks in businesses and government offices from destruction and disruption. Free alternatives might work, but you should ensure that you have done adequate research to determine the best possible protection solution for your particular situation.

ethics project//

Content Control: Censorship to Protect Children

In this exercise, you'll research and then role-play a complicated ethical situation. The role you play might or might not match your own personal beliefs; in either case, your research and use of logic will enable you to represent the view assigned. An arbitrator will watch and comment on both sides of the arguments, and together, the team will agree on an ethical solution.

Problem

Many parents use web-filtering software (also known as content-control software) to protect their children from objectionable content on the Internet. However, the software is also widely used in libraries, schools, and other public places where people other than parents are making decisions about what information to restrict. In 2000, the U.S. federal government began requiring libraries to use content-control software as a condition to receiving federal funds under the provisions of the Children's Internet Protection Act (CIPA). Libraries that don't receive federal funds don't have to install filtering software unless their state (like Virginia) passes laws requiring them to do so to receive state funding. Upon installation of the software, it's up to the library administrators to decide what content is restricted, as guided by the provisions of laws such as CIPA. Therefore, content restriction can vary widely from library to library.

Research Areas to Consider

- U.S. Supreme Court case *United States v. American Library Association* (2003)
- Content-control software and First Amendment rights
- Violation of children's free speech rights
- Children's Internet Protection Act (CIPA)

Process

1. Divide the class into teams.
2. Research the areas cited above and devise a scenario in which someone has complained about objectionable content not being blocked or about innocuous content that was inappropriately blocked.
3. Team members should write a summary that provides background information for their character—for example, library patron, library administrator, or arbitrator—and that details their character's behaviors to set the stage for the role-playing event. Then, team members should create an outline to use during the role-playing event.
4. Team members should arrange a mutually convenient time to meet for the exchange, using a virtual meeting tool or by meeting in person.
5. Team members should present their case to the class or submit a PowerPoint presentation for review by the rest of the class, along with the summary and resolution they developed.

Conclusion

As technology becomes ever more prevalent and integrated into our lives, more and more ethical dilemmas will present themselves. Being able to understand and evaluate both sides of the argument, while responding in a personally or socially ethical manner, will be an important skill.

Glossary

adware A program that downloads on your computer when a user installs a freeware program, game, or utility. Generally, adware enables sponsored advertisements to appear in a section of a browser window or as a pop-up ad.

antivirus software Software specifically designed to detect viruses and protect a computer and files from harm.

backdoor program Program that enables a hacker to take complete control of a computer without the legitimate user's knowledge or permission.

backup A copy of a computer file that can be used to replace the original if it's lost or damaged.

biometric authentication device A device that uses some unique characteristic of human biology to identify authorized users.

black-hat hacker A hacker who uses his or her knowledge to destroy information or for illegal gain.

boot-sector virus A virus that replicates itself into the master boot record of a flash drive or hard drive.

botnet A large group of software applications (called *robots* or *bots*) that run without user intervention on a large number of computers.

computer forensics The application of computer systems and techniques to gather potential legal evidence; a law enforcement specialty used to fight high-tech crime.

cookie A small text file that some websites automatically store on a client computer's hard drive when a user visits the site.

cybercrime Any criminal action perpetrated primarily through the use of a computer.

cybercriminal An individual who uses computers, networks, and the Internet to perpetrate crime.

cyberloafing Doing anything with a computer that's unrelated to a job (such as playing video games) while one's supposed to be working. Also called *cyberslacking*.

data breach When sensitive or confidential information is copied, transmitted, or viewed by an individual who is not authorized to handle the data.

data file A file that contains stored data.

denial-of-service (DoS) attack An attack that occurs when legitimate users are denied access to a computer system because a hacker is repeatedly making requests of that computer system that tie up its resources and deny legitimate users access.

distributed denial-of-service (DDoS) attack An automated attack that's launched from more than one zombie computer at the same time.

drive-by download The use of malicious software to attack a computer by downloading harmful programs onto a computer, without the user's knowledge, while they are surfing a website.

e-mail virus A virus transmitted by e-mail that often uses the address book in the victim's e-mail system to distribute itself.

encryption virus A malicious program that searches for common data files and compresses them into a file using a complex encryption key, thereby rendering the files unusable.

firewall A software program or hardware device designed to prevent unauthorized access to computers or networks.

geotag Data attached to a photograph that indicates the latitude and longitude where you were standing when you took the photo.

grey-hat hacker A cross between black and white—a hacker who will often illegally break into systems merely to flaunt his or her expertise to the administrator of the system he or she penetrated or to attempt to sell his or her services in repairing security breaches.

hacker Anyone who unlawfully breaks into a computer system (whether an individual computer or a network).

identity theft The process by which someone uses personal information about someone else (such as the victim's name, address, and Social Security number) to assume the victim's identity for the purpose of defrauding another.

image backup (system backup) A copy of an entire computer system, created for restoration purposes.

incremental backup (partial backup) A type of backup that only backs up files that have changed since the last time files were backed up.

inoculation A process used by antivirus software; compares old and current qualities of files to detect viral activity.

keystroke logger (keylogger) A type of spyware program that monitors keystrokes with the intent of stealing passwords, login IDs, or credit card information.

logical port A virtual communications gateway or path that enables a computer to organize requests for information (such as web page downloads and e-mail routing) from other networks or computers.

logical port blocking A condition in which a firewall is configured to ignore all incoming packets that request access to a certain port so that no unwanted requests will get through to the computer.

logic bomb A computer virus that runs when a certain set of conditions is met, such as when a program is launched a specific number of times.

macro virus A virus that's distributed by hiding it inside a macro.

malware Software that's intended to render a system temporarily or permanently useless or to penetrate a computer system completely for purposes of information gathering. Examples include spyware, viruses, worms, and Trojan horses.

master boot record A small program that runs whenever a computer boots up.

multipartite virus Literally meaning "multipart" virus; a type of computer virus that attempts to infect computers using more than one method.

network address translation (NAT) A process that firewalls use to assign internal Internet protocol addresses on a network.

packet analyzer (sniffer) A computer hardware device or software program designed to detect and record digital information being transmitted over a network.

personal firewall A firewall specifically designed for home networks.

pharming Planting malicious code on a computer that alters the browser's ability to find web addresses and that directs users to bogus websites.

phishing The process of sending e-mail messages to lure Internet users into revealing personal information such as credit card or Social Security numbers or other sensitive information that could lead to identity theft.

polymorphic virus A virus that changes its virus signature (the binary pattern that makes the virus identifiable) every time it infects a new file. This makes it more difficult for antivirus programs to detect the virus.

pretexting The act of creating an invented scenario (the pretext) to convince someone to divulge information.

program files Files that are used in the running of software programs and that do not store data.

quarantining The placement (by antivirus software) of a computer virus in a secure area on the hard drive so that it won't spread infection to other files.

rootkits Programs that allow hackers to gain access to your computer and take almost complete control of it without your knowledge. These programs are designed to subvert normal login procedures to a computer and to hide their operations from normal detection methods.

scareware A type of malware that's downloaded onto your computer and that tries to convince you that your computer is infected with a virus or other type of malware.

script A list of commands (mini-programs or macros) that can be executed on a computer without user interaction.

social engineering Any technique that uses social skills to generate human interaction for the purpose of enticing individuals to reveal sensitive information.

spam Unwanted or junk e-mail.

spam filter An option you can select in your e-mail account that places known or suspected spam messages into a folder other than your inbox.

spear phishing A targeted phishing attack that sends e-mails to people known to be customers of a company. Such attacks have a much greater chance of successfully getting individuals to reveal sensitive data.

spyware An unwanted piggyback program that downloads with the software you want to install from the Internet and then runs in the background of your system.

stealth virus A virus that temporarily erases its code from the files where it resides and hides in the active memory of the computer.

surge protector A device that protects computers and other electronic devices from power surges.

time bomb A virus that's triggered by the passage of time or on a certain date.

Trojan horse A computer program that appears to be something useful or desirable (such as a game or a screen saver), but at the same time does something malicious in the background without the user's knowledge.

virus A computer program that attaches itself to another computer program (known as the host program) and attempts to spread itself to other computers when files are exchanged.

virus signature A portion of the virus code that's unique to a particular computer virus and that makes it identifiable by antivirus software.

white-hat hacker (ethical hacker) A hacker who breaks into systems just for the challenge of it (and who doesn't wish to steal or wreak havoc on the systems). Such hackers tout themselves as experts who are performing a needed service for society by helping companies realize the vulnerabilities that exist in their systems.

whole-house surge protector A surge protector that's installed on (or near) the breaker panel of a home and that protects all electronic devices in the home from power surges.

worm A program that attempts to travel between systems through network connections to spread infections. Worms can run independently of host file execution and are active in spreading themselves.

zombie A computer that's controlled by a hacker who uses it to launch attacks on other computer systems.

Index